Tantrika

Tantrika

TRAVELING THE ROAD OF DIVINE LOVE

Asra Q. Nomani

 HarperSanFrancisco
A Division of HarperCollins*Publishers*

OCT '03

HarperCollins books may be purchased for educational, business, or sales promotional use. For information please write: Special Markets Department, HarperCollins Publishers, Inc., 10 East 53rd Street, New York, NY 10022.

HarperCollins Web site: http://www.harpercollins.com

HarperCollins®, ■ ®, and HarperSanFrancisco™ are trademarks of HarperCollins Publishers, Inc.

FIRST EDITION

Library of Congress Cataloging-in-Publication Data has been ordered.

ISBN 0–06–251713–9 (cloth)

03 04 05 06 07 RRD(H) 10 9 8 7 6 5 4 3 2 1

On this earth, to my mother who gave me life
My father who let me live
Bhaya who revealed to me the complexity of life
Bhabi who showed me love waxes in life like the moon
Safiyyah and Samir who taught me so much, most of all play
And precious Shibli who allowed me to touch the divine in this life

In the heavens, to dear Danny
You made me laugh so much while you were among us
May you and the Little Prince now laugh a plenty at us from the stars

Contents

Introduction   *ix*

1   Learning American Tantra   *1*

2   Leaving My Old Life   *15*

3   The Man I Married   *31*

4   From the West to the East   *45*

5   Worshiping the Lingam   *57*

6   A Cremation Ground   *65*

7   My Devoted Muslim Family   *72*

8   Implosion   *84*

9   Finding Freedom Again   *95*

10   Pilgrimage to the Himalayas   *104*

11   From the Bay of Bengal to a
Train Berth   *119*

12   The Village   *132*

13   The Sick Man   *144*

14   Finding New Shakti   *147*

15   Durga on Her Tiger   *159*

16   Dharamsala   *177*

17   Morgantown   *185*

18 Thirty Days in a Spiritual
    Prison Camp   190

19 Riding into the Village   197

20 Wannabe Goddesses Cry   207

21 Out of Morgantown   219

22 Parrots over a Safe House   235

23 Child of Truth   256

    Epilogue   267
    Acknowledgments   283

Introduction

The sounds of flutes in the bamboo grove
When the winds blow
Rustling of pipal leaves
Singing of crickets
Falling of streams
Croaking of frogs
Hissing of snakes
Hooting of owls,
All this deepens the mystery of dark.
The whole of creation is awake,
Even the stones and plants meditate.
 — "MY VILLAGE," IFTIKHAR AZMI

T HE VILLAGE ELDERS had never before set their eyes on a blossom-headed ring-necked parakeet like Cheenie Bhai.

His head was an iridescent shimmer of plum and rose. His beak, the color of sunflower petals. A goatee of black fell to his full chest, the green of lime. His necklace, a fine strand of dark purple pearls uninterrupted. From it burst turquoise light found in the most tranquil sea. Gentle ruby red marked his wings, each a soft reminder of the frailty of creation. His tail feather was the blue of the most precious lapis, trailing behind him in a dignity no royalty could imitate.

My friend Anaya, whose real name was Deborah, rescued him from a *shikarwalla,* a bird catcher, as we traveled on the road outside a city called Jhansi, and gave him to me before she returned to America. He traveled with me through India, by foot, train, car, auto rickshaw, and bicycle rickshaw. I brought him with me to my ancestral village of Jaigahan tucked amid the fertile farm fields of Uttar Pradesh, a wide expanse of a state in northern India. Anaya kept calling him Sweetie Pie, and I could find no better translation for *sweet* than *cheenie,* which means sugar in Urdu. Anaya called him Cheenie Pie. Our driver kept hearing her say, "Cheenie bhai." That's how Sweetie Pie became Cheenie Bhai, or "sugar brother."

Alas, he was a caged bird without his flying feathers. Anaya had clipped them so he wouldn't have to be imprisoned, but that act meant that he was grounded, even though I wanted to free him to the skies above. Cheenie Bhai gave me the excuse to learn how to say "parrot" in my native language of Urdu, the language spoken by most Muslims of the Indian subcontinent. *"Tho-thah."* It wasn't something I'd had much occasion to learn during my childhood in West Virginia, where the bright red cardinal and the full-bellied robin were the birds of the wild.

One morning, Cheenie Bhai's distinctive twerp mixed with the *azan,* or call for prayer, as the village muezzins told us that it was time for *fajr namaz,* our predawn prayer. *"Allahu Akbar, Allahu Akbar, Allahu Akbar-Allahu Akbar,"* rang from one *masjid* to the next. "God is great" four times if you didn't get the point the first time around.

Cheenie Bhai had kin that I rescued from the Nah Kaus bird market in Lucknow. I named her Cheenie Apa. "Sugar Sister." I didn't clip her wings but kept her with Cheenie Bhai so she could remind him of the way of parakeets.

Her shrill call pierced the crisp air.

"Twoight! Twoight! Twoight!"

For four days, as I hauled water from the well and ate purple carrots at night by lantern light, they twerped into the clear air.

On the fifth morning, an amazing thing happened. A flock of blossom-headed, ring-necked parakeets swooped over the village houses. The birds were wild, *jungli.* They were barely visible in the predawn light. But their distinctive twerps swept from the southeast over the fertile wheat fields to the northwest, where the birds landed on the thick branches of a bael tree that stands like an age-old sentry beside my ancestral home. There was a shine on the leaves from the rains that had lulled the village to sleep the night before. The tree stretched its branches toward a balcony where the Cheenies danced upside down in a stainless steel cage I had hung from an awning. The leaves, the bale fruits, the ants, the bulbul birds, the sun witnessed the glorious reunion of the *junglis* with the Cheenies. They erupted into the magnificent song of nature recognizing itself.

I sat on a *charpai,* a low bed with rope strung tightly around a frame, in the room off the balcony. I sat under the same *machardani,* dani mosquito netting, that used to protect my maternal uncle, Iftikhar Azmi, who was a Sufi poet. I didn't want to frighten the Cheenies and *junglis.* A pink organza sari with a golden border fluttered above me like a royal canopy. The dawn light cast itself through the sheer fabric, creating the illusion of silver thread where there was none.

These parakeets showed me an amazing truth—that the essence of all creation reveals itself. We might be disguised. Our feathers may be clipped. Outwardly, we may be caged. But we will triumph over our cages. We will turn ourselves upside down. We will cry out. We are part of something greater. Ultimately, our fundamental essence will demand liberation.

Ultimately, we can be freed if we give ourselves voice and hear our own singing. In Sanskrit, it's called *mahamudra,* a state of enlightenment in which we know the expression of divinity that lies both within us and outside us as a single breath, much like the sweep of the wind upon our faces. We are not defined by boundaries. We embrace the beauty in the present moment without judgment, expectation, acceptance, or rejection. It is as pure and clear as the flight of the *junglis* before me, whose wings in flight touch nothing, but it is filled with everything that is glorious. It is a state of liberation, *moksha* in Sanskrit.

I sat watching this play during the gentle spring after a winter chill, just before the summer *loo,* the hot air that embalms you and sucks your life force out of you so that you are raw electrical wiring ready to ignite. I was sitting in my maternal home, Latif Manzil. It was a palace of endless rooms. When my uncle, Iftikhar Mamoo, first brought a beautiful young British woman named Rachel here to wed, she rounded the dirt alley that leads to Latif Manzil's gate and thought, "It's like a wedding cake lost in the jungle."

It was a curious thing that I should find clarity here, but it was a curious mandate that had brought me here. I had come to India to uncover the secrets of the ancient art of Tantra, a philosophy that weaves sexual energy into its unique brand of spiritualism and religious devotion. It is a mysterious practice that is said to have sprung from goddess worship in the ancient Indus Valley civilization, weaving its way into Hinduism and spreading into Buddhism through Tibet.

One of the aims of Tantra is to recognize the divine perfection of the world by visualizing it as a celestial mansion, a mandala that is *vimana,* Tibetan for a "measureless mansion" in the middle of Buddhaland. Latif Manzil was my mandala.

When I first came through the same alley through which Rachel Momani had traveled, it was as if God had put this house here as a palatial gift to his subjects. The jungle had been stripped away, leaving mile after mile of fertile land. My mandala rose from the earth with a wide expanse. It towered to the sky with a large center veranda over which hung carvings like *jalee,* or netting. Each side was balanced with a balcony from which I imagined princesses could drape their tresses. Three solid pillars held up the majestic roof under which our white Ambassador rolled to a stop with my sheer green *dupatta,* a scarf, holding closed the driver's door. The front gate was bent awkwardly on its hinges, but it didn't matter. The window was cracked on the door in the middle of the front veranda, but it didn't matter. The white of the walls was yellow from the monsoon rains. It didn't matter. I walked through doors that led to more doors with more rooms.

With my cousin-sisters Lucy and Esther, I walked the corridors. They were born to Iftikhar Mamoo and Rachel Momani in England, but they were daughters of the village, their bare feet touching the soil of their ancestors as toddlers. They were now spirited, mystical young women, guiding me into this magical place with our elderly aunt, the sister of their father and my mother, as our chaperone.

"I'm walking through my own dream," I told them.

This home was the living incarnation of a recurring dream through which my subconscious had led me for years. Sometimes I was in an apartment. Other times I was in a house, but I always discovered rooms I didn't know existed. Each led me to more doors that led me to more rooms. Each time, the dream left me amazed. I thought my dream was the fantasy of a modern-day urban dweller, but a yogini in Gujarat explained to me, "The dream is a walk through the endless rooms of your soul." Maybe she knew. Maybe she didn't.

When I first began my exploration, I was thirty-three and had the legacy of a modern Western woman's quest for happiness: ill-suited boyfriends and a failed marriage of three months. Tantra, as it was sold to me, had an appeal: creating a spiritual partnership with a man in which he worships you and you worship him. The Sanskrit texts said that through specific Tantric yogic practices done with a partner, *karmamudra,* we can reach *maithuna,* a sacred union that moves us toward enlightenment.

Who could have a problem with that? I was rebounding most recently from a relationship with a man I thought was the soul I was destined to worship. I was mistaken. He was a twenty-nine-year-old technical virgin without plans to upgrade his twin-sized loft bed that I called a bunk bed. I was an urbane New York City single with boxes of Kenneth Cole shoes piled in a walk-in closet in my sweeping apartment in Brooklyn Heights, a neighborhood where Truman Capote wrote *Breakfast at Tiffany's* and Walt Whitman printed *Leaves of Grass* long before President Clinton gifted a copy to sex siren Monica Lewinsky. I thought my journey began that summer when things went so wrong with him.

But with each passing day I realized the journey had begun long before. Tantric teachers say that we can't achieve liberation in mystical union with another until we begin to deconstruct our ordinary selves. We must liberate ourselves from the doubts, fears, duplicities, and confusions that make up our unenlightened selves, the ego. Then we release into a philosophical nonself that is our *sunyata,* Sanskrit for emptiness, our absolute nature. I had a dream early in my exploration that I was wandering the streets naked. No underwear. No nothing. I awakened wondering, knowing I would have to strip myself like that if I were to continue. I remembered what a friend told me when I began: "Asra, you're going to have to tell the world everything."

I chose to continue following the trail without censor. That was the Tantric way. To practice Tantra well is to be a Tantrika, a woman who isn't defined by anything, living compassionately, lovingly, blissfully, and fearlessly with appropriate wrathfulness when necessary. To master Tantra is to become a *dakini,* a woman who dances in the sky, flying free of the things in life that keep her hostage to ego, fear, and boundaries. She is a sky dancer whose flight takes her through a spiritual voyage of clarity, fearlessness, and ecstasy that liberates her from worldly existence. A Tantrika is a divine creation, a goddess with a small *g*, respected, honored, and worshiped, liberated from shame, fear, expectation, exploitation, and suppression. She is free to be adventurous, aggressive, and bold in her efforts to find enlightenment. She is a yogini who has awakened her inner fire and helps others light their own.

She isn't defined by the dualities of worldly life. Man. Woman. Old. Young. Good. Bad. Sane. Insane. East. West. She moves beyond those boundaries to a place of nonduality where she exists with simple honesty, compassion, and wisdom.

It was in the stillness and emptiness of Latif Manzil that I started to find clarity. I saw the dualities that had torn me apart, and what it was that I was freeing myself from in this odyssey taken in the name of Tantra. The heavens were my canopy. I stared at the glittering sky before I slept and felt my ancestors shoot over me in the stars that darted across the sky. I could feel their spirit when clouds floated overhead against the darkened sky.

It was here a young widow taught her daughter decades earlier the rituals and code that would make her a good Muslim girl. That girl became a virgin bride married to a man she didn't see except for a glance until three days after her wedding. Both of their ancestral histories held secrets and mysteries little spoken about, reaching into the worlds of Hinduism, alleged murder, and madness. Together, they journeyed across the ocean to create a home fashioned out of a World War II barrack painted bright red at 208 Bevier Road in Piscataway, New Jersey, a honeysuckle bush outside the window of a bedroom painted to resemble a jungle. They left behind in India a young son and daughter. These two later crossed the ocean on a TWA jet with only each other for company.

I was that four-year-old girl. Except for two summer trips to my homeland, my connection to my roots was limited to my parents' efforts to teach me my culture and the adventures I read about in Nancy Drew's *The Mystery of the Ivory Charm,* in which Nancy tries to reunite a circus boy, Rishi, with his father, a lost maharaja of an imaginary wealthy Indian province.

I was to grow into a woman whose journey into the ancient art of Tantra would become a discovery of one of the key ingredients to Tantra, *atman,* or true self. And with that true self, Tantra teaches, we can realize *raga,* passion, and *kama,* sexual desire, on the path to enlightenment with another. Little did I imagine that Tantra would turn out to be a path that allowed me to uncover my secrets as a native child born of India, a girl raised in West Virginia, and a woman who felt like an immigrant in both cultures.

Liberation. Equanimity. Mindfulness. Fear. Ego. Samsara. These words that meant little to me would make me give away my Aveda face toner, make peace with a former boyfriend named Paulo, and transport me to a land where peacocks run wild in the fields. I started my travels to India with the clearest of mandates, spelled out to me during a commercial break during *NYPD Blue* in the living room of a friend outside San Francisco.

"It's about finding the force within you," I told her and her husband borrowing the Star Wars mantra of our generation.

How could I know that it would take a confrontation with the most ugly and dark in this world for me to know the meaning of divine love?

Tantra comes from the Sanskrit verbal root *tan,* meaning "to weave." It is not about leaving life but about weaving the realities of life with honesty, sincerity, compassion, and truth. *Tra* comes from *trayate,* which means "to liberate" in Sanskrit. It is about freeing ourselves from suffering by freeing ourselves from illusions, or *maya.* I didn't know the literal meaning of *maya* until one evening when my feet kicked up the sand beneath me at the Maha Kumbh Mela where millions of Hindu pilgrims had descended upon the confluence of the Yamuna, Ganga, and legendary Saraswati Rivers. I looked at the blazing sun, descending in a flare of orange that made a silhouette of the pilgrim tents.

"It is *maya,*" said the man beside me. Illusion.

I was to remember later, here in the courtyard of my ancestral home, what I had forgotten from sixth-grade science class: the sun does not set.

We orbit away from it. This was a truth about the nuance of what we know as reality.

"Twoight!"

"Twoight!"

My eyes open. Sunlight spills onto the balcony. I am transported back to this reality, to the mystery of life unfolding. The *junglis* have dropped half-chewed green grapes to the balcony floor. The grapes seem like diamonds fallen from the stainless steel cage. A squirrel ventures onto the balcony to grab one of the grapes. The *junglis* flutter their wings with a flurry and skate into the clear sky. Cheenie Apa chatters in a frenzy, wondering where they have gone so quickly. Cheenie Bhai stays calm. He tugs at his red string over and over again, as if saying a mantra on a *mala,* a circle of beads.

The bamboo trees stir. In their wind dance I can feel my soul stir. I have flown far not only in body but also in spirit to sit here now. There is a psychic legacy that we inherit when we are born—our karma, the accumulated energy of our past incarnations. But there is another deep legacy that pulsates within us. It is something like our ancestral karma. Our journey toward liberation means freeing ourselves not only from the impulses and momentum of this incarnation but also from the lives that make the subconscious with which we were born. It is then that we can join in blissful union with ourselves and another so that we can know the kiss of the wind upon not just our faces, but also our souls, with a richness and a beauty that is as natural and raw as the flight of *junglis* is to a Cheenie Apa and a Cheenie Bhai.

The doors to the veranda open like the doors within my soul. Before me, the sun hits the roof of the house that used to be the home of my maternal great-grandfather, before he built this palace. It is as if they took a thousand clay pots, broke them in half, and laid the halves upon that roof across the way. The fields stretch out behind the house. The wind stirs the trees in the bamboo orchard. Everywhere, birds chirp and dart and call to each other.

I close my eyes to remember from where I flew.

CHAPTER I

Learning American Tantra

M Y SEARCH FOR TANTRA, sex, and love began with a gnarly foot wash in a forest of pine trees in the Canadian countryside.

I washed the scaly feet of a lanky stranger, cloaking them with soft soap suds and warm water. We sat on the porch outside a sprawling log house, the sun draping itself over us like the gentle touch of a velvet glove. The scent of home cooking wafted toward us from the kitchen inside and mingled with the lavender smell of the soap that I caressed on the bottom of this stranger's feet. I massaged each toe separately, stretching them under my fingers, pressing my thumb into the small dip where his ankle began. As I slid my hands underneath, he flinched. My touch tickled him. He giggled. I smiled politely and averted my gaze.

"What am I doing here?" I asked myself, trying not to look at his gangly toes and smashed toenails.

I had been living in a bird coop of an apartment in Manhattan's Upper West Side.

I had just finished writing an article about how gorillas in Chicago's Lincoln Park Zoo lived in cages with more square footage than the apartment of a couple who recently moved to Manhattan. I hated my home. The windowsills were splattered with bird droppings. I was in a miserable relationship. A metal safety gate spread across the windows like an accordion, reminding me of the *jahlee,* or screen, through which my Muslim sisters in purdah peer when they are hidden from the outside world.

I wasn't hidden, but I wasn't happy. I had been looking for love in all the wrong places, first my failed marriage, then a string of bad relationships. Now, in humiliation, I was finally letting go of this latest boyfriend when I escaped to a new apartment across the Brooklyn Bridge. When I arrived, my cat, Billluh, sat in the window, his nose twitching at the gentle

waft of a summer breeze that swept into the apartment, the first fresh air
he had breathed in months. I breathed in at last when my nineteen-year-
old cousin-sister Lucy Ansari arrived in Newark, New Jersey, on an early
morning Continental Airlines flight. In India cousins, especially first
cousins, are considered brothers and sisters. All her belongings were
packed into a knapsack on her back. It made me yearn for a life in which
things could be so simple. She came to visit me at the tail end of her adventures around the world. Her father, who had died of a heart attack a few
years before, was my mother's eldest brother. I called him Iftikhar Mamo,
and had helped me unfurl my wings. When I was a college freshman considering journalism, an unorthodox field for a child from India, he
encouraged my mother to support me. At one low point in my life, he
reminded me of the power within me.

"You are creative," he told me. "If the real world is bad, you can create
a new world. Through your writing, you can create a new world."

Now, his doe-eyed daughter, a long-legged gazelle of a poet in flip-
flops and cargo pants, brought the beauty of the world to me again. She
helped me recover what the damaging relationship had obscured. Lucy
cooked *dal* and *chawal,* lentils and rice, for me. She stirred me awake
before work to run through the tree-lined brownstone streets of Brooklyn
Heights, down the Promenade. Step by step, life began again, but I was
disillusioned by romance. I wondered if I could ever find love.

Then Ken Wells, one of our page-one editors at the *Wall Street
Journal,* came to me with a reporting assignment. "We want you to look
at the business of Tantra. Go find Mr. and Mrs. Tantra." Ken told me
Tantra was America's hottest new fad. It was a natural assignment for
me. I'd earned an informal reputation on the tenth floor among my fellow reporters as the *Journal*'s sex reporter, the rising incidence of "Mile
High Club" sexual misconduct on airplanes among my page-one stories.

In my cubicle at the World Financial Center in lower Manhattan,
adjacent to the World Trade Center, I tapped *www.tantra.com* into the
address line of my Web browser. The browser led me to steamy pictures
of men and women in different sexual positions. Clicking further, I came
across ancient images from the Kama Sutra of men and women in acro-
batic positions of lovemaking.

I punched *T-A-N-T-R-A* into the search line on dejanews.com. A crazy world unfolded before me as I clicked from screen to screen. A man talked about introducing something called his lingam into his wife's yoni. He held his wife still and focused on her *ajna* chakra and meditated. Another Tantric explained the chakra *puja,* where a guru picked eight couples to randomly pair up for a night of "passive copulation" in a circle around a guru and his *shakti.* What did *shakti* mean? What was a *puja?* And was it really something *Wall Street Journal* readers needed to know?

I called my experts on India, my parents, in Morgantown, West Virginia. "Have you ever heard of Tan-trah?" They didn't know what I was talking about.

"You know, Tan-trah?"

They finally figured it out. "Thun-thruh," my mother said. They didn't even pronounce it the same way. In India, it turned out, Tantra was considered a cult of black magic used by evil people. It was to be avoided. It had mantras that were like spells. I didn't know any mantras. I certainly didn't know the word was actually pronounced "mun-thruh" instead of "mahn-truh." As a Muslim, I didn't even know the spiritual significance of the dots Hindu women in India wear on their foreheads. I just knew I wouldn't be caught dead with one. Little could I imagine that I would one day enter the cave where the Hindu god Ram supposedly meditated and emerge with a smear of vermilion red pasted smack in the middle of my forehead. I was an Indian Muslim who recited Arabic verses from the Qur'an but never tried the downward dog or upward dog of modern American yoga, let alone anything that ended "Om Shanti."

I began to think that perhaps I had too quickly dismissed the secrets of my culture because of a misjudgment in what I believed to be my destiny, my marriage to a man from the Indian subcontinent. Through trial and tribulation, my parents' marriage had survived over thirty years, though I had never once seen them hold hands. My brother, Mustafa, had his marriage arranged to a gentle young woman named Azeem. Now, his beautiful children, Safiyyah and Samir, filled the walls in my childhood home with Crayola scribbles. Maybe I needed to learn more about the traditions of my motherland, even if they were a part of Hinduism and I was a Muslim.

To be Muslim from India meant to be cut off from the world of yoga, meditation, and karma that were parts of Hinduism and Buddhism. Muslims believe in one God, Allah, and for that reason we shun the many deities that Hindus worship. I knew nothing about Kali's fright, Shiva's might, or Ganesh's knowledge. To me, Hindu temples were a blur of bright colors on the sides of the mountain passes we rode from Bombay to our home in the hill station of Panchgani. Buddha was more a stranger to me than George Washington, whom I at least had studied in ninth-grade American history class. I wasn't even sure whether Buddha was a real person or not.

There was an unspoken line between Muslims and Hindus. My childhood friend Sumita told me that in her extended family she was told there would be separate plates for Hindus and Muslims. Most of my relatives snickered at all the Hindu gods. In Hyderabad, my father's sister, Ishrat Aunty, had a friend, Vijaya, who was Hindu. It was a friendship accompanied by exclamation. Sumita and I were more united by our junior high admiration for a cute blond-haired track star named Kurt Erickson than separated by modern-day religious rancor. Maybe that was the secret of the melting pot.

But even in America, although Muslims and Hindus intersected, we still stayed away from each other's cultures. To Ken, I was Indian and therefore the perfect person for the assignment. But for me, pursuing the article meant I had to abandon generations of my inherited ignorance and abhorrence for Hindu beliefs, many of which turned out to be founded in Tantra. I tried to keep an open mind. I certainly wasn't having success as a Muslim woman in the man department. Maybe researching this article would help me find my soul mate. Gathering my hopes with my doubts, I ventured to find out.

I raced through the countryside to make my date with other couples and singles at the Omagaki Wilderness Centre outside the sleepy town of Pembroke, an hour's drive west of Ottawa, for a weekend workshop that promised to teach "Sacred Sex."

A rush of greenery whipped by me. I nosed my rental car over a stretch of bumpy dirt road and edged into a gravel lot next to a looming log building. I gingerly walked into a cavernous room with vaulted ceilings. A towering woman with a frenzy of blond hair and dark roots left a circle of men and women seated yoga style in the corner to greet me. Her gauzy shirt floated behind her. Her name was Beverly, but she went by Pala. "Welcome. Welcome!" she said in a soft voice meant to be soothing. (It was, in fact, raspy and eerie.)

She handed me a folder with a blazing headline: "It's all about Sacred Sex. Lovers in Mind, Body, and Spirit."

"Thank you," I muttered. "But I'll be watching. I won't really be participating."

"Oh, no! You'll get a lot out of this for yourself."

Just then, her husband bounded over in a bleached-blond Mohawk, bouncing his head enthusiastically with the energy of an anxious puppy. "I'm Al!" Together Pala, and Al Copeland promised to reveal to me the ancient secrets for finding romantic, spiritual, and sexual fulfillment.

Tantra.com had told me that Tantra is a quasi-religion that dates back some six thousand years. Its first texts were in Sanskrit. Its original adherents practiced ritual copulation—essentially, for them, a form of yoga meant to achieve an arrest of all mental processes en route to a mystical bond with the "oneness of the universe."

It was believed that by retaining their semen, men would reach higher states of ecstasy and live longer. Men and women trained themselves to move their sexual energy through seven energy centers, called chakras, to bring themselves to higher states of intellectual, creative, and spiritual expression. As part of those beliefs, women were goddesses meant to be worshiped by men on the path to mutual cosmic bliss, just like the mythical god Shiva worshiped the goddess Shakti. It was in their love story that Tantra was rooted.

Shiva was a great god living in the jungles of India as a yogi. He had transcended all worldly passions and existed in a constant state of meditation. His hair was uncombed. He went naked except for a piece of animal skin covering his loins. His skin had a bluish gray tint from the sacrificial ashes he had used during his sacred meditation. He became Lord of the Universe because his advanced yogic practices made him a symbol of transcendence.

The Mother of Creation, the goddess Devi, looked at Shiva and decided it was time to bring him down to earth. Time to get him to hurt like the rest of us. But first he had to love. She sent Sati, a beautiful woman with long shiny black hair and large brown eyes. Shiva saw Sati. He fell in love. They married, living in bliss on the sacred Mount Kailash.

One day, Sati died. Shiva was grief-stricken, wandering aimlessly. This was what Devi wanted. She wanted Shiva to feel human sorrow and absorb Sati in the deepest caverns of his soul. Shiva believed love had to be wed with meditation and contemplation to create a blissful union. The other gods took pity on Shiva and reincarnated Sati as Shakti, an even more enticing woman. When they met, Shiva and Shakti united in bliss and marriage. Shakti's name came from *shak,* the Sanskrit word meaning "power," for she was a great yogi herself. The great source of her power came from her yoni, her "secret garden." Shakti epitomized the female energy of creation. The story went that both Shiva and Shakti knew they were nothing without each other. They needed each other's energy to awaken themselves.

Shakti accepted Shiva as her guru. The marriage of their energies liberated both of them. They became spiritual partners and soul mates. Shakti taught Shiva to temporarily let go of asceticism, to weave the art of love and sexual union into his spiritual meditation. They began the path of yoga that became known as Tantra, the yoga of divine love.

Shiva and Shakti learned new ways to channel their orgasmic powers through the pathways of their energy centers, their chakras. They incorporated music, astrology, massage, painting, dance, poetry, visualization, ecstatic ritual, and meditation. The teachings spread through scriptures called Tantras, taught through a conversation between Shiva and Shakti. The message of the Tantras was that by loving and worshiping each other as Shivas and Shaktis, all men and women could live in blissful union.

"Look upon a woman as a goddess whose special energy she is, and honor her in that state," wrote the early Tantra texts.

I didn't feel quite ready to be a goddess. I still thought my butt was too big.

Three couples sat before me on the edges of their chairs, next to three single men, one of them handsome. "We're going to learn how to move your sexual energy through your body," Al said.

"It's the passion pump," Pala guided us. "Close your eyes. Squeeze your butt. Squeeze, squeeze, squeeze. Inhale through your nose. Breathe in deep into your belly. Keep the rest of your body real relaxed. Move the energy up your spine to your head. Clench your teeth. Press the flat of your tongue against the middle of your palate and the tip of your tongue where your lower front teeth and gums meet. Push your chin slightly backward. Look up and roll your eyes to the top of your head. Now, breathe out."

She lost me somewhere between my teeth and my tongue.

"Squeeze, squeeze, squeeze," she began.

It wasn't enough to move the sexual energy with breath. Al slipped a cassette into the tape player as we cleared the wide floor. We were to use the blindfolds we'd been told to bring. I had forgotten. I borrowed one and immersed myself in darkness as a gentle sound spilled into the cavernous room. We danced blindfolded to something called Kundalini music. I crashed into a chair.

We assembled again on the floor.

"The thought of surrender is terrifying to a lot of people," Pala told us. "But to enjoy sacred sex, you have to open your hearts. Write a word on a piece of paper. Tuck it under your pillow."

Why not try? In my cabin, by the light of a flashlight, I scrawled one word, *Surrender,* and slipped the paper under my pillow.

I wondered if I could surrender. Was it possible to release my heart? Maybe it was I, not the men I chose, who feared intimacy. It didn't take much past Psychology 101 to realize that I wasn't choosing good mates. My twenty-nine-year-old who couldn't discuss his virginity wasn't quite material for a spiritual love connection.

One activity spilled after another in the weekend training schedule. Blindfolded, we ate food fed to us by our foot-washing partner. My partner was kind. He spared me the Tabasco sauce.

Blindfolded again, we thrashed coiled towels against the floor to unleash our anger. I thrashed and thrashed. We gazed into the eyes of the stranger next to us. My partner had gentle eyes that lingered. John Travolta taught us how to thrust delicately in a movie clip from *Saturday Night Fever.* This was a trick for men to keep themselves from ejaculating. Thrust, pause, thrust again. Men could do the Kegel exercises, too, we were told. Like women, all they had to do was tighten the muscles that stretch like a hammock from the base of the spine to the pubic bone, supporting the sexual organs, the urethra, and the rectum. Al called the exercise "push-ups for the penis."

We moved to a grassy lawn beside our log cabin retreat center. We were about to learn one of the most critical parts of Tantra, how to release and move the energy through our body through the seven chakra centers. They were the chakras Shiva and Shakti used in their lovemaking. I wasn't a believer. I sat on the edge of my seat as another Tantra student, Robert, pressed a finger into the soft of my skull.

"This is your crown chakra," Al told us. "Hold the pressure. Hold it. Hold it. Hold it."

How strange. I felt myself relaxing. Maybe this actually worked.

Robert moved his finger then to a dip at the base of the back of my head, the "Wind Mansion." Then, he moved to the dips of my shoulders, "Heavenly Rejuvenation." Then, right below my clavicle bones. I could feel my entire being release. It worked. I was a convert. The energy flowed down through me as if by some magical force of nature. My head collapsed. I could barely bring myself to pay attention. I pressed my own finger into the dip below my sternum, between my breasts. This was "The Sea of Intimacy," the heart chakra.

"Press here to overcome your fears. To open your heart," said Al.

We lay on mats on the grassy field. The teachers told us to put our hands on our waists and press our fingers into the dips there, "The Sea of Vitality."

We slipped our hands behind our lower backs so that our knuckles pressed into the dip right above our butts, at "The Sacral Point." Pressing on it was supposed to release raw energy. Naked energy. Lust. The idea was to unleash our energy so that it brought us to higher levels of ecstasy.

After a candlelight dinner together, we saw the sky had filled with bright stars. I walked down to the dock with Robert and the handsome weekend student, Frederic. Darkness had descended upon this lake, leaving glints of light on the water like sparkle dust cast from the skies. Robert breathed in deep and then left. The crickets chirped. A cloud floated over a star.

Frederic and I studied the white flashes in the woods to figure out if they could be lightning bugs. It was quiet except for the sound of chirping and our breathing.

"May I?" Frederic asked, reaching for my hand.

I was silent as he took my hand. I wondered what was coming next.

"Immerse yourself in the sound," he whispered dreamily.

A smile crept over me in the darkness. Never heard that line before. I waited a polite moment. I withdrew my hand from his. He walked me back to my cabin.

I went in alone.

My next stop was Santa Cruz, California, the birthplace of many a New Age fad.

I stepped into the dimly lit ballroom of the Best Western Seacliff and, scanning the fresh faces and eager smiles, felt as if I'd walked into an Amway convention. But we weren't there to learn how to sell soap. We were there to learn how to create ecstasy. With fifty-six couples and thirty singles, I settled into one of the small circles as we bowed heads toward each other and gazed into each other's eyes.

"Feel the circuitry of love. Breathe love to your organs," encouraged a middle-aged man, Charles Muir, sitting in the front of the ballroom in tight blue silk pants, floral Hawaiian shirt, and bare feet.

His partner, Caroline, looked like Olivia Newton-John. She welcomed us in a singsong voice. Together, they sat yoga style with hands on their knees, facing palm up.

"Joy is part of your inner nature," Charles pronounced. "Tantric lovemaking is the sweetest of meditation. I am loving. I am lovable. You all are. This isn't just about sex. It's about loving sex."

Like the other women at the workshop, I was a goddess, here to be worshiped like Shiva worshiped Shakti. It's her powerful energy that runs through women, and it's this energy we're supposed to harness to create "the divine feminine." I pressed the palms of my hands together, fingers upward against my chest, in the Hindu ritual of greeting, more foreign to me as a Muslim than it was to some of these northern Californians who had learned the gesture in yoga classes.

"*Namaste,*" I said, not even knowing what it meant. Charles explained, "It means, 'I bless the divine within you.'"

Charles continued with his instructions. "Be the little girl. Now, men, be cute. Be the little boy. Show her your Doberman eyes." I felt a kinship with the man across from me. I hurt for his hurts. I thought of the boys in the men that I've known. And I thought of the little girl in me.

"Hey, beautiful!" The shout came from the yellow school bus that had just dropped me off near my home in Piscataway, New Jersey, when I was about eight.

I turned around.

"Not you! The tree!" The shout turned into snickers as the bus drove away.

I let go of this memory as Charles instructed us to draw closer to each other. I stepped toward the man across from me. Following directions, I pressed my right hand onto his chest and my left on his back, to create "a circuitry of love." The stranger was Harrison, a California native, thirty-seven, single, seeking his soul mate. Drenched in sweat, he started weeping.

"This is kindergarten Tantra," said Charles, a Bronx native.

"We all have the ability to release unlimited sexual energy, to have wave after wave of glorious, easy release," Charles cooed.

"Inside every woman's vagina is a sacred spot. If a man is willing to take the time, he can learn to touch this spot in a way that will pleasure and heal his woman," Caroline purred.

Charles took over. "In the yoni is stored a conglomerate of mixed energies. It may feel bruised. It may feel burning. There may be emotional tensions as layers of fear and guilt come up. This is the energetic entry point that enables people to access past experiences that caused them to close down their sexual energy."

With a partition splitting the men and women, Charles coached the men on how to "awaken the goddess" by massaging a woman's "sacred spot," the mysterious G-spot that has eluded scientific confirmation since its apparent discovery. "It's a sacred duty for you guys to awaken an energy that seems to lie dormant. This is not just for bodies. Sexual love is a sacrament that will bring you closer to your god, as well as to each other.

"Use the third or fourth finger. Palm upward, reach into the yoni and curl the finger toward you in a kind of come-hither gesture. First, just hold the contact without movement. After one minute begin linear stroking, experimenting. Gradually proceed to all the other strokes, pulsing, tapping, vibrating, using a circular motion or going side to side. After trying all these strokes, make a dance of all of them."

On the other side of the wall, over tears, the women whispered tales of abuse and dejection and neglect. Rape, sexual abuse, depression, emotional walls. I thought of all my hurt through the casual and episodic relationships I'd had over the years, filled with dreams that never crystallized.

It was my turn to divulge why I was sitting at this workshop. I returned from my daydreaming. I told them what I dared: my life started in the country where Tantra began, and though this was a reporting assignment, I was hoping to gain something from this personally for I, like everyone, was in pursuit of the things that touch our souls. There, I thought, that was enough.

The partition slid away, the married couples retreating for "homework." The single men assembled into a *puja* circle, sitting cross-legged with their eyes closed, while the single women stood inside the circle.

Charles instructed the women to hold hands, "breathing energy" out their right hands, and told us, "Honor the goddess within you. Here are your choices. You can go home alone and experiment by yourself. Or you can say, 'I'd like to experience sacred-spot massage, and I'm willing to trust someone to do it with me.' If you choose to stay you will have a memorable night."

Over a vegetarian meal, earlier that day, one of the single men, Ben, a local with a business card that read "sexual healer," had volunteered to give me "a sacred spot massage." "I'm excellent," he'd said. I stepped out of the circle. The other women paired up with the men, retreating into the night together. One woman feasted that night with a man she had just met. They drank Bartles and Jaymes wine coolers and ate coconut macaroons he bought from 7-Eleven. She solved one mystery. She discovered she had a G-spot.

Over avocado soup, the Muirs wove the tale of their ascent in America as Mr. and Mrs. Tantra. The Muirs launched their Tantra teaching business even though neither one of them had been to India. The business enjoyed years of success. But the Muirs now carried a secret. They had separated two years earlier and gone on a "relationship sabbatical" because Charles wanted to do "research" on healing other women.

We walked the curving sidewalk to an intersection that led the Muirs to their room. Caroline cast me a smile. "Two years ago, we would have asked you in to have sex. If I wasn't here, Charles would ask you now."

I smiled politely and scurried away.

A few months later, I experimented privately with the art of sacred spot massage behind the white lace curtains of the Grand Hotel du Nord overlooking the main plaza in Reims, France's capital of champagne production. My boyfriend was a twenty-four-year-old French-Algerian my childhood friend Sumita had introduced me to at the corner of Montague and Henry Streets in Brooklyn Heights in front of John's Pizza when he was visiting America and earning money scooping Italian ice out of a cart marked Italian Queen.

"Surrender," my Western Tantric teaching told me.

With no instruction from me, my boyfriend did the things Charles had instructed the men to do to worship women. It was both painful and ecstatic. But my boyfriend hadn't gone to college, he was nine years younger than I, and his father couldn't read or write. I pressed upon my heart chakra to release my fears. No surrender could transcend doubts about a career in Italian ice.

I returned to America for my friend Sumita's wedding. She was marrying a Muslim friend of mine from Iran whom I'd introduced her to after meeting him on the volleyball courts on the Washington Mall. Her grandmother didn't know she was marrying a Muslim, but it mattered little to Sumita, who always lived with a pure heart, transcending the judgmental tendencies that seeped into our immigrant culture from India. In her home, appropriately, I experienced my first *puja,* not the kind I'd seen in Santa Cruz, California, where singles paired up, but a prayer to a Hindu god, Ganesh. As others used their hands to waft smoke from the fire ritual upon their faces, I hesitated. "Go ahead," her father encouraged me. I did and breathed in my first blessing from a Hindu prayer.

I discovered the mysticism of my roots through Sufi poetry, especially that written by the poet Jalaluddin Rumi, born in 1207 in modern-day

Afghanistan, sparking even more of my experimentation with surrender to the mystical. A man of Colombian descent followed, leaving me to reread his love poetry to me while his former girlfriend visited from her native Madrid to surprise him for his birthday.

My casualties accumulated with an intern I met when I arrived at NBC studios for an on-air interview by anchor Brian Williams. The intern called me to go out. I dreamed great thoughts about his rise on TV, my book, our future. I used my Tantric principle of surrender to release my soul to him. While I daydreamed about our future, he rose from bed. "I've got to get up early in the morning."

"How are you getting home?"

The subway, he said. I figured it would be too dangerous at that late hour. He said he was out of money. I reached into my wallet and pulled out a twenty for him to get a taxi. I remembered another twenty-something I'd dated in Washington. We'd rendezvoused in front of the Lincoln Memorial. We were breaking up. I cried. He cried. When we parted, he asked me if he could borrow a twenty to get home. As I gave the bill to this NBC intern, he turned away from the doors with the words, "I'll call you." I never got a call.

I still believed in love. Though I wept over these men, I was grateful to them for teaching me lessons of dharma, what Buddhists call "knowledge." They crystallized for me a realization that I had been approaching for some time now. This path upon which I was treading was not the one I wanted for myself. Every few months I met a man with whom I thought I could start a relationship. But, sure enough, each time my judgment was wrong. American Tantra taught surrender, but the philosophy of surrender as I understood it was foolish and filled with suffering.

I was ready to leave this life. I had departed from family tradition as a woman. I had moved away from home alone at the age of twenty-one, earned my master's degree, and then pursued a prestigious journalism career at the country's largest newspaper. I'd set up homes for myself in San Francisco, Chicago, Washington, D.C., and finally New York, criss-crossing the country, jetting into strange cities for assignments, renting cars and navigating my way for everything from interviews in a

Minnesota maximum security prison to the crash site of TWA Flight 800 off the coast of Long Island. While I had broken new frontiers, my life of single abandon had left me with a longing for home and a sense of belonging. I needed the emotional support of my family.

I called my mother. "I'm coming home."

CHAPTER 2

Leaving My Old Life

I DRAPED SILKEN SARIS over my curtain rods. My wedding *dupatta* went over the sofa. I pushed my mattresses into my walk-in closet, clearing the bedroom floor for my Tantra going-away party.

I bought dozens of Catholic religious candles from the grocery store emblazoned with the images of Jesus and the Holy Mother. I scored a keg and poured Jell-O mixed with vodka into Dixie paper cups for Jell-O shots. A man on the Internet claiming to teach Tantra came by the office so we could meet beforehand. He didn't seem to know very much, to tell the truth. I asked him to teach PG-rated Tantra since the guests were mostly friends from work. Little did I realize they'd appreciate an R-rated lesson.

The party was a wild mix of jokes with Larry Ingrassia, the *Journal*'s handsome third-section editor, and his beautiful wife, Vicki, cuddling during the Tantra workshop. I wrote the invitation with a Tantric pun: The last to come would get a special door prize.

On a cold winter day after Christmas, my father arrived in our blue Chrysler minivan to help me escape New York single life.

Samsara is the Buddhist concept of worldly attachments. Although I left many of these behind when my father and I packed our rented U-Haul truck, somehow the truck was still packed with boxes filled with the symbolic representations of samsara.

This was the beginning of my lesson in nonattachment, a word I didn't even know yet. To me, Buddhism taught detachment. My father told me Buddha was detached when, as Prince Siddhartha, he left his wife and newborn son in his kingdom so he could wander and find the answer to relieving suffering.

"It's not detachment," a dear friend of mine, a student of Buddhism, told me gently but firmly. "It's nonattachment." I thought she was just being a highbrowed stickler for words, but my departure from New York was my first step in understanding this principle by which I could exist engaged with the world but not obsessed, possessed, or consumed, a tall order for a woman in a culture where every other friend, including herself seemed, to be battling OCD, obsessive-compulsive disorder.

Tantra says that the base chakra, called the root chakra, is located at the bottom of the spine. Its Sanskrit name is the *muladhara* chakra. It's supposed to be the force that empowers us by grounding us to the energies of the earth. Its color is supposed to be red. The organs associated with the *muladhara* chakra are the body's physical support, the base of the spine, the legs, bones, the feet, the rectum, and the immune system. The mental and emotional issues associated with the *muladhara* chakra are safety and security, kinesthetic feelings, movement, and the ability to provide for life's necessities. Not paying my Time-Warner cable bill on time meant, I figured, I'd failed on this account.

The other emotional issues include the ability to stand up for yourself, feeling at home, feeling a sense of belonging, emotional support, survival, self-esteem, social order, familial conditioning and beliefs, superstitions, loyalty, instincts, and physical pleasure and pain. I struggled with most of these emotional issues and knew that it was in Morgantown, my hometown, where I could start to bolster my *muladhara* chakra. The physical dysfunctions associated with this chakra are chronic lower back pain, sciatica, varicose veins, rectal tumors and cancers, immune disorders, and depression. Depression. That one I knew well.

As I saw the last bit of the Manhattan skyline in the rearview mirror, I thought back to the world from which my family and I had catapulted into this reality.

It was 1962, and my mother and father stood on a railway platform in Hyderabad waiting for the train that would take my father to Bombay to catch a plane to America. Garlands of jasmine flowers lay over my mother's arms like a shield in front of her belly swollen with her unborn first child. My father had won a fellowship from the U.S. Agency for International Development to study at Kansas State University in Manhattan, Kansas. His teachers at Osmania University's Agriculture College in Hyderabad had earned their PhDs at universities from Ithaca, New York, to Wales, United Kingdom. Kansas State University had a partnership with the college to transform it into a land grant university in the spirit of American universities in which the government gives land for research.

Images of pink flamingos danced in my father's head as he embarked for America. One day when he had gone to class as a student at Osmania University, his professor had showed the class slides from America. Pink flamingos perched on their skinny legs filled one slide. Another showed a long bridge on the Overseas Highway, U.S. 1, connecting the mainland to thirty-four islands in the Gulf of Mexico, ending with Key West, Florida.

He had stared at the bridge, surrounded on both sides by clear water, and marveled at the manmade creation. Many years later, we ventured to Key West on a family vacation, and my father asked eagerly, "Where are the flamingos?" We didn't find them.

For now, at night in Kansas, he read his wife's letters into the night on the top bunk in the room he shared with his best friend from Hyderabad. Aftab Ahmed watched him curiously from below. "Go to sleep, Zafar," he said before rolling away from the light.

My older brother was born during my father's absence. My father returned to India after a year in America. I was born two years later just before the monsoon on June 7, 1965, at Noor Hospital on Mohamed Ali Road in Bombay, the "hospital of light," bundled into a red-and-white checkered outfit. I belonged to India's first generation born after independence. What was I to learn about freedom?

In the tradition of new mothers returning to their maternal home, my mother took me to Bella Vista in the hill station of Panchgani a few hours outside Bombay. An elder cousin, my Choti Momani, "small aunt," who had raised her, greeted her with a cold glass of *hareera,* a mix of buffalo milk, pistachio, and almonds.

My mother's first cousin, whom I grew to know as Baray Mamoo, "big uncle," gave me an Arabic name rarely chosen: Quratulain. *Ain* meant "eye." *Quratulain* meant "coolness of the eye," a description of calm. My most famous namesake was a legendary Urdu novelist named Qurratulain Hyder, who wrote poetically about identity, spirituality, and India. The ritual in Islam is to recite the first verse of the Qur'an and slaughter two goats for the new name of a boy at an *aqeeqa,* a welcoming and naming ceremony. One goat for a girl. Two goats were slaughtered at my *aqeeqa.*

But I discovered years later that only one was dedicated to my name. The second was for food because there were so many guests in the house.

We returned south to my father's house in Hyderabad. My maternal grandmother, Dadi, didn't like my name. She changed it to Asra, meaning "to travel by night," guided by the divine hand of God. Pronounced "Us-ruh," it is mentioned in the first verse of surah Isra, the seventeenth chapter of the Qur'an. It told the story of a mystical journey by the Prophet Muhammad from the Sacred Mosque in Mecca to the Farthest Mosque in Jerusalem, where today al-Aqsa Mosque sits next to the Dome of the Rock. I'd always heard that it was so timeless a journey Prophet Muhammad's bed was still warm and his doorknob still shaking when he returned. Prophet Muhammad first flew to the seat of the earlier revelations in Jerusalem, then through the seven heavens, even to the Sublime Throne, where he was initiated into the spiritual mysteries of the human soul struggling in space and time. It's said that this great mystical story of the ascension, al-Mi'raj, reflected the journey of the human soul in its spiritual growth in life. A Spanish scholar, Miguel Asin Palacios, credited this tale with inspiring the medieval writer Dante to create *The Divine Comedy*, the wonderous human journey through the netherworlds.

We lived together those two years in Hyderabad. My father returned to his job as an assistant professor at the agriculture college. But he didn't lose sight of America. It wasn't about the lure of this new country. It was about getting a good education. The sad truth, too, was that not all of India welcomed his type. One day as he sat with a Hindu colleague, a friend, on campus, he was shocked at what he heard.

"*Ahray,*" Hindi slang for "c'mon," "Muslims should just leave and go to Pakistan."

It was a constant chorus that stung the heart of a boy born of India. So one day, at the airport, I sat perched in my father's arms next to garlands of white flowers draped over his dark suit. It was a moment of celebration captured in a black-and-white photo in front of a sign for BOAC, the precursor to British Airways. Not one smile broke across the grim faces. Indians hadn't yet learned to smile for photos.

My father was leaving to earn his PhD at Rutgers University in

America. He was part of the brain drain out of India of those seeking advanced degrees in the West. The Indian diaspora. Not long after, my mother also left to join my father. My brother and I stayed with Dadi and Dada. U.S. immigration laws and my father's paltry student wages kept us from crossing the Atlantic Ocean. Every night for two years, my mother wept for us in a tiny apartment my father had rented at 10 Union Street in New Brunswick, New Jersey. By day, she baby-sat kids named Eda, Laura, and Kerry to eke out a tiny savings to buy my brother and me tickets for futures in America she could never imagine. One day in 1969, it was our turn to make the journey. My parents had saved the $593.60 they needed for the tickets.

"Bhaya! Bhaya!" I called after my brother, using the honorific for older brothers in India.

We wore outfits stitched from the same striped fabric so that we could be reunited easily if we lost each other on the TWA plane. My brother was six. I was four. We stared into the camera with the dazed look of children who didn't understand.

When we arrived at John F. Kennedy Airport, my brother vomited. At least that's what he always remembered.

I didn't remember a thing. My mother said I looked over my shoulder for Dadi because my grandmother had told us she would be following us on the next plane. Apparently, I didn't recognize my own mother.

In the tradition of India, my date of birth was written incorrectly on my passport, making me a year older, so that I could go to school earlier. I was not ready.

I came home from kindergarten every day crying. My mother was sympathetic. She let me stay home. The principal called. "Mrs. Nomani, it's against the law to keep your children at home and not send them to school." Back to school I went.

I didn't feel pretty there, where girls had lovely names like Elizabeth and Sarah.

English was my second language at this school named after Martin Luther King Jr. in Piscataway, New Jersey. I made the new language my first. In the tradition of lonely children everywhere, I turned to books as my best friends.

I caught fireflies with a neighbor girl, Pinky, who was also from India. We punched holes into jar lids and stuffed the bottom with grass, as if we could imitate nature for these creatures so gentle they would let us catch them so easily in our pudgy hands. I refused to answer back in anything but English when my parents talked to me in Urdu. It was a poetic language with influences from Persian. I didn't care. I just knew it didn't sound American. I rejected some things American, too. On my way home, I'd ditch my mother's bologna sandwiches in an open basement window.

"AAAAAAAhhhhhhhssssssssssss-ruh," sang the taunts at school in Morgantown, West Virginia, where my father took a position at West Virginia University as an assistant professor. I headed down the stairwell at Evansdale Elementary School as a sixth grader to the annoying sound of my name being abused. Our school was a squat three-story yellow brick building just across University Avenue from the faculty apartments where we lived.

At home, it wasn't easy for my mother, either. My father, now forty, worked long hours in his new job. English was his second language, too. Succeeding as an immigrant was harder for him than for me. One night I found my mother sobbing. She had been softly singing Indian film songs lately, often as she stood at the sink washing dishes. My brother and I usually begged her to stop.

"They're so depressing!" we whined.

As my mother wept, I wrapped my arms around her to comfort her. At ten, I wondered if the women of our culture always had to quietly suffer. Finally, after midnight, my father came home. He had been at work, anxious to win tenure and job security.

For me, God became my refuge. In the solitude of being strangers to a new city, my mother taught me to do *namaz*. At the end of each prayer, I followed her instructions. I turned my head to the right to wish peace upon the angel whom my mother said sat there to jot down my good deeds.

"*As-salam-u-alakum wa-rahmatullah wa-barakatuh,*" I said in Arabic, evoking, little did I know, one of the fanciest of greeting. "May the peace, the mercy, and the blessings of Allah be upon you." I then turned my head to my left shoulder to wish peace upon the angel who sat there and noted my bad deeds. My mother didn't tell me it was also a part of something called hatha yoga. She wouldn't have known. Yoga. That was foreign to her. I finished my *farz namaz,* my mandatory prayer, the same way each time. I joined my open hands together in front of me, buried my face in my palms, and asked God for the same thing every time.

"Allah pak hum kho suhkoon dho," I said in Urdu. "Dear God, please give me peace of mind." I would add, "Please give my mother, my father, my brother peace of mind."

One sunny afternoon a family that looked like mine stopped their Honda station wagon at the traffic light beside the WVU faculty apartments.

The father spotted me and yelled to his family, "Look! An Indian girl!"

A nine-year-old girl in the backseat popped her head up. Her name was Sumita. She had been reminiscing about the friends she'd left behind in Providence, Rhode Island. She wondered what kind of friends she would make in this new town. I was playing Wiffleball, focused on the game. When they pulled into the parking lot, the father called out to me.

They needed directions to the Pierpont Apartments. It was a towering building right behind the faculty apartments. I pointed the way. And then I invited them into our house.

My young mother stood in front of the stove and kneaded dough into balls to flatten into *rotis* for this family of six, the Sinhas, who had just walked into her home.

The friendship I was to forge with the nine-year-old girl in the backseat would be an unusual bond given the post-Independence divide between Hindus and Muslims in India. Circular scars the size of nickels sat on our left upper arms, reminders of the smallpox vaccinations we had gotten as children, much like children in America. But because they seemed to scar so much more distinctly on our brown skin, we considered them markings for our gang of child immigrants from India. Our friendship started with American baseball. The Sinha children, my brother, and I challenged the neighbors—the Wolf clan of nine brothers and sisters—to baseball. Indians versus Americans. We weren't the Americans.

One day I came home from school with a permission slip. This one would allow us to learn to square-dance in Mrs. Gallagher's sixth grade. I begged my mother to sign it. In orhtodox Islam, though, after the age of nine, boys and girls were barely allowed to mingle if they weren't related. Dancing was definitely out. My mother finally relented. And I learned to square-dance with a boy named David Stitzel. This was my last close encounter with a boy until I turned nineteen.

The next year we moved into our first house, set in the middle-class neighborhood of North Hills in Morgantown, a tract of development cut out of a mountain that sloped into a lush green valley. Our town was a classic small college town where drivers braked for college students crossing the road, townsfolk converged on High Street for the annual Christmas parade, and it made local news when the town hung plastic poinsettas on the lightposts for the holidays.

Two balconies with black steel railings balanced the back of our two-story house with pink aluminum siding and wall-to-wall carpeting. From the balconies, we looked into the valley and across to the swath of mountain that bordered it on the other side. We had a small community of families from India. Somehow, being thrown together in a town where everyone bought groceries at a store called Kroger, the aunties and uncles crossed geographic, religious, and caste boundaries that in India only the rebellious would touch. Baby-sitting Bobby and Misty, the children of a Hindu family named Majumdar, and walking their Pekingese dog named Pluto, I grew up not knowing these boundaries existed even though I washed my hands carefully with Ivory soap afterward. My mother had taught me the Muslim way. Dogs were dirty and *haram,* forbidden.

My family floated between the Hindus and Muslims, and I could see the contrasts in the two cultures. I dashed freely in relay races one Saturday night with Indian girls, my new friend Sumita among them, during a celebration of the Hindu festival of lights, Diwali. We arm-wrestled and waited eagerly during a raffle for three twenty-dollar J. C. Penney gift certificates. None of us won them. A J. C. Penney executive actually won one. We didn't like the food, but freedom burned in our lungs with the yelping we did during our Diwali hall Olympics.

The next night I entered another world. We rode down Riddle Avenue to the Medical Center Apartments for a Muslim Student Association dinner for our holiday, Bukreid. A bearded man directed my mother and me upstairs to a tiny one-room apartment packed with Arab women in head scarves and robes. The men carried food to our room in casserole dishes. We weren't allowed downstairs, where the men were gathered with the main spread. My head hurt from the foreign sounds of Arabic echoing in my ear. I felt as if we were in a jail. My mother and I were both relieved to leave.

When the Majumdars, Sinhas, and Yusuffs, another Muslim immigrant family in town, came to dine at our house, the men sat in the living room and the women settled in the kitchen. There were no public displays of affection. I never saw my parents kiss, let alone hold hands. The couples arrived and left in the same cars, but, mostly wed in arranged marriages, they skirted nimbly around each other as if they had conceived their children through divine intervention. My mother invited the men first to the spread she had placed on our Montgomery Ward dining table. Chicken *biryani,* flat hand-kneaded *roti,* and plates of other steaming dishes. The women filled their plates after the men cleared out. Women and men intermingled only when they went for seconds.

In America, symbols of my religion expressed themselves in the strangest of places.

"What's this?" Miss Lafever, my phys ed student teacher, asked me one afternoon at Suncrest Junior High School as I curled my body into stretches. She pointed to three squiggles I had made on the top of my health quiz.

It was the Arabic numerological shorthand, 786, for the first line of the Qur'an: *"Bismillah ir-rahman ir-raheem."* I was supposed to recite it before I ate, before I ran the mile race, before I did anything. Okay, I didn't know what it meant in English.

"What's it mean?" I asked my mother at home that evening.

"In the name of God, the Most Gracious, the Most Merciful," my mother told me.

I vowed to tell Miss Lafever the next day, if I could remember during eighth-grade Grubby Day.

Whatever the limits, or because of the limits, my religion gave me a personal discipline. I wasn't tempted to date, party, or even wear skirts. I wore pants over my legs. I read *Go Ask Alice,* the tale of a teenage girl who beat drugs only to die anyway. I was grateful to have been born a Muslim. I saw it as a privilege. Whenever I was faced with a dilemma, I asked myself whether my choice would comply with the Qur'an. I was grateful to faithfully do *namaz* for the relief it gave me. I knew better than to ask permission to go to the Drummond Chapel dances where girls like the McCroskey twins sealed their popularity.

I always knew when I had broken one of the rules. Once, when I was thirteen, I went out with Minh, my best friend Karen's adopted sister from Vietnam. Her mother only let her see her boyfriend on double dates. I joined her, set up with a blind date. When my date called me afterward at home, I was flattered, even if his face was pocketed with pimples.

My brother picked up the other phone line, listened in, and swore at my teenage suitor. "Don't ever call here again!" He never did.

We had our cultural breakthroughs. My mother layered slices of pasta carefully above cheese, tomato sauce, and *halal,* or Islamically kosher, ground beef for our first lasagna. We made our first turkey dinner when I was thirteen. My visiting cousin-sister, Ruby Apa, promptly vomited. A young Indian daughter of my parents' friend disco-danced surreptitiously in the hallway for Ruby Apa and me when we visited her family for dinner.

"That's great!" I shouted.

"Shhh!" she whispered. "My father doesn't let me."

I wondered what it felt like to know love. Did my parents really love each other? I didn't know. I didn't think so. What were the chances of finding love in an arranged marriage? What about harmony?

I wondered if maybe I should find religion again. I had stopped lifting myself from bed to pray my nighttime *Isha namaz* before sleeping. I now appealed to God to help me with the struggles being waged inside me. When my mother taught me Islam, she would tell me, "It is the right path."

But what was my path? Even when I ran, training for cross-country, I skirted the way trod by others and found my own.

I started at West Virginia University because my parents didn't believe a daughter should leave home even for studies. I remained an obedient daughter, but one night during my freshman year I challenged our understood order without even intending to do so.

It was just after 2 A.M. on a Friday night when I turned our purple Pinto station wagon into our driveway off Cottonwood Street, bouncing as the car rolled over the gutter. My brother bound out the front door and down the steps to meet me in front of the car in his white *kurta* and *py-jama*, flailing his arms in the air.

"Where the fuck were you?" he screamed as he lunged to open the passenger-side door and slammed it shut. He followed me into the house with a string of profanities. "You could have been raped!"

I tried to hold my ground. "I just went to a party."

My father picked up the phone. "I just reported my daughter missing. She has come home now." My first party, and my father called the police.

My mother sighed loudly in the living room. I heard the sighs from my bedroom.

"We should return to India," my father said.

My mother agreed.

As the clock neared 3 A.M., I heard my brother cough. He was still awake. My mother sniffled. She was still awake. I tried to sleep off the pain vibrating inside me from the reception I'd received when I got home. Maybe my brother knew something I didn't know. Later he told me he was just scared something had happened to me.

In the fall semester of my sophomore year, I arrived late one morning to my class, Women in Technological Development. The lights were out for a movie. I slipped into a seat next to a stranger and whispered to the darkened figure next to me, "Did it just start?"

A twist of fate that would uproot centuries of ancestry sat me there that day. When the professor switched on the lights, I saw I was seated next to a blue-eyed man with dirty-blond hair, a very American name, Michael, and a can of Coke on his desk. He spit Skoal chewing tobacco into it. He was in my Arabic class, too. He was a Special Forces medic in the Army Reserves, a Green Beret, who wanted to run covert operations in the Middle East while I wanted to work in the region as a journalist.

The temptations of the West overtook my family's shelter. Michael became Mike. He was the son of an engineer who worked with the Trident submarine. He started giving me rides home in his two-door Celica with a spotty gray paint job. I had him stop a block away from my house at the intersection of Headlee and Briarwood Avenues, where the McCroskey twins once challenged me to a race.

"Drop me off here," I told him.

I was too afraid to go closer in case my parents or the Majumdars saw me emerge alone from a man's car.

He slowly initiated me into my first touches of intimacy with a man. *"Ki 'tab,"* we mouthed to each other behind adjoining carrels at Colson Library, practicing the Arabic word for book. He slipped his shoes off and played with my bare toes. I crossed a line I'd never dared before.

One night I studied with him in his room at the Pierpont Apartments, to where I had once directed the Sinhas. Pierpont was one of Morgantown's tallest buildings, with its nine floors spread like three spokes from a center. He massaged my shoulders. He massaged my feet. He led me to the lower mattress of a bunk bed. My feet hung over the edge. He leaned over me. I closed my eyes to his face closing in on me. He kissed me. It was sloppy, but it was my first kiss. I was nineteen.

My junior-year fall semester began. Mike wanted a more physical relationship. I didn't. He told me, "I think we should break up."

I couldn't let that happen. I'd kissed him. I'd made a commitment. I relented. One night we dined at Wings & Things, a local Mexican fast-food restaurant. I didn't want to leave him. We returned to the trailer he shared with a friend from his Army Reserves Special Forces unit to watch *Hill Street Blues.* During a commercial, the axis of my life took a turn. He led me to his bedroom. I could see the white circle on his Levi's pocket left by his can of Skoal chewing tobacco.

I told him, "Turn off the light."

I pressed one of my hands against the thin cardboard wall of faux paneling that separated the bedroom from the living room. It was a far cry from the cherished wedding night when I was supposed to lose my virginity. I was two years younger than my mother was when she first looked into my father's eyes. The closest I got to silk was his polyester camouflage blanket. Still, afterward, he said, "I love you."

I loved him, but I was speechless. I felt happy, but I wept. This wasn't how I was supposed to lose my virginity. What was I one day going to tell my husband? At home, I told my parents I'd spent the night at my friend Christina Toh's house.

A year passed of these lies. At Western Sizzlin' Steak House on Patterson Avenue, next to the Kroger where we'd shopped since my childhood days for Wheaties, sacks of onions, and bright orange tins of oregano, turmeric, and red pepper for my mother's *masala,* or mixes of ground spices, I told my father, "I want to move out."

He was heartbroken. No proper Muslim girl left her family before she wed. My mother was not present, having gone to India to rescue my brother. Our family in India had been reporting worrisome tales of bizarre behavior. He had gone to India to play soccer, but he was now traveling aimlessly from one relative's house to the next, daring to grow his hair long and mingle with Hindus.

When they returned, my father and I went to New York to pick them up at the airport. We rested at the midtown Manhattan apartment of my mother's elder brother, Anwar Mamoo, off Lexington Avenue. It overlooked a *halal* meat shop that sold kosher meat to Muslims. My father told my mother that I was staying out late. That I wanted to move out. My mother had just gone through a hell that I couldn't appreciate. I was making another hell come to life for her. I admitted to her that I had a boyfriend.

She was clear about what I had to do. "Stop dating him."

The rules had always been clear to me. No dating allowed. But, having taken a bite out of the forbidden apple, I defied the rules. I started living a double life. I moved into an apartment on Wiley Street with friends. One day my father dropped off a letter, a pink rose gracing the bottom of each page. He wrote, "Asra *baytee,*" meaning "Asra, dear," on the envelope, centering *786* in Arabic letters upon the top of the first page. "I am not a psychologist or a politician or a double talker," he wrote. "In my very own way I would like to express my feelings to my daughter, whether it makes any sense to her or not."

He wanted to tell me that friendship did not have to be expressed with sex and marriage. He asked me whether my lifestyle wouldn't destroy my parents, close relatives, and even myself. Did I think differences in religion, culture, and values would hold my husband and me together? My family and my husband's family? Love, he told me, should be viewed realistically, not with a blind eye.

I could hear his voice echoing as I read his words. "Number seven. If you walk in a coal mine, you expect to get coal dust on you and not perfume. In the same way, if you move in a perfume factory, your body will expel fragrance."

I wondered, did I want coal dust? Or perfume?

Across town in my childhood home, my mother sat on a wing-backed chair in the living room, trying to distract herself with *General Hospital*. Tears that she thought had dried up streamed down her cheeks. She propped a yellow legal pad on her lap and penned a New Year's admission of the hurt that consumed her.

"What did I do wrong that you have rebelled against me to the extent that I cannot handle?" she asked me. She sought the same divine comfort that had helped her deal with deep pain before. "May God help me in this ordeal."

The truth was that I was staying in a bad relationship because of the loyalty that my culture had taught me between a man and a woman. Throughout our relationship, Mike had made me feel bad about myself as he lusted, one time, after the bouncing breasts of a coed crossing the street in front of our car and other times trying to convince me that a ménage à trois would be exciting, slipping his *Playboy* magazines in front of me hoping I would develop a lust for other women. One night he confessed to me that he had slept with someone else. I ran down High Street in the rain, my hair dripping. I wept. And I took him back. I thought that was what a woman was supposed to do, even though he came from a world in which I was an outsider. He told me a ROTC friend called me "a sand nigger."

The poet Maya Angelou came to campus. She had a message for the young women who were gathered in a classroom in Woodburn Hall. "In your lifetime," she said, "men will come and go. But you will always have your work. Always stay dedicated to your work."

I dedicated myself to a vision of becoming a great writer and journalist. The previous summer my father had broken tradition and allowed me to live on my own so I could be a summer intern at *Harper's Magazine*. The next summer my father drove me to Washington, D.C., to State's News Service, a scrappy operation that gave me clips in newspapers from the *Allentown Morning Call* to the *South China Morning Post* and a regular stint, snaking through the Pentagon to write about military affairs. My parents lifted their worries about my studying away from home and sent me with their blessing to do my master's degree at American University in Washington. There I spent my days working for Reuters news agency while going to school at night. Mike wanted me to have more sexual experiences. "You can sleep with other men. Just don't fall in love."

I fell in love. My boyfriend was a gorgeous and doting classmate from graduate school, a surfer from San Luis Obispo, California. When I asked him if he wanted me to do a ménage trio with him, he answered, "Why would I want to share you with anyone else?" Then, after I moved to Chicago to start my career with the *Wall Street Journal,* I met a man who made me swoon with CD serenades by Randy Travis, bouquets of flowers, and adoration so gentle and thorough I was always strong and secure with him.

My mother had to be wrong. This dating business was working out after all.

It was 1989, and my family was returning to India. My aunt, Nuzhat Phuppi (phuppi meaning "father's sister") had arranged my brother's marriage to a Hyderabadi girl born in 1969, the year my brother and I had left India. My mother and I went to see her. She was demure and young with wide eyes cast down. She spoke not a word to us. My brother saw her for the first time after they were married when he looked into a mirror into which she also looked. He saw her reflection. She didn't dare to look for his reflection.

I returned to Chicago wondering what my reality should be. In Morgantown my father was getting his own pressure. Dadi had written again asking when I would marry. He was powerless between the expectations of our culture and a daughter who wouldn't abide by the unspoken covenant into which she was born. Dadi wanted me to marry one of her other grandchildren. I protested whenever my mother made the suggestion. "It'd be incest!"

My father stirred my mother awake one night. "When is she going to be married?"

"I don't know! Ask her," my mother murmured, rolling over.

"Either she gets married or I'm leaving the house!" he yelled. "It's time to start looking. If you don't apply for research grants, how will you do any research?"

Didn't they realize it wasn't a simple question for me to know with whom I would want to spend my life? Besides my mother's brother, Iftikhar

Mamoo, who had wed the British girl Rachel, I only had one example in my family of a relative who had married outside of our culture, my mother's cousin-sister, a woman I called Anjum Khala, *khala* meaning "mother's sister." She visited me in Chicago with her husband, Tim, and I stole time away from my workaholic life to tour the Art Institute of Chicago with them. I liked Tim's gentle nature, and the two loved each other deeply, but his white skin beside her brown skin didn't seem like a match to me.

Our family's first generation in America was born on May 30, 1991, to my brother and his wife. Safiyyah Zohra Nomani. Safiyyah means "best friend" and "tranquil" in Arabic, and this smiling bundle of joy was just that to all of us. Zohra was the name of my maternal grandmother, my nani. My mother sang again, but she wasn't singing the sad songs I remembered. Safiyyah's arrival stirred desire in my heart for marriage and motherhood.

My Greek girlfriend Vasia was dating a Greek man for the first time. "It is so beautiful to make love in your own language," she told me. English was the language of my fluency. But how nice would it be to share my native language at the most intimate of times?

Even the Grimm fairy tales of my childhood had instilled in me an early message to love my own. In the tale of the hare and the hedgehog, the hedgehog outwitted the hare for mocking hedgehogs as slow. He accepted a challenge to race the hare. They started off together. When the hare reached the finish line, the hedgehog's wife was there waiting in a leisurely way, tricking the hare into believing she was her husband. She clinched the victory even though her husband had ridiculed her when she protested that he was racing the hare. "Woman," the hedgehog had cried, "don't try to understand the affairs of men! This business doesn't concern you. Just do as I say."

She stood dutifully at the finish line, repeating as her husband told her to say, "Here I am already."

The hare finally accepted defeat after their seventy-third race. The moral of the story, the Grimm brothers told me, was that "when you marry, be careful to marry someone just like you. Especially if you are a hedgehog, you should make doubly sure that you marry no one but another hedgehog."

I started searching for my hedgehog. He needed to speak Urdu.

CHAPTER 3

The Man I Married

O N A CRISP DAY in January, I got a voice mail at work. "It's Omar. Remember me?"

I replayed the message twice to make sure I'd heard it right.

I did remember. Omar was the handsome man with a bounce in his step and an easy smile that I remembered meeting on the steps of the American University Mary Graydon Student Center. He was the first man from my culture who intrigued me. Before I even talked to Omar, I confessed to my boyfriend in Chicago that I was distraught over how to resolve the most intimate question of my identity: whom to love?

My boyfriend was more noble a man than I could imagine. But I couldn't commit my future to him. I was anxious to find a man from my culture and religion. That's what my father wanted. That's what my mother wanted. That's what my brother wanted. I thought that was what I wanted. I tried to explain to him the pressures upon me as we walked through Chicago's Lincoln Park.

"A dark cloud hangs over me."

"I'll convert. I'll learn Urdu," he told me. It wasn't enough. He looked different. He was a Lutheran blond of German ancestry.

"It wouldn't be the same. I have to decide what I want." The next day he was distant with me.

"It's not fair you're so mad at me."

But he wasn't even angry. "I'm not mad. I'm sad." My heart shattered for the hurt that I was causing.

Not enough, though, to stop me from calling Omar back. We seemed to have lived parallel lives in Muslim families divided by the border of the Indian subcontinent. We were born the same year, he in Karachi, Pakistan, I in Bombay, India. His mother was born in Lahore in the province of Punjab, an important fact to some, but it meant little to me.

His father was a native of Delhi whose family migrated to Pakistan after the partition. As a Pakistan International Airlines executive, his father moved the family around mostly outside Pakistan in Saudi Arabia, Bangladesh, Turkey, and France, where Omar studied at École Anglaise de Paris S.A.

He ran around his apartment, his two cats, Sylvester and Tweety, chasing him. I did the same with my two cats, Billlie and Billluh. He knew *khatoon* meant "lady" when I told him my sister-in-law's name was Azeem Khatoon. He knew the name of the silver paper laid atop the *burfi,* a dessert made on the subcontinent. His parents lived in the F/8 neighborhood of Islamabad. My phuppi and phuppa, my paternal aunt and uncle, lived in F/9 next door. When he was eight, his mother taught him how to cross-stitch cushion covers and handkerchiefs for his home economics assignment. He pronounced my name right. I cross-stitched roses onto a table cover in my mother's childhood home in Panchgani.

His mother, too, sang when she was sad.

It was 3:36 A.M. when we finally got off the phone. I whispered to myself, "I think I'm falling in love again."

Daydreams captured my mind. I saw him clearly by my side in a delivery room, leaning over me as we both held our newborn baby. I couldn't see my boyfriend and me like this. It was as if he was the answer to my questions. An angel of God. Torn between the loss of my boyfriend and the possibility of Omar, I pulled out my first self-help book, *The How to Survive the Loss of a Love Workbook.*

"Describe your pain," this book demanded.

"It is numbness now."

Words sat upon the page like blood spilled from the heart. "Circle or highlight the ones you're feeling now." I pressed hard around *Pain* with my blue felt pen. Muddled? Yes. Overwhelmed? Yes. Beaten? Yes. Self-hatred? Yes. Fear? Yes. Inferior? Yes.

Lost? I circled it so many times I must have thought I would find myself in one of my circumambulations of the pen.

Angry? I didn't circle it.

"Is there some magic to carry all of us home?" I wrote. "To bring us to a point where we can live with ourselves and our lives? Where is the magic? I want some. I need some. Or shall I spend my life as lost a soul as I am? Please let me journey toward that magic."

I admitted my struggles to my mother. She stayed awake until dawn with the weight of this sadness upon her. She confided my struggles to my father.

They called me together, and we talked into the night. I told them the truth of my struggle between East and West. My relief was unimaginable. My father didn't disown me. He didn't even have a heart attack. Instead, he told me, "I love you."

I invited Omar to be my date at a friend's engagement dinner celebration in Washington two weeks later on Valentine's Day.

First, I went home to West Virginia. Bhabi, my brother's wife, pulled out the *shalwar kameez* suits she had gotten as her wedding outfits. The *shalwar* resembled baggy pants like the kind worn by women of harems. The *kameez* was a long tunic. A *dupatta,* or long scarf, topped the *kameez*—or the head, for a more modest look. We settled on a suit with a hot pink silk *kurta* with gold embroidery and shiny smooth stones decorating the front. She was giddy with excitement. I descended into the Bombay Palace on K Street, blocks from the White House. My date waited at the bottom of the steps. He turned his brown eyes shaped like almonds up the stairs toward me. His wide face with angular cheekbones filled with a smile. I fell for him instantly.

We went to the movies that weekend. Indian director Mira Nair's *Mississippi Masala,* of all things. It was the story of a beautiful Indian girl who emigrated from Uganda. To her family's chagrin, she fell in love with a boy who wasn't from India but was rather an African American carpet cleaner, played by Denzel Washington.

During a sultry phone scene, the girl lay back on her bed, a bumper sticker behind her, "My dharma ran over your karma."

Omar jetted to Chicago two weeks later.

"You are like a miracle," I told him after a dinner of tandoori chicken and Coca-Cola. "My bridge between the East and the West."

By Sunday morning, we were high on the euphoria of falling in love. He turned to me and said, "I never want to lose you."

"What do you mean?"

"I want to spend the rest of my life with you."

We laid our *janamaz,* prayer rug, upon the floor facing east. After doing *namaz* toghether, we cupped the palms of our hands together and said our *dua,* prayer, into our hands. I asked God again for the *suhkoon,* Urdu for "peace of mind," I'd been seeking since I was a child. We washed our faces with the palms of our hands and then *phoonked* upon each other. It meant to blow a breath of blessed air. Our mothers had done this to us ever since we were children.

When I told him that he was my *chand ke tukrah,* he knew it meant "a piece of the moon, a saying of admiration."

I called my parents, giddy with new love and happiness that I had ful-filled my familial obligation. "I feel such relief," I told my father. He told me, "A weight has been lifted off my shoulders." A few days later, my brother woke up with a panic attack at 6:30 A.M. and jolted awake my parents.

"Who is he? My sister calls one day, says she is going to be married, and we say, 'Okay?'" he screamed. "You're so immature!"

Little did we recognize my brother's wisdom.

With my engagement, I felt as if I had created a modern picture of that old black-and-white image of my parents on their wedding day, completing the circle of our immigration with an Eastern marriage even though I was raised in the West. Not many of even our generation dared love marriages. I was one of just a few of our cousins who married in the name of love. One insisted until her parents relented. Another evaded her brother's chase down the New Jersey Turnpike to marry in a *masjid,* a mosque.

We dreamed of an outdoor wedding. I wanted it in my home state of West Virginia. His mother argued ill health. She had always dreamed of the day she would open both her front doors to welcome her daughter-in-law to her new home. I agreed to wed in his hometown of Islamabad. I tried to accept this idea.

I was in such mania. My brother had a nervous breakdown for me, becoming seriously ill. I asked God, "Why?"

Why this calamity upon my brother? I sat on the *janamaz,* the prayer rug, my *dupatta* pulled tightly over my hair and tucked behind my ears.

Was he haunted by the curse I'd made when we visited India years earlier? "I wish you'd die!" I had said, jealous because I was sick and he was outside enjoying himself. Could trauma from the malaria that he got soon after have stayed with him for years? Allah, I was repentant.

"Please bring peace and balance to my brother's mind."

Even though my fiancé had had sex with girlfriends, he and I chose to do everything but. Afterward, one time, I told the man I was about to marry, "I'm so in love with you."

He stirred. What sweet words would come from him?

"I think I'll jump in the shower."

My heart fell to the pit of my stomach as he rolled away from me.

I wrapped my drinking glasses in the *New York Times* Sunday newspaper and tucked them into juice boxes I picked up from Jewel, my neighborhood grocery store. I was turning my life upside down in one month's time. I had just left my sweet blond boyfriend. I had gotten engaged to another man. I was about to leave my dream apartment in a 1920s building off Chicago's Lake Michigan and move into my fiancé's apartment in Chevy Chase, Maryland, on the fifteenth floor of Highland House West, opposite a Jewish community center. It was the kind of sterile high-rise apartment building I had told my Chicago real estate agent never to show me. I went shopping for the first time at the professional woman's store, Ann Taylor, to buy a dress to interview for a new job that I got in the *Wall Street Journal* Washington bureau.

I went through with a traditional engagement ceremony on the new wooden deck built onto my childhood home. Bhabi wrapped my girlfriends in her and my mother's silk wedding saris. My girlfriends were worldly adventurers, Vasia from Greece, Chiyo from Japan, Pam from Seattle, Nancy from Birmingham, Alabama, and Sumita from Morgantown via her ancestral in Bihar, India. I centered paste-on paisleys, called *bindhis,* my mother brought from her store, Ain's, on their foreheads, between their eyes. I had no idea what these markings meant, but my friends looked like exotic princesses.

"You put one on, too!" Sumita coaxed me.

"Nooooo! That's okay." I was a Muslim girl. We didn't wear *bindhis.*

When my fiancé put the engagement ring on my finger, my friends and family applauded. We were bold. Traditionally, the boy's mother put the engagement ring on the girl, since the bride and the groom saw each other for the first time on their wedding day.

Bhabi was returning to India for the first time. She would take Safiyyah, her and my brother's first child. Safiyyah crawled on the ground and tried to eat the cat food. She was to be parted for the first time from her dada, dadi, and father. She cried and refused to sleep. I consciously knew for the first time the depth of emotions of a girl less than two.

My mother did something I hadn't heard her do since I shushed her into silence. She sang. I heard her through the door to the living room. Somewhere inside of me the song was familiar. It was as if I could remember the gentle lullabies she sang to me as a child before she left India. Tears sprang from a well I didn't know existed.

By day, I was a warrior. After Bill Clinton won office, I switched beats to cover international trade, exposing a behind-the-scenes smear campaign against a trade attorney vying for appointment as U.S. trade representative. I ran around town, digging up details for the story, including a document slipped to me in a brown envelope in an elevator. At home I was a different person. I sobbed, readying myself for this wedding I was beginning to understand should not happen. But suffering was what I saw staring back at me in my mother's eyes in her bridal photo. The understanding and devotion showered upon me by my last boyfriend haunted me. I tried once to reach out to him in a postcard on which I added "P.S." from Billlie and Billluh in the crooked handwriting of my left hand. It was meant to look like the scribbles of a cat if he got a pen in his paws. I never heard back.

I wept as I packed, but I figured if I endured this marriage would endure. It was the path of the Indian woman, to suffer, to survive, to endure. I plucked a white sweater studded with white beads from the rack at Neiman Marcus. It was long enough to cover my butt when I landed in Islamabad, Pakistan, an act of modesty.

The three days of wedding festivities took on a momentum beyond my control. I allowed my relatives, mostly my father's side, who had migrated to Pakistan from India, to drape a bright golden yellow *dupatta* over me like a shroud. It was for the *mehndi* ceremony where my first cousins gathered on the ground to sing songs making fun of the family into which I was to marry. The other family retorted with their own songs. I only knew because I peeked out from beneath my veil. I sat on a chair with tall cardboard tubes tied to the back and decorated with bright gold wrapping paper and green tinsel to make the chair resemble a throne. I wore only *kajal*, kohl eyeliner, and pink lipstick. This was supposed to be the plain me before I was decorated for my wedding.

Much later, I looked again at the silver ribbons sewn like endless diamonds on the fabric of my *dupatta*. I saw in them the shimmer that glittered from the stainless-steel wires around Cheenie Bhai's cage. Golden sequins were strung in the middle of each diamond with orange thread. They reminded me later of the shiny grapes I tucked between the wires of Cheenie Bhai's cage. At that time in Islamabad, though, I saw only a blur of yellow and orange in front of me.

I tried to talk to one of my cousins from under my golden veil. A phuppi, my father's sister, came over to scold me. "Stay quiet for at least one night."

I felt sick to my stomach.

Two days later, I sat in a chair at the Mee Lee Beauty Parlour run by an immigrant from China, Mrs. Lee Chu Liu. A hairdresser caked foundation on my face like I'd worn only once before, when I'd had a free makeover at a Merle Norman beauty salon in New York City. My mother watched anxiously as they sprayed my hair into a high bun five inches above my head so that my heavy wedding *dupatta* wouldn't lie flat upon me, making me look more peasant girl than princess.

"Now, we wax your arms and bleach your face," the hairdresser told me, ever so enthusiastically.

I protested.

"Yes, yes, you'll look more fair and more beautiful," she said.

My cousins uttered not a word. No one jumped to my defense to shield my arms from this violence and my face from this violation. I did it myself, refusing a tradition meant to beautify me in the ways that were important here, smooth skin and fair skin.

It was more a wedding factory than a beauty parlor. Brides in various stages of preparation sat around me like tulip bulbs ready to pop open under the sun lamps of hair dryers. We resembled each other. Red streaked their cheeks. And mine. Glossy strawberry lipstick enflamed their lips. And mine. Pitch-black *kajal* lined their eyes. And mine. It was something my dadi had put on my eyes and even my brother's eyes since we were infants to ward off evil.

I walked with stutter steps and a beaming smile to the front door of the Margala Motel, white lights strung upon its edges like bead necklaces. I was getting married in a motel? I tried to forget that fact. Traditional brides weren't supposed to beam. But I didn't want photos without a smile, like in my mother's wedding. I wore six rows of shiny twenty-four-karat gold necklaces from a wide jeweled choker down to the heavy necklace my mother-in-law had worn on her wedding day. I resembled a dark ruby set in gold. The *dupatta,* embroidered heavily with gold, lay like a weight upon my head. A golden *teeka,* like the one my mother wore, rested in the middle of my forehead. The *dupatta* flowed over a heavy velvet *shalwar kameez.* My doting phuppis flocked around me like peacocks in bright saris, wearing twenty-four-karat gold jewelry pulled out of their safe deposit boxes for the night.

"*Bay-toh, bay-tee,*" they instructed me. "Sit, dear."

They urged me onto a royal red sofa with golden curls edging it like a gilded frame that should have encircled a black velvet Elvis painting. Instead, it was I sitting inside this golden frame like an actress upon a dais in front of three hundred guests assembled in rows as if they were about to watch a theater production. I refused to sit in the side room where the bride usually waited for the *nikah nama* papers of a Muslim marriage to be signed, the bride and groom traditionally separated from each other in different rooms. In front of me were more strangers than familiar faces. The celebrity guest was the wife of the Pakistani army chief, a general and a phuppi's brother-in-law. I sat quietly under instructions to utter little.

The *barat,* the groom and his party, arrived, leading the man I was to marry into the side room usually reserved for the bride. Since I insisted I wouldn't be shuttled to the side room, he went there.

A few days before, I had told my father and Baray Abu, meaning father's eldest brother, "I want women witnesses." Under Islamic law, I had to have two witnesses. In Islamic law, two women equaled one witness. "We'll see," he'd told me.

Now, as they brought the *nikah nama* to sign, an uncle, my grandmother, and youngest aunt, Ishrat Aunty, gathered beside me. My eyes scanned this curious document. Line number five asked, "Whether bride is a vergin, widow or divorced," *virgin* spelled incorrectly. VIRGIN was typed in capital letters as if writing it boldly would make it true. Line number thirteen asked, "The amount of Mahar."

FATIMI was typed beside it in bold letters.

It was said the Prophet Muhammad asked his future son-in-law, Ali, for only a small wedding dowry, the proceeds from the sale of a shield, for his daughter Fatima. Doing the same now wore her name, as if making it virtuous. I signed. My dadi signed as half a witness, her hand grazing the page from right to left as she wrote her name in Urdu script. Ishrat Aunty followed, as the other half of a witness.

Moments passed.

A flurry of action filled the room. Seated there alone, my head bowed under the weight of my *dupatta,* I had just been wed to the man in the next room. My fiancé had become the man I married. It was sometimes the bride led to the groom, a heavy *dupatta* veiling her face. This time, it was the groom led to the bride. He wore garlands of red roses and white jasmine flowers over his dark *sherwani* with its high collar and regal air. His father led him into the giant ballroom, surrounded by my uncles, cousins, and my pensive father. A cone of a towering silver turban sat on his head with a gold ribbon coiling around its base like a serpent, a stiff plume over his left ear reaching to the sky.

When our eyes met, I smiled. My marriage was the completion of my struggle to bridge my culture with my adopted country, I thought. Brides are supposed to cry when they walk toward the car that will take them to their groom's house. I didn't cry. I figured he should cry. We were returning to America. He was the one who would be living far from his family. Not me. My father's wrist curled from the weight of a Qur'an he held for us to walk under. As someone else took hold of the Qur'an, it slipped and fell on my head before Ishrat Aunty, my father's youngest sister, caught it. Was God trying to tell me something?

With huge ceremony I was led to my in-laws' house. The doors were massive wooden double doors with intricate carvings. Red rose petals showered upon the man I married and me as we stepped out of a gray Honda. A black *bukrah,* a goat, on a chain greeted me. It was the goat to be sacrificed for the wedding. My new *sas,* my mother-in-law, opened both doors as she dreamed of doing. The man I married carried me inside in his arms. My mother-in-law fed me milk, a symbol of fertility. His relations handed me gifts of jewelry and envelopes of cash that I was told to pass to my father-in-law. I did.

The man I married led me to the wedding room that had been decorated for the night. Garlands of white jasmine flowers hung from the bed as if it were wearing a thousand strands of pearls. A few days before, I had asked Omar to arrange to have us spend the wedding night away from his parents' house. When I saw the bed I wanted to stay there. It had the magic and scent of romance.

But he had already hatched an escape plan. He sneaked me away from the relatives strewn like a big slumber party in the front hall. We arrived at the Marriott Islamabad, a sweeping hotel with brass doors leading to a glittering lobby. He took me upstairs and opened the door on a sterile room with two double beds and without the garlands of jasmine. I lay on the bed closest to the window. He pressed a button on a tape player. The theme song from *Beauty and the Beast* dripped out, as we did that which we had avoided during our engagement.

The next day I went to another hairdresser. I was told this one was where Benazir Bhutto supposedly had her hair curled before her marriage to a mediocre polo player. Now she was under house arrest for crimes aplenty during her tenure as Pakistan's first and only woman prime minister. I insisted on light makeup. Subtle pink lined my lips tonight. It was my *walima,* the reception thrown by the groom's family to mark the consummation of the marriage. I broke tradition and walked around the reception. Traditional brides sat quietly. I couldn't do that.

We returned to my husband's house. It was quiet when his father turned to me, as we sat in the front hall.

"You are a Muslim. You must speak Urdu. You are Pakistani," my husband's father told me.

I stayed silent, but his proclamation infuriated me. My identity was instantly being remade to mimic the bumper stickers I'd seen in the bazaar proclaiming national pride. "PROUD TO LIVE IN PAKISTAN." "GOD BLESS PAKISTAN AND PLEASE HURRY!" I didn't like it.

The man I married turned out to be my emotional nightmare, and I his. We were incompatible. I had too many ghosts to be patient with his emotional distance. He was too young to know how to soothe me. The black-and-white image of my mother, her eyes downcast in her wedding picture, haunted me.

Within four months, I'd borne all I could bear and slipped into depression. I dispatched my friend Rachel Kessler, a buoyant, cheerful pal, to buy me books about overcoming depression.

My parents took me to a psychiatrist. He recommended a psychologist, Dr. Donna Kozuch, whose name my father scribbled on the back of a flyer advertising a four-session program, STEP, Systematic Training for Effective Parenting. She was next door to the Holiday Inn in a sterile office building. But she filled her office with antiques and magazines like *People* and *Good Housekeeping*. She was commanding as she welcomed us with a firm handshake. Her hair was a wildly tousled mix of blond and brown. Her face had the seams of a woman who had stitched much fun in the sun into her life.

Dr. Kozuch heard my story. "You don't have depression," she told me. "A woman who's depressed doesn't get a pile of books to research depression. You're just in a depressing situation. Get out!"

I was stunned and shocked. Get out? But we didn't do that. We suffered. We endured. But I wasn't enduring. I was suffering.

I feared the wrath of failing my parents. I was clearly not yet wise about such things. "We don't care about the marriage," my father told me, his face twisted in anguish, but his eyes gentle with love. "We care about you."

I went home to Morgantown to recuperate. When I returned, I still wasn't ready to leave my marriage. The man I married agreed to meet me. He picked Hoolihan's behind our apartment building. It was the kind of chain restaurant that I avoided. But I agreed. I made sure I looked pretty, putting some pink lipstick upon my bare lips.

I walked past the bar and cheesy wall prints and saw him waiting for me in a side room at a table for two, his back against the wall. His eyes looked vacant. His face, weary. Bags hung from his eyes the way they sometimes hang from the underbelly of a woman's behind. I took a seat across from him and offered a weak smile. Wary. Weary. I, too, had gone through hell.

I started, gingerly: "I'm willing to give it a try."

He was flat in his response. "I'm not."

"What?"

"I'm not. It's too much work."

"What?" I couldn't believe my ears.

He pushed his chair back, as if about to leave.

"You're walking away?"

"It's too much work."

"What about the promise to make this forever?"

"That was then. This is now."

"This is now?" I was stunned that he was abandoning the marriage.

He pushed his chair back completely and bolted. He ran out onto the patio. There was no way out. Even more stunned, I watched him hurdle over the black metal railing around the patio. And he kept on running. I ran around the side entrance, chasing after him. I didn't know that I wasn't supposed to do such things. This was my marriage. I couldn't let go that easily. I made a commitment. He couldn't just run away. But he was running away. Literally.

Forever never was.

Defeated, I turned around and returned to my apartment where my parents listened to my tale, as stunned as I was as I related it to them.

I moved out. Some days later, I made an appointment to return to my apartment with my childhood friend Sumita to collect some of my things. The man I married appeared at the door rumpled and sluggish. He dragged himself back to a mattress laid in the corner of the living room upon the parquet floor. He lay in a crumble. I wanted to help him.

Ingrained in me was the message that suffering was the natural destiny of the women of India. We didn't leave our marriages. My heart still belonged to the man I wed. I didn't want to abandon him.

I stayed the night, massaging his headache away and nursing him with Sudafed. Cautiously, I lay beside him for the first time in weeks, our bodies barely touching as I drifted in and out of tense sleep. In the darkness of the night, I felt him edge closer to me. My heart rose in hope. Perhaps the vision that brought us together could be realized.

I allowed myself to be available to him as a wife to her husband. His familiar breath lay on the back of my neck as he breathed heavily upon me. When he collapsed and lay still, my heart hoped his intimacy consummated both of our desires for reconciliation. Then, he slowly crept up from the mattress.

I lay alone. I heard the bathroom door click shut. Moments passed. I waited for him. He didn't emerge. The morning sun crept in through the slits in the blinds. It cast a shadow over my heart. I gathered my strength to rise, and I tapped on the door. I heard his voice, muffled by the door. Two words emerged: "I'm sorry," punctuated by a meek plea: "Don't hold it against me."

Then, uttered with the next breath, the finality: "Leave."

The sun had risen and set on my heart. It was my first one-night stand. And it was with my husband.

His parents flew into the country. I had moved with Sumita into an apartment with just the style I liked on Seventeenth Street in the heart of Washington's Dupont Circle. Wood floors, high ceilings, and an eclectic street of gay bars and the 7-Eleven. Our apartment was in a historic building called the Whyland. My therapist didn't miss the irony of its name at this juncture in my life. My father and his father talked over the phone. My parents didn't want me to meet his family in person for fear they would try to humiliate me by having their son declare his divorce, Muslim style, uttering the words, *"Talaaq. Talaaq. Talaaq,"* meaning, "I divorce you. I divorce you. I divorce you."

His father asked, "Did she cook breakfast, lunch, and dinner for him?"

My father explained, "This is America. Both of them work all day. At home, men and women share jobs."

"If my son ever cooks, I will chop off his hands!" his father shouted into the phone.

I didn't understand what was happening. Much later, my mother told me that a cousin-brother who had once criticized me for baring my arms in my Morgantown High track uniform told her, "No matter if you're a journalist or a medical doctor, you have to cook for your husband."

Not long after, I got a call from his father. "It's over," he told me in a deep voice. "Omar doesn't want to try."

I didn't know what to say. "This is an unusual way to hear the news." I paused. His father said nothing. "If this is the way Omar wants to do it, fine. I don't have much more to say."

I collapsed into my bed, in tears. My father prayed two *rakats,* or complete prostrations, of a prayer called *shukranah,* meaning "thanks." He was grateful to God that I had survived the emotional prison of this marriage.

My parents took me to the Masjid Al Hijra in the suburban Virginia neighborhood of Falls Church. A Sudanese imam told me that a man seeking divorce couldn't have sex with his wife. I was finally starting to understand that a life with the man I married was not the life for me. I also knew that I was a gem that he had thrown back into the ocean. My luster would radiate forever. I made a pledge that it must. I had to believe my own pep talk.

CHAPTER 4

From the West to the East

"**N**EXT!" I SHOUTED.

I had abandoned any hope that the East offered me a spiritual union of anything to do with love and sex. I was finding my new life at the Mall behind the Lincoln Memorial in Washington, D.C., with the most unexpected of activities: beach volleyball. I'd played volleyball at Morgantown High, making the team not because I had any talents but because Coach Rice liked the way I sacrificed my body to reach balls before they hit the gym floor. I was perfect for volleyball on the beach.

The Mall to D.C. volleyball players is a grassy inlet tucked between a triangle of roads that lead to Rock Creek Parkway, the Arlington Bridge, and downtown D.C. Dug into the lawn are rows of volleyball courts filled with a mix of sand and gravel. I ventured down to the Mall one Saturday morning with my new pal, Danny Pearl, who had just moved to Washington from the *Journal*'s Atlanta bureau. The child of immigrant parents, like me, he had a father who was also a professor, and he was tall and handsome with a playful smile and a ready laugh. We discovered an informal hierarchy on the courts. The outer courts closer to the Lincoln Memorial were left for beginning B-level players. Farther from the memorial, the play got better. We started on the outer courts, Danny helping me unleash the leftover rage from my marriage and heal with one of the best therapies possible: play. Danny hurled himself at any ball, sacrificing leg and limb just so the ball wouldn't hit the sand. "You fly!" I exclaimed as Danny shocked me with one soaring defensive save after the next.

"Mine!" I screamed, to claim the ball, when a serve came across the court to me.

Meanwhile, I tried to find bliss the modern Western way, dating a trail of ill-suited boyfriends who followed my ill-fated marriage. Danny helped me host the first party I ever threw, the theme, "A Midsummer

Night's Prom," for the high school prom I had never attended. In all ways visible, I counteracted my upbringing. I sent my mother the billowy "Made in India" cotton skirts I'd been wearing since my graduation day as a college senior, the first day I wore not only a skirt but also nail polish since my childhood. Like the skirts of my twenties, it fell to my ankles. "Make them miniskirts, please," I asked my mother. She complied, even though her legs had never seen the sun.

In volleyball, we called "Next" when we wanted to play. I applied that principle to my love life. At my Wednesday morning sessions with Dr. Kozuch, I learned an important lesson—to do what I wanted to do, not what I should do.

I ran as far away from the Marriott Islamabad as I could get. A DHL package sat inside my mail slot one day at work. I took it back to my cubicle and pulled out a brown paper envelope. Inside the envelope was a single page marked at the top with the crescent and star, the symbol of Islam. The words FIFTEEN RUPEES spread like a flag fluttering over ornate scrolls. That converted to about twenty-five cents. The man I married declared that he said before witnesses the magic words of *talaaq,* divorce, in Islam: "I divorce Asra Nomani. I divorce Asra Nomani. I divorce Asra Nomani."

The document minced no words: "She is a stranger to me." I saw my husband's familiar signature below the words. I tucked the divorce paper back into the envelope, relieved. After work, I did what came naturally to me now. I ran down to the volleyball courts and called, "Next."

Years of play followed until I moved to New York to be near the virgin boyfriend and my cousin-sister Lucy arrived to rescue me from my despair.

When Ken approached me with the Tantra assignment I remembered what Lucy's father, Iftikhar Mamoo, had told me about the power of my writing: "If the real world is bad, you can create a new world." I realized that I had to create a new world for myself. I decided to make Ken's assignment my road map to a new future with the hapless stops in Canada and Santa Cruz, California, as the first on my itinerary.

If I was going to do this right, I had to go to the source. I set my eyes on India. Writing about Tantra became the excuse with which I could journey back in time across the Atlantic to my native land. At first, it truly wasn't much more than an excuse. Tantra's principles about finding the divine within a soul mate and the self appealed to me, but I was by no means a convert.

When I left New York to return to my home in West Virginia in the hills of Appalachia, my sister-in-law, Azeem Bhabi, wanted to see the Golden Temple that the controversial Hare Krishnas had built years earlier in a West Virginia rural enclave just hours north from us in a town called Moundsville.

We set off in our blue Chrysler minivan, my mother, Bhabi and her children, Safiyyah, now eight and Samir, now six, and me, winding our way over narrow West Virginia roads. Along the way, we pulled over to watch the sun descend into the hills, and joy welled up within me, for the company I had with me was purer than any I could imagine. *Shakti,* the Sanskrit word, is supposed to be divine female energy or power. To me, this car was filled with shakti. My mother sat beside me. To me, she was my raw shakti.

When I read about the goddesses of Tantra, I thought of my mother. I learned of Lakshminkara, who represented a female deity known as the Severed-Headed Vajrayogini. In my mother's family, as in most of traditional India, the women tied their hair in a single braid that ran down their backs. Islam considers hair a symbol of seduction, thus ordering women to hide their hair. It's a tradition in Hindu and Buddhist cultures, too, to plait the hair. Lakshminkara freed her hair from a braid. My mother, too, loosened her hair during my teen years as she saw me standing up for her and challenging the rules as she knew them. The severed head meant the slaying of dualistic thinking. Like Lakshminkara, my mother reached deep within herself to liberate herself and others, in ways small and big. One night, when my mother and I were tired, we saw there was only enough food for a full meal for either us or my father and brother. "Let's eat it," I said, rejecting the tradition of feeding men first. We ate part of it, leaving enough for my father and brother. A friend of my mother's laughed heartily at the tale when my mother recollected it for her later. "You're more liberated than all of us," she told my mother.

My mother freed my father from the traditional definition of manhood by refusing to accept the roles that her culture told her would make her a devoted wife. She ran a boutique, which gave her economic independence none of her sisters ever experienced. Her personal determination gave her a will few women in her family asserted. To me, she was the female Buddha, beheading herself to slay the dualities that otherwise define men and women in my culture—the wife who sacrifices her personal self for her marriage and family, the husband who is obliged to financially support his extended family and cloak his emotions. More than anything else, my mother freed me. For my mother, her choices were not without detractors. My father's sisters judged her critically, and his nephews, staying at our house, made jokes at her expense about her control over my father, although he never complained. He always said his mother's strength made him respect powerful women.

When I entered a Mother's Day contest to write about my mother in twenty-five words or less, I wrote, "Coming from India in sari and sandals, she gave me the life she couldn't imagine. She inspired by example, breaking cultural boundaries, setting me free." My mother laughed that she didn't literally wear sandals because of America's winters, and I lost the contest to a boy with cancer whose mother took care of him, but my appreciation was solid.

I looked over at Bhabi in the backseat with her children, and I was in awe of the personal journey she had traveled. Until she was married, Bhabi never emerged in public without first cloaking herself in her black *burqa,* following the rule set by her father, a kind but orthodox Muslim. A young beauty with lush black hair and infectious laughter, she accepted without protest an arranged marriage to my brother that would send her thousands of miles away to America to live with a stranger and his family. My liberal parents freed her from traditional restrictions, and, in an ironic way, while my brother loved her dearly, his delicate situation propelled her toward even more independence. She didn't completely understand this stranger who was her husband, but she was intuitively compassionate to him beyond anything I had ever seen. Fittingly, she was studying at West Virginia University's School of Nursing, destined one day to trade in her black *burqa* for the white uniform of a nurse.

In Tibetan Tantric Buddhism, I had learned there were twenty-one female deities manifested in the form of a goddess named Tara. She was the most adored of the deities. The ancient tales said that she was a woman just like any woman. Many ages ago, she took the bodhisattva vow to work for the benefit of all beings until all were enlightened. Embodying compassion, she was known as White Tara. Bhabi was the White Tara I knew in my life.

We snaked through the hills and found the Golden Temple, a place where the men and women walked in robes with shaved heads except for tails of hair descending from the crown. One of the men told us the story of Krishna. We didn't buy his exaltation of this god my mother spoke disparagingly about because of his many dalliances with women and girls who were *gopis,* or goat herders. "A playboy," she called him. What I didn't know was that Krishna is supposed to represent the aspect of God, or the divine, that attracts us, whether it's his creation of the moon or the latest BMW series. And the dalliances are supposed to symbolize the way God loves all creation. The man led us into a large room lined with statues, just like Virgin Mary manger scenes, only these statues were shimmering with gold and silver, devotees decorating them with garlands.

A chant and buzz rang through the air. We looked around, trying to figure it out. The Krishna devotees were breaking into a frenzied dance. Bhabi always wanted to dance, something not allowed in her conservative upbringing. I figured no time better than the present. We jumped with the disciples to their chants of "Hare Rama Hare Krishna Hare Hare Rama Hare Hare Krishna." What was this all about? My mother jumped with us, too, flailing her arms around and ticktocking her head. If only her mother could see her now.

I didn't know it, but we were flailing ourselves in something called a *kirtan.* Unlike a *bhajan,* which is organized singing, a *kirtan* is supposed to be an ecstatic, free form of expression, much like the Native American sun dance and Sufi dervish dancing, which changes the state of awareness, much like meditation is supposed to do.

Let's admit it. The Nomani family wasn't quite ready to flow for too long without reservation. But we danced enough to have smiles on our faces as we slipped out of the room. Safiyyah bought herself a little purse to dangle on her wrist with "Hare Rama Hare Krishna" stitched onto the side in cursive. We didn't know she was supposed to drop her prayer beads inside and chant her mantra quietly to herself, using the bag to hide the movement of each bead under her fingers. She figured it'd be a cute place to put her Barbie lipstick.

Before leaving, we pulled our minivan close to a lake where devotees were gathering. A bonfire raged at lake's edge. The stars splashed overhead, turning the sparklers passed to us into starbursts. Bhabi, my mother, Samir, and I twirled them. Shivering, Safiyyah wilted in my arms but still twirled her sparkler. Swans glided in small patches of water not frozen over on this lake. Then flashes of fireworks ignited the blackened ceiling of stars. I couldn't have scripted the beauty of this celebration, bringing in the new millennium for the Nomani family.

With the new year, I started asking my parents about roots I had never cared to pull at before.

I learned it included a rich mystical past. I was the twenty-second generation traced back on my paternal side to Raja Turloq Chund, a Hindu prince who ruled the state of Rajpathuna between Gujarat and Rajasthan in western India, on the southern edge of the Indus Valley where Tantra began.

The Rajputs were a warrior caste with a committed and almost fanatical belief in the principles of chivalry, both in war and in running the state. It was their obsession with honor that helped me understand my stubborn difficulty in excusing what I deemed dishonorable acts. They were like the knights of medieval Europe. The Rajputs fought foreign intrusions into their land but couldn't coordinate their powers enough to battle superior forces over a long time. They became folded into the Mogul Empire, but their skills in battle were much appreciated and they were considered among the best of the warriors in the emperors' armies.

My ancestors spread from the north of India to the state of Uttar Pradesh, where temple bells echo over farmlands, dark-skinned peasants till fields, and the city of Agra sits in the western corner with the Taj Mahal as its crown jewel. It is a region known as the Hindu Belt for its coveted place in Hinduism. It is India's most populated state with a population the size of Brazil, producing many of India's prime ministers. The

Ganges River, the holiest river in Hinduism, cuts a swath through the middle of the region. Four of Hinduism's seven holy towns are in Uttar Pradesh, the most important of which is Benares, renamed Varanasi by Hindu leaders.

The soldiers of the Muslim sultans conquered lands in India. And great sheiks, or *pirs,* of the Sufi orders converted Indians to Islam from Hinduism. The Sufis were the mystics of Islam, most commonly known to the west as the whirling dervishes of the Ottoman Empire. Their spiritual philosophy taught followers to be aware of the presence of the divine in each moment.

It wasn't Tantra. But it had a similar message that followers should experience ecstasy of the divine to the fullest. The sheikh taught *zikr,* or remembrance of God, sometimes simply by repeating words like *Allahu,* meaning God, the divine essence, to a prescribed pattern of breathing and head movements, much like the teachings of Tantra.

The special teachings also descended from the sheiks to the disciples, some of whom the sheiks would anoint to teach others, as in Tantra. Because of Islam's strong disapproval of celibacy, the sheiks had a strong chain of succession from father to son, and Sufis established orders that usually spread through different territories. The tombs of the order's saints became centers of pilgrimage, like temples became holy sites to Tantrikas.

In the 1700s, I estimated, an encampment of Sufis settled just a mile outside my ancestral village of Bindwal. "Wherever you turn there is the face of God," I imagined the sheik told the men and women gathered in the darkness around a campfire of branches and cotton rags. Six generations before my birth, on my father's side, Thakur Shivraj Singh lived as part of the Rajputs. Thakur was the common name for landowners, and Shivraj was a blending of the Hindu god Shiva and *raja,* meaning "lord." Late one night, family folklore went, after a day of hunting in the jungles surrounding the village, Thakur Shivraj Singh jumped off his horse at his home and rushed into the kitchen, mindlessly keeping his boots on from his day's journey rather than respecting the Hindu tradition of leaving the shoes at the door. His brother's wife saw this insult with horror and questioned whether he had adopted the ways of the Muslim invaders who most often did not leave their shoes behind them.

"Are you a Turk?" she asked him, scolding him with her eyes.

Thakur Shivraj Singh stopped in his tracks. He studied her face, contorted in disrespect. While crude, her question went to the heart of where his identity and soul lay. He stared at her as she kneaded the dough for *roti* beneath her knuckles.

"I do not belong here," he told himself. "This is not my place."

He felt a peace with the Sufi dervishes with whom he had talked for hours around the campfire. His hunger for food left him. He rushed outside onto his horse and galloped to the campfires.

"I submit to the will of Allah," he proclaimed to the dervishes, who welcomed him into their encampment. That dark night by the light of only the moon and the campfire, he changed his name to the Muslim name Sirajuddin.

I listened to my father tell me the story and couldn't help but feel like a modern-day Rajput Sufi princess.

In a strange way, Thakur Shivraj Singh led me to Honesdale, Pennsylvania.

After my Tantra story ran in the *Wall Street Journal,* a marketing man, Bill Boos, sent me a copy of a book, *Tantra Unveiled,* by a man called Pandit Rajmani Tigunaut, spiritual director of a place called the Himalayan Institute. He was a University of Pennsylvania PhD graduate who taught Tantra according to the Vedic principles. The book mentioned sex only once as something that purist Tantrics didn't practice. I had had the book for a year without cracking it open, until I began planning my trip to India and pulled it off the shelf. I called the institute. That coming weekend, there was an "Introduction to Meditation" workshop.

I talked to the pandit. I didn't even know that *pandit* was an honorific that said this man came from the highest Hindu caste, the Brahmins, who were the scholars and caretakers of temples in India. I just figured it was his first name. He invited me to come. "Bring your *mataji* and *pitaji,*" he said. I didn't know who he was talking about.

My dad agreed to go with me. Turned out he was my *pitaji,* or "father" in Hindi, the language of Hindus. The Urdu spoken by Muslims is very much the same as the Hindi spoken by Hindus, although Urdu writing is like Arabic text, compared to the Sanskrit text of Hindi. But I found that some important words differentiate Hindus from Muslims. *Pitaji* is *abba* to a Muslim. *Mataji* is *ammi.*

The guru of the Himalayan Institute was a man called Swami Rama of the Himalayas. A big tennis player and smoker, he came from India and set up the Himalayan Institute in the eastern Pennsylvania mountains in a small town called Honesdale. There, Swami Rama was simply "Swamiji." The institute said he had died a few years before. A dark secret lurked on these grounds about Swamiji. Few dared mention it, but the Himalayan Institute had lost a $1.9 million lawsuit filed by a young woman who testified that Swami Rama had seduced and raped her as a nineteen-year-old virgin, claiming he could heal her of physical ailments when she came to the institute.

My father drove our Chrysler minivan over the roads blanketed with a fresh snow. We turned into the compound, where a staffperson ushered us to a comfortable home. We went straight to our first session and folded our legs beneath ourselves on the floor. My father sat beside me in Western shirt and pants.

We learned about something called *sadhana.* It was a part of Tantra, and it was a Sanskrit word that meant "means for attainment" of a state somewhere between relaxed and concentrated. I was looking for a practice that could just make me a lot less irritable. And I didn't want to find the answer with Prozac. When we returned to our chalet without the ski resort, I scolded my father, "Why do you have to ask so many questions? This isn't your classroom! Don't talk so much!" I wasn't proud of my relationship with my father. I didn't understand him well.

My questions about sacred and divine love were leading us, as a family, into territories usually left untouched. My father was a man brave enough to bare his soul. He threw his body to the ground and wept. "When I first had sex with your mother I thought she was my spiritual soul mate." But my mother, it seemed, didn't like having her virginity stripped from her without her being ready.

"She has taunted me for thirty years for having sex with her on the wedding night."

Since I started the Tantra assignment she had stopped, he said. "Maybe she sees that sex is a normal thing." I thought about my *Journal*

front-page middle-column story the year before about the demise of sex
on the wedding night as more couples, already having consummated
their relationships, spent the night partying with the friends they hadn't
seen for years. Maybe my mother read that story and saw that most couples
are expected to have sex on their wedding nights. The truth was that I
also understand my mother's sense of violation. She went into her wedding night with romantic notions of her husband's devotion to her. What
she heard was his loyalty to a mission serving his family and humanity.
Not the words of the Barbara Cartland romances my mother read growing up in Panchgani.

But my father was always a man trying his best. My mother told me
the story that not long after their wedding night, my father showed her a
Buddha calendar that sat beside him as he studied. She didn't care about
Buddha. She wanted romance. My father finally put it away. But that
didn't mean he kept Buddha's philosophies out of his heart. With a belly
in his early thirties to match that of the Happy Buddha and principles of
serving humanity, my father was always like a selfless Buddha, struggling
like any man with the frustrations of life on this earth.

For the next session, my father changed into the white *kurta* and *py-
jama* that is the traditional attire of Muslim men on the subcontinent.

Luke, the meditation instructor, advised us to move our breath from
our mouth through our body. My dad raised his hand. No. Not again.

"The breath doesn't actually move. You should say, 'Visualize your
breath moving.'" I had to admit that my father made sense. His advice
stayed with me every time someone told me to move my breath through
my body.

The pandit met with me privately in his office.

My father had told him about our ancestry. The pandit had advice for
me as I traveled in India: Many of the Hindu pandits wouldn't want to
teach a Muslim. He looked at me from across his desk, his hands folded
together, and offered his suggestion for my Tantra travel: "Tell them your
ancestor was a Rajput, Thakur Shivraj Singh."

I nodded my head, accepting his advice.

On the way home, following snowy roads, I got impatient as my
father drove slowly. I wrote into my notebook that I didn't want enlight-

enment. My only goal over the next year was to simply stay calm even when my father braked for green lights. I looked over at this amazing man who had driven these treacherous roads to help me expand my mind. I wanted to one day be able to express my appreciation to my father with the simple act of showing him respect and patience. Could I accomplish such a humble, yet distant, goal?

Stress consumed me as I readied for this pioneer journey to India on my own. I wheeled a shopping cart through Wal-Mart, throwing in Cover Girl lipsticks and barrettes marketed by *Sixteen* magazine as gifts for my vast network of relatives.

What clothes to wear? Western? Traditional? *Shalwar kameezes?* What sandals to wear? I didn't want to be obviously Western as I traipsed into temples. I was a wreck, but a wreck with a day-timer. At Office Depot, I bought my first day-timer, figuring the one marketed by *Chicken Soup for the Soul* was an appropriate theme. In Buddhist Tantra, a yogini often carries a knife with a carved handle and a blade shaped like a crescent. It's not meant to harm. But it is a meditative tool for slicing through illusion, negative energy, and ego with the sharp edge of wisdom. My father came through the door at my mother's store as I stood behind the counter. He handed me a bag from Pathfinder, a store down High Street. I pulled out a shiny red Swiss Army knife with sharp silver blades. I didn't have a blade the shape of a crescent. But I had scissors that flipped up.

A stranger walked through the store doors before my departure, a tall and slender man who seemed as if he could stretch himself into a pretzel. He wanted to see if there might be a market for handicrafts his wife might bring from their native Nepal if she got her visa approved to enter the U.S. He introduced himself as Deepak Pant.

I started talking to him about my study of Tantra. To my surprise, he told me he had studied Tantra. I couldn't believe my good fortune. Here, in Morgantown of all places. His wife's family had a Tantric guru. "Vishnu Uncle," he said.

I was excited, but Deepak warned me that walking down the path of Tantra could lead to a confrontation with dark realities that might not be pleasant or easy to endure. I had heard that in India, the most extreme of Tantrics spent their nights at cremation grounds, practicing rituals meant to overcome one of the greatest fears of humans, fear of death, even seizing the energy of the dead for their own energy. It wasn't much spoken about, but the most brazen of Tantrics were said to even have sex with the dead body of a woman, setting the body upon them as they sat in meditation posture. There were other dark elements, Deepak told me during visits to our house, that I would discover for myself.

Shivarathri was a Hindu holiday, he told me, important to Tantrics as a celebration of the god Shiva. Tantrics and disciples traveled by foot, bus, and train from throughout India to converge upon an ancient Shiva temple in his native Kathmandu, where his wife and family lived. Vishnu Uncle would likely be there, too.

He gave me a gift, a necklace of dark brown beads. "It is a *rhuda raksha*," Deepak explained. "Every Tantric must have a *rhuda raksha*." It was a protection of sorts. I sat at the top of the stairs to my childhood home as he wished me farewell and good luck on my journey. He turned around and looked at me earnestly. "Be careful." It's a dangerous world.

I giggled. "I will."

He said, "I'm serious."

CHAPTER 5

Worshiping the Lingam

MONKEYS WITH PINK-RED BOTTOMS glided from a temple rooftop to overhanging branches. A small rock stood before me where people stopped to pay their respects, touching the fingertips of their right hand first to the rock and then to their third eye. I did, too, though I didn't know why.

I was in Kathmandu on the occasion of Shivarathri with a brother of our Nepali friend Deepak and Prakash Joshi, a friend of Deepak's who taught at the chemistry department at Kathmandu University. Prakash paused in front of the rock and explained, "It's a Shiva lingam." At my Santa Cruz workshop I'd learned about the lingam, the Sanskrit term for a penis. This rock, then, was the phallic symbol of Lord Shiva's power. Worshiping the lingam amounted to worshiping Shiva and the male energy residing in all of us. But try to tell someone at Wal-Mart that you just bowed your head to a penis, and it doesn't translate so well.

I wove with Prakash and Deepak's brother on narrow pathways until we came to a long row of stone steps lined with skinny men naked except for loincloths covering their lingams. They were the babas and sadhus of Hinduism and Tantra. We sat on a brick wall across a slow, narrow, dirty creek from two-storied temple houses that resembled pagodas with gold-plated roofs. The buildings made up this temple, Pashupathinath, upon which thousands had descended. Hindus consider it one of the most sacred shrines in the world. A sign outside banned non-Hindus. Eastern Nepalese Kiranti rulers built the temple before the fourth century, but the temple got its current shape and design in the early eighteenth century. Inside sat a sacred lingam, although I couldn't pretend to really understand its significance.

Thousands of devotees stood in lines snaking around the main temple, waiting to go inside.

I was staying at the home of Deepak's wife, a modern, pretty woman named Nabina. At home, a middle-aged man in a saffron robe sat with Nabina's mother. He looked like he was in his forties but youthful. I whispered to Nabina, "Who is he?"

She answered, "Vishnu Uncle." I felt a bit in awe being so close to him. I didn't quite know why. I sat beside him on the *takht,* a wooden platform for sitting and sleeping.

I tried to introduce myself, explaining my acquaintance with Deepak back in Morgantown and my mission to learn about Tantra.

After I finished, he asked, "Who are you?"

I was confused by his question. I figured there was a right answer and I didn't know what it was. He gestured to a string around his neck to ask if my father wore a string like the one he wore as a Brahmin. I remembered what Pandit Tigunait advised me to say. "I am the descendant of a man named Thakur Suraj Singh." I even fumbled on his name, mispronouncing his middle name, Shivraj.

Vishnu Uncle smiled, pleased. He asked what I would give him for imparting knowledge to me.

"Love from my heart." This seemed to please Vishnu Uncle even more. Nabina clapped her hands in amusement. I was confused that somehow I had stumbled upon the right answers, but I felt like a fraud, not admitting I was Muslim. This truth burned inside me.

The Tantric texts say that a Tantrika has to be initiated by a guru, male or female, who belongs to a Tantric lineage. "If merely by drinking wine, men were to attain fulfillment, all addicted to liquor would reach perfection. . . . If liberation were to be ensured by sexual intercourse with a shakti, all creatures would be liberated by female companionship," says a text called the Kularnava Tantra. Followers of Tantra seek to adore these gurus. I had misled my potential guru with an inauthenticity about myself. I didn't think you were supposed to do that.

A commotion awakened me at 4 A.M. Vishnu Uncle was storming out of the house with his suitcase. I sat up and quietly watched. He was drunk. He said he didn't know what he could teach me.

He sobered up under the gentle coaxing of Nabina's mother. He told me, "We'll now go to the temple." I eagerly rose. Nabina's mother dispatched a nephew of hers as an escort. We slipped out into the dark early morning. Few people were on the street. As we walked past a karate school, Vishnu Uncle held my left hand with his right hand. It was a strange gesture in a culture where married men and women didn't even hold hands in public. But I didn't know the ways of these gurus, so I kept my hand in his.

As we arrived at the temple's gate, Vishnu Uncle gestured for me to cloak my head with my *dupatta*. He put his fingers to his lips. I was to stay quiet. He thrust into my hands a bowl made of leaves, filled with a garland of flowers and other bright objects. I walked past the sign that banned non-Hindus from the temple, glancing at it just slightly, and stepped through a set of silver-coated doors into the Pashupathinath Temple, an act that could have had me arrested and jailed because of my religion.

A haze of smoke inside the temple grounds hit us. Virtually naked babas lay sprawled on the ground, their skinny bodies stretching in all directions. We turned to the left where a crowd pulsed in front of a small door. Women pushed each other, holding onto shoulders with one hand and brandishing offerings with the other. The push of the crowd finally landed me at an opening to a shrine, only no one was allowed to enter but could only peer through the open window. A bleary-eyed boy sat on the ledge, his eyes dilated, staring at me. I wondered if he was high. The smell of marijuana was thick in the air. I watched the other women and mimicked them. Like them, I thrust my offering at the boy. He took it, tossed it behind him toward a statue so festooned in garlands I couldn't make out whether it was a man, woman, or lingam. He smeared my forehead between my eyebrows with a thick paste. It's written in Tantric ritual that Shakti dips her finger in red powder mixed with a little soapy water and oil. She places a red mark on the eyebrow center of those before her. She is given a mark, too. The mark symbolizes the levels of concentration and participation of the *ajna* chakra, or the psychic eye in the center of the forehead between the brows. It's written that if the *ajna* chakra is awakened, you will participate in the Tantric act without tension and without being blocked by emotions or shame or frivolity. The crowd pushed me away from this moment of illumination as quickly as it had thrust me there.

Vishnu Uncle beckoned me toward him. We swept past bodies strewn around, smoking water pipes, *hookas,* filled with hashish and tobacco. I knew I didn't want to experiment with drugs. Before I left New York, I'd had a night of morphing doors and pulsating lights after I'd tried brownies baked with marijuana. Before that, I'd ended a snowboarding vacation in Telluride, Colorado, after doing mushrooms at the Beaux Art Ball, a costume ball where I, along with other women, dressed in lingerie. It was my first time. I flew back to Washington, D.C., wearing shades the entire flight to shield myself from the light. My father drove my mother from Morgantown to nurse me back to health. One afternoon, as I sat outside the Dupont Circle Starbucks, I studied the flowers planted outside and muttered to my mother, "The flowers are soooooo pretty." I'd had enough bad experiences with illegal drugs. I didn't need a bad trip in Kathmandu.

We returned home in time for a Sunday outing Nabina and a sister had planned for me. I just got in the car, not knowing quite where we were headed. Vishnu Uncle wore his orange robe. Nabina and her sister, who had never traveled outside Nepal, were more modern in jeans and shirts than I appeared to be, still drowning in the tentlike *shalwar kameez* I'd been wearing when I stepped off the plane the day before. What was wrong with this picture?

On the ride there the lush green vistas were beautiful. They told me we were going to the Dakshinkali Temple, where every Tuesday and Saturday the local people give offerings of live animals—hens, goats, and buffalo—to the goddess Kali. The pandit's feet were said to bathe in flowing blood those days.

On the road outside the temple sat rows of stalls, where women sold flowers and other offerings to the goddess. Vishnu Uncle bought offerings and put them in our hands. He led us up many stairs that wound around the side of a steep hill. He gestured for me to go forward into an open-air room with a shrine at the end. I watched Nabina. She handed her offering to the man to the right of the statue and bowed her head to a goddess statue meant to be Kali. The man was the *pujari,* who oversees the rituals at the temple. I followed Nabina's cues and bowed my head to Kali. The *pujari* smeared the third eye on my forehead. I could feel the quake of my Muslim ancestors, for whom this was an unthinkable act. What would I tell my mother?

Nabina's sister sat in a corner of the room, her legs crossed in lotus position, eyes closed. I sat beside her, crossed my legs, and rested my hands on my knees, though I wasn't quite sure what I was doing. I figured she was meditating. I still didn't have a quiet practice, and the scene was strange to me.

Vishnu Uncle settled into a small veranda behind the Kali statue. He opened his cloth bag and pulled out a bottle of Bagpiper Whiskey.

He did what looked like hand tricks over the bottle. I discovered later they were *mudras,* symbolic hand gestures meant to harness energy. He insisted Nabina's sister take a shot. He insisted that I drink some, too. Images of villagers made blind by moonshine liquor deterred me. I insisted that I didn't want to join his drinking. Nabina's sister slipped Vishnu Uncle some money. I followed her lead and slipped him a thousand Nepali rupees.

Vishnu Uncle sat with me in his room later that evening, drinking more Bagpiper Whiskey and asking me what troubled me. It was stupid, but I told him that in transit to Kathmandu my mother had told me over the phone that my cat Billluh was lost. It was a crazy obsession, I admitted, but it was on my mind. He smiled patiently. "All will be fine."

At that moment, the phone rang. "For you, Asra," Nabina said.

It was my mother. "Billluh came back home!" My niece and nephew, Safiyyah and Samir, had spotted him from the backseat of the family minivan as my father pulled into the driveway. I was relieved. I had to wonder if Vishnu Uncle had special Tantric powers over lost cats thousands of miles away.

Vishnu Uncle and I walked again to Pashupathinath by rows of bazaar shops. We stopped to step into a tiny gem shop. He studied the gems and handed me one. "It will give you special powers." And then he told me a mantra. "Keep this for yourself."

I really didn't understand the phenomenon of mantras. A mantra is a name, syllable, or word used to connect with the mind. The sound of the mantra is supposed to create a vibration that is supposed to strengthen and relax the mind. The word is derived through Sanskrit from two

Indo-European words. *Man* means "to think" and comes from *manas,* which means "the mind." *Tra* comes from *trayate,* which means "to liberate." Mantras actually struck me as a bit freaky. I couldn't see myself actually believing in a mantra. That was something hippies did. Still, I wrote my new mantra on a brown paper bag I borrowed from the gem *walla,* seller.

We navigated through the grounds and ended at a small temple. In the center sat a brass lingam larger than any I'd seen in reality. I felt strange. Vishnu Uncle gestured for me to circle the lingam. I did. And then he told me to say my mantra over and over again in front of the lingam, as he continued to circle this huge brass penis, muttering mantras, I presumed, out of a small book he was holding. I had to admit, I didn't get it.

We slipped into a room facing the Pashupathi River where one very old man sat, coughing and hacking.

Vishnu Uncle introduced him as Pagal Baba, *pagal* meaning "crazy" in Hindi and Urdu. Water dripped from his eyes. A young man stood nearby as his attendant. Vishnu Uncle whispered something to him. He ran off and returned with *bhang,* a home brew mixed with *cannabis* and a favorite of the babas, along with Bagpiper Whiskey.

These babas were the saints of the subcontinent. What little I knew about sadhus made me leery of them, but here they became men with hometowns and families. As a child, I had seen them, walking slowly along the edge of the roads, leaning on crooked sticks, sometimes begging for money. They were also the bogeymen of India. When my mother was a child in Panchgani, the elders yelled, "The sadhu is coming! The sadhu is coming!" when they wanted to quiet the children down.

When I was nineteen years old, my brother, who was twenty-one, declared he was a sadhu. He had gone to India to explore our homeland. Encouraged in part by me, my parents allowed my brother's journey as an inquiry into our culture. If the Americans did it, shouldn't we? That was the year I was on my own journey, kissing for the first time. India claimed the brother who had brought me safely to America's shores. When he returned to Morgantown, doctors diagnosed him with a serious illness of the mind. "I've lost my brother," I cried one night, staring out the window of my friend Eric Maclure's apartment in Pierpont House, overlooking the faculty apartments where we had once played baseball games of Indians versus Americans.

My brother had wandered from home to home among our relatives, his raven black unkempt hair growing down his back and falling like a tangle over his eyes. He would whisk it away from in front of his protruding eyes with fingernails that he wouldn't cut. He would stare with piercing brown eyes on his hollowed face, certain of his mystical powers. He would declare to those who dared to ask, "I am a sadhu."

Hearing the reports from our relatives, my mother had journeyed to India to rescue him. She appeared before him in a black *shalwar kameez.* "Are you a jinn?" my brother asked, absorbed in the black of her clothes. They were the spirits written about in the Qur'an, souls who return to earth to do both good and bad. I had heard about them since my childhood, usually as something to fear. But I chose to consider them my friends. My mother wept at the sight of her son. The doctors said he had a genetic predisposition to the illness, but its onset was most probably aggravated by the trauma of his return to India. It made me fear the consequences of my return.

For now, I sat behind Nabina's brother-in-law, Keshab, as he skirted me through Kathmandu to an old section of the city, Darbar Square, on his scooter.

We sat at a rooftop restaurant. I studied the menu and wondered aloud, "Do they have *samosas?*"

They didn't, Keshab Bhai said. "Let's have *momos,*" he said. It was something Deepak called traditional Nepali food. When they arrived, they looked to me like Chinese dumplings. Keshab Bhai crossed one ankle over a knee. "Reebok" peeked out from upon his socks. The sun beat upon us. American tourists sat nearby. Keshab Bhai told me the story of his spiritual quest. He had been a teenager involved in Nepal's democratic movement. He realized, he told me, that freedom was a principle vital to existence. He had gone across the border and spent a year in Benares at an ashram. There, he realized the universal truth about what we needed. "Freedom for the soul." He paused. "It means freedom for the woman, too."

This was a simple man whose logic I could follow and also embrace. He took me to the home of a famous Nepali artist, Romio Shrestha, painter of Buddhist *thangkas,* ornate depictions of deities often used as points of meditation in Tantric practices. A photo album was filled with pictures of him beside the likes of models Naomi Campbell and Iman. Romio was struggling with pressure from his family to take money he said he'd received from Deepak Chopra for building a meditation center and invest it, instead, in the family's carpet business. "What do I do?" he asked me. I thought he should get the quiet guidance of a man such as Keshab Bhai.

On the road again, Keshab Bhai said he learned to create a peaceful vibration within his body through meditation and mantras. It gave him balance. He didn't look for special Tantric powers. "I'm only happy," he said. We headed out. I wasn't certain where we were going.

We parked on a busy street and slipped into a narrow alley where I ate two of the most delicious *samosas* I'd ever had, not counting the ones made by my mother or Bhabi. They were spicy and fresh, just pulled out of a vat of hot oil.

He told me, "You wanted *samosas.* In Tantra, your every desire is fulfilled."

I bit into my *samosa,* its mix of spices and warmth spilling through me. I was breaking the code of safe international travel by eating something off the streets, but I indulged. I had immersed myself quickly and deeply into a world foreign to me. I had to flee now with what I had learned. I didn't find a teacher in Vishnu Uncle, but he made me confront the most essential question of understanding my identity. And Keshab Bhai inspired me in the ideals of my search, freedom. I boarded an Indian Airlines flight to New Delhi, a string of *rhuda raksha* prayer beads given to me by Vishnu Uncle around my neck, knowing that to free myself I must begin to be able to honestly answer the question Vishnu Uncle posed to me: "Who are you?"

CHAPTER 6

A Cremation Ground

THE WAILS OF WOMEN emerged from the house. Relatives and friends streamed past me to go inside to pay their respects to the man who had died the night before.

I wanted to go inside but thought it would be more polite to stay outside. Friends of my family, Nandi Uncle and his wife, Chawla Aunty, let me accompany them to this corner of Old Delhi to the cremation of a relative. The houses were narrow and close together, unlike the neighborhood of sprawling houses and wide yards where I'd been staying with the Chawlas, their young servant girl, Poola, and their big dog, Rufus. From Kathmandu, I had jetted into Delhi without a plan or a place to stay. I slept the first night at a five-star hotel, spending what felt like an eternity in the shower, trying to wipe away the grime of my inauthenticity in Kathmandu. My one principle in travel was to always have the phone number of a personal contact wherever I might be visiting. For Delhi, my mother's brother, Anwar Mamoo, gave me the name of his good friend from the garment industry, Nandi Chawla. When I called him my second night in Delhi, he gave me a boisterous greeting.

"Come over in fifteen minutes!" he bellowed into the phone. "We're going to a wedding!"

I found myself at a festive outdoor Punjabi wedding on the lawn of a military club. It was a free-spirited scene like none I'd ever seen in the more sober settings of my family gatherings. Aunties and uncles danced together, drinking gin and tonics and rushing to the buffet when the waiters brought out the chicken *biryani*. A long-legged niece of Nandi Uncle's swept across the lawn, her shimmering *dupatta* flowing behind her. "She's a model," Nandi Uncle told me. I wore my best *shalwar kameez*, but I felt inadequate. I had no secrets about my identity with the Chawlas. They knew that I was Muslim because they knew my uncle,

Anwar Mamoo, so well. And it wasn't a dividing line for them. Nandi Uncle had a clear philosophy about religion, he told me between sips of Scotch. "I believe in universalism."

The music got louder, and Nandi Uncle pushed me to dance. "Have fun!"

The Chawlas were a modern Delhi couple whose daughters had left the nest and settled into new lives with their husbands in nuclear family homes, not the extended family arrangements of my mother's generation. "These educated girls are writing new rules," Chawla Aunty explained to me. Their only son studied in the U.S., and one of his friends set up the computer in their home so Nandi Uncle could e-mail him regularly. Chawla Uncle was a vivacious businessman with charm and enthusiasm. His name, Nandi, came from the name of a bull that protected the god Shiva. Devotees at Shiva temples rub the bull's loins and haunches to have some of his strength rub off on them, much like the way tourists have always rubbed the testicles and haunch of the bull that stands at Wall Street in lower Manhattan, making these appendages the shiniest part of the bull. Nandi the Bull also represents the Lord of Joy, loving music and dance, not unlike Nandi Uncle.

Born into an old Delhi family, Chawla Aunty was a more simple and quiet woman with great patience for the bad eating habits that threatened her husband's health, like his love of barbecued chicken wings. He had diabetes but at the time of my visit wasn't doing much to watch his weight, despite all of the sweet, fresh papaya she fed him for breakfast. Over the next days, Chawla Aunty took me into her private world of Hindu devotion. Ducking her head, she led me into a tiny alcove of a closet underneath a stairwell. Her mother-in-law used to pray there until her death. Chawla Aunty kept a pile of thin books on a shelf opposite the alcove door, spiritual guides by Indian philosophers and saints. She sat down on a small stool in front of a shrine with images of Hindu deities. I sat on the mat behind her. Although Chawla Aunty was inviting, I felt like an interloper. This was my first time in someone's personal *mandir*, temple. She pulled the thin books from the shelves, touching each one to her third eye in a gesture of respect when she picked them up. Her rituals were foreign to me, but she practiced them quietly, lighting incense before starting to read.

From the safety of their house, I explored Hinduism, Tantra, and the fine art of doing business in India. Plenty of warnings accompanied my search. A woman named Pravati activated my mobile phone account. When she heard that I was researching Tantra, she squealed. "Be on the safe side. Don't just carry a phone. Carry a gun."

Another day, Chawla Aunty took me on a short walk through the neighborhood to visit her pandit at Shri Sanatan Dharam Mandir in the F-block of Nanak Pura, a neighborhood. He sat behind a desk in a small building next to the *mandir,* a simple structure with a quiet ambiance. I asked him about Tantra. "It's *very* bad," he said with a look of disapproval. Chawla Aunty, too, didn't think highly of Tantra because of its modern-day reputation for black magic and scams, not spirituality.

On our slow walk home past wide houses, Chawla Aunty told me about the law of karma, which defines Hindu philosophy, plucking one of the simple analogies found in the spiritual guidebooks of her *mandir.* "It's like a bank account," she said. "All of your good deeds are credit. All of your bad deeds are debit. At the end of your lifetime, you hope to have a positive balance. That is the karma that follows you into your next lifetime."

I thought I might be in trouble. I could never balance my checkbook.

One morning, I opened the Tata white pages to see what I might find under "Tantra." The "Tantra Foundation" jumped out at me. The man who answered my call said to come by. I hailed an auto rickshaw for this ride, and it dropped me off at a huge billboard of a sign so cramped with writing it reminded me of the rambling letters we'd get at the *Wall Street Journal*'s Washington bureau, cursive filling every bit of the page with allegations of FBI conspiracies and CIA surveillance. The billboard claimed this was the site where former Indian prime minister Indira Gandhi came for a special fire blessing.

A man outside directed me to a room. When I entered, a terrible smell hit me. The man who had talked to me on the phone lay before me like a reclining Ganesh with a potbelly, the revered son of Shiva and Parvati, created out of a father's rage. Jealous at the presence of even a boy in his wife's room, Shiva, just back from a trip away from his palace, chopped off his son's head. When Parvati told him this was his son, a distraught Shiva put an elephant's head where his son's head had been.

This sleeping Ganesh pointed to a rock in front of me. "Do you know what this is?"

I didn't.

"It's a Shiva lingam!" he yelled at me. "The entire power of the universe is here. All of the world will follow Hindu dharma," he said.

I listened to him silently. His dogmatism scared me.

Still seeking—elsewhere—I found myself some days later in a place that felt like a spiritual waiting room.

The spiritual doctor was the son of a man I'd found on the Internet, a man called Revered Gurudev Dr. Narayan Dutt Shrimaliji, leader of the Mantra Tantra Yantra Vigyan. Beside me sat my driver, an earnest, clean-shaven, balding man named Deepak Soni. On our ride over in a big white Ambassador, he had told me he read Dr. Narayan Dutt Shrimaliji's magazine in Hindi whenever he could afford to buy it.

We found ourselves at a house in a neighborhood outside Delhi. Around us, the floor was packed with about a hundred men and women sitting shoulder to shoulder. To our right, a man stood behind a counter selling Dr. Narayan Dutt Shrimaliji books, buttons, and scarves, things I'd just dropped money to buy. The day before, we'd paid 520 rupees each to get blessed by Dr. Narayan Dutt Shrimaliji's son, a man we were allowed to meet privately for just a few moments. An Indian woman who took my money spoke with admiration about "girls" like me who kept Indian tradition alive, wearing *shalwar kameezes* instead of "jean and shirt." I knew this judgment call well. A good girl wore the clothes of her culture. A bad girl didn't. When I met the son, he looked so bored I wondered if he would rather be napping. As I sat wondering what was to come next, a disciple called the driver and me forward. For our *diksha,* or initiation, my driver and I ascended a few steps into a room with a larger-than-life-sized photo of Dr. Narayan Dutt Shrimaliji.

We sat cross-legged on the floor. Beside us sat a young man, Abhishek Chandra, who lived outside Delhi, the son of a retired colonel, A. C.

Chandra. The son came for a blessing to help him fight an evil spirit that had taken over his body after, he thought, a man jealous of his father had cast a Tantric spell upon him. He had already paid Mantra Tantra Yantra Vigyan thousands of rupees for protection mantras and his *diksha,* which symbolizes rebirth. Now he was back for more.

After we'd gathered, the son of the guru walked somberly forward and took a seat in a chair in front of us, the picture of his father behind him. He looked as bored as the day before. He chanted with glazy eyes, vacant without emotional expression, and flicked water on us with his fingertips. He called us *bachchay,* or children, and sent us on our way to practice every day a mantra he'd given us.

The colonel and his son were pleased. Deepak the driver smiled broadly on the ride home. We passed posters plastered all over Delhi with the cherubic face of a woman called Mataji Shri Nirmala Devi. She was at Ramlila Ground at Delhi Gate holding a teaching about "Self Realization Through Kundalini Awakening." Her posters called us to "Attain Freedom from Physical, Mental and Emotional Problems." I considered going, but I was tired. I didn't have the energy to have my energy awakened.

I sat in my room instead, pulling out a bright red book on meditation by Dr. Narayan Dutt Shrimaliji. I started going through the exercises, the breathing, focusing on a fixed point. I exhaled hard, as one exercise told me to do. It was weird. I felt power with his exercises. "Close the eyes. Count the breath in. Count the breath out," I read, and then I did. I felt a calm and a power. White light filled my closed eyes.

When I went to brush my teeth, I looked down at my toothpaste. It was "Colgate with Shakti power."

Now, as I stood outside the home of Nandi Uncle's relatives, watching somber-faced mourners go by me, I wondered about power in life, especially when faced with death.

My thoughts were interrupted when the dead man's daughter emerged from the house, wailing and weeping, crying out to the sky. Tears rose within me as I watched her cry. I thought of my own father. How would I mourn if he died? How much would I regret the impatience I had shown him when he stopped at green lights? A flurry of activity awakened the street, as a procession of men came outside with the body of the man strapped on wood planks and hoisted on their shoulders. The daughter set out behind the men, along with a few young women. I followed. Nandi Uncle was in the procession, a plank on his left shoulder. They shouted to a Hindu god. I shouted with them, not knowing what I was saying.

The girls drifted back from the procession. I was neither with them nor with the men up ahead and continued to follow the procession. Nandi Uncle faltered. He stepped to the side to catch his breath as the other men continued with the body. I caught up to him. "Are you okay?"

He didn't answer but started walking again behind the men. They reached a van, and I arrived as they all piled inside. They invited me to sit inside, and I climbed onto the edge of the seat, the lone woman with these men, Nandi the Bull, and the body of his cousin.

We reached a gate that was the entrance to a cremation site. Women filtered out of cars. The men carried the body to an open-air expanse held up by pillars, open-air walls on three sides. Here were the pits where bodies were cremated. In Hinduism, bodies are cremated rather than buried to free the soul from the body, which, the philosophy goes, has only been a vessel for our souls in our lifetime. Fresh orange-colored flower garlands surrounded one pit, thrown by friends and family mourning a rich and powerful industrialist cremated earlier in the day. Smoke filtered from his cremation pit, the remains of his body mostly gone. The men laid the body of Nandi the Bull's cousin into a simple pit, decorated with nothing.

His daughter arrived with the other women and stood beside the pit. She wailed and wailed and wailed. "Papa! Papa! Don't go!" An elder relative pulled her away. I learned later that, as in Islam, at burials it's Hindu tradition for women to stay away from cremations for fear they'll get too emotional.

A young man stood beside the pit, a stoic contrast to the daughter. A white *kurta* flowed elegantly down over his white *pyjama*. A woman told me he was a nephew of the girl's father. He was so close to his uncle, he had the duty of lighting the cremation fire, an act usually done by a son, but his uncle had had no sons. He had the facial growth of a man who hadn't shaved in days. He uttered not a word and silently walked around the pyre, performing rituals I didn't know but mourning with a dignity I could recognize as the effort of all of us to accept the reality of death. He shook some oil into the fire with a long-stemmed ladle. It reminded me of the dignity with which Rachel Momani, Lucy, and Esther buried my uncle when he died in Maidenhead, England, while his daughters were teenagers. They broke orthodoxy to the gentle acceptance of the British Muslim immigrant friends of my uncle, and Lucy and Esther helped carry their father's casket, wearing the *sherwanis,* the long dignified jackets that were his standard wardrobe. Before the burial, they told their mother they wanted to put the plastic pigs that had been special to them in the casket with their father. Such an act would have shocked many a Muslim, for whom the pig is considered *haram,* Arabic for "forbidden." But their mother laughed her gentle laugh and told her girls, "Why not?"

At this cremation, there was soon little difference in what remained in the pits of the industrialist, decorated with garlands, and the young man's uncle. Similar wafts of smoke emerged from both.

Nearby, Chawla Aunty wondered where her husband might be. She hadn't seen him at the cremation site. In the parking lot, the wife of Nandi Uncle's brother acted secretive. She suggested we follow her to her house. We set out behind her car, only to end up in front of a hospital called Malhotra Heart Institute.

Nandi Uncle's brother broke the news to Aunty. "Nandi had a heart attack."

So that's what happened when he stopped to catch his breath. I scanned Aunty's face for a reaction. She didn't cry. She didn't lose her breath. She didn't even flinch. She responded with stoicism.

When she returned home from the hospital, I didn't see her for a while. She had slipped into her alcove beneath the stairs. All I heard was the singing of her mantra filtering out, her dog, Rufus, also listening quietly nearby.

CHAPTER 7

My Devoted Muslim Family

THE BLACK FABRIC covered me from head to ankle, only my eyes peering out from behind the veil.

I slipped through the alleys of Aligarh with my two cousins, also clad in black *burqas*. I had decided at the last minute to visit my cousins in Aligarh, a two-hour train ride from Delhi, for our Muslim holiday of Bukreid. It was a holiday marking the Qur'anic and biblical tale of the prophet Ibrahim, "Abraham" in the Bible. Ibrahim loved Allah so much, the story went, that when he heard voices from Allah telling him to sacrifice his son for his love of God, he took a sword to his son's head. The hand of God stopped Ibrahim before he killed his son.

The *Wall Street Journal* travel agent told me that it was too late to get a reserved train seat. I thought about hiring a car but chose to risk an adventure on the train instead, despite all the warnings I'd heard about the dangers of traveling alone as a woman. My taxi pulled up to the station. Before it pulled away, a gaggle of men had swooped upon me like vultures. A rip-off artist suggested I give him money to buy me a ticket. I refused. I was flustered and near tears. Making my way to the station platform, I found a mess in the tangle of travelers, porters, and the tea-selling boys yelling, *"Chaichaichaichai."* I jumped into the first-class compartment on the train and slipped through a door into a private cabin. I sat down without a ticket. A fast-talking man in his thirties, a lanky Indian with crooked teeth, recited poetry, philosophies, and tales from his life in Norway all the way to Aligarh. I was the only woman in my cabin.

When the train pulled into Aligarh, the crooked-teeth philosopher insisted I share a bicycle rickshaw with him. When we arrived at my relatives' doorstep, he told me to stay behind in the rickshaw so I could surprise my cousin. He knocked at the door, his appearance frightening my teenage cousin-brothers. And then I heard him say, "Won't you give me some money for dropping her off?" The gall. I bounded out of the rick-shaw, spat some words at this loser, and bade him farewell.

When I walked through the door, I realized I could be in Gaithersburg, Maryland.

My cousin-sister, Nasheed Apa, the daughter of my mother's older sister, Shahida, had moved her furniture from her home in suburban America to this bungalow on the campus of Aligarh Muslim University. The living room was the same as their living room in Gaithersburg. It was the same flowered cream sofa. The lamps were the same. The drapes were the same though the bells on the cords had gotten dusty here. It was the same carpet here with leaping horses woven upon the orange. Even Nasheed Apa's oil painting hung here, as it had done in Gaithersburg. Outdoors, I saw Nasheed Apa still had an amazing green thumb with an English garden filling her front yard with bright colors and a vegetable garden off the side with herbs and plants whose Ayurvedic remedies she recited like the scientist she once had been. But there was one huge difference. I wore a *burqa* as a social experiment; for them, it was a way of life in which baking a Betty Crocker cake in their kitchen in American suburbia was a distant memory.

Nasheed Apa was like an older sister to me. When I was ten years old and living in Piscataway, New Jersey, I had ventured away from my mother for the first time since we were reunited to help Nasheed Apa with the birth of her first child on April Fool's Day. The newborn was a beautiful girl named Arina. In Gaithersburg, Arina had grown up to be a precocious girl. But as she entered her teens, her father went through a transformation. He would invite Muslim men into his basement for meetings of Tablighi Jamaat, sort of the missionary Mormons of Islam. His wife would labor late into the night, frying snacks for the men, even as she battled ill health from diabetes. He brought stricter codes of Islam into the house, banning entertainment TV, forcing Nasheed Apa and his daughter to watch *General Hospital* in secret and snap off the TV when they heard Zafar Bhai's car pull into the driveway.

We visited often. When my aunt, Shahida Khala, stayed with her daughter once for medical treatment, I massaged her feet, which were aching from diabetes. "Your hands are from heaven," she told me in her gentle voice. Her affirmation of my healing power gave me confidence in the power of my touch. She watched quietly as she saw her daughter's life increasingly restricted by her son-in-law's Islam. "I've never seen Islam practiced this way," she once told my mother, shaking her head.

One day, while I was at work in the *Journal*'s Chicago bureau, I picked up the phone. "Zafar has kidnapped Nasheed and the children," my mother said. "He has taken them to India and won't let them leave."

The story went that Zafar Bhai took his wife, daughter, and two sons to India for a vacation, confiscating their passports once they'd arrived and telling his wife that he had made the unilateral decision to migrate back to India. I spent days gathering all their documents together so they could return, but his wife decided not to live the life of a single mother divorcee in America. Over the years, I sent Arina, her brothers, and a new sister born in India reminders of America, including Halloween cards. I bought Arina a sweet sixteen charm for her birthday but never sent it.

Now I didn't know what to expect when I walked into their home. How had Nasheed Apa and Arina adjusted to this life that began with a virtual kidnapping?

Nasheed Apa greeted me with the broad smile I remembered from my childhood. It was always wide and welcoming, but it concealed dark stories she would confide to you only in the wee hours of the morning. Arina was a taller version of the cute young girl I had last seen. Zafar Bhai hadn't changed much. He filled our meal conversation with lectures about devotion to Allah and surrender to God. He was a constant proselytizer, preaching about Islam with a smile and a grin and without a breath's pause.

Zafar Bhai enforced strict purdah in his house. No men outside the immediate family were allowed to see Nasheed Apa's and Arina's faces. When they walked out the door, it was only cloaked in black. Twenty years earlier, Nasheed Apa had moved freely in Gaithersburg, nosing her family car from the grocery store to her job as a researcher in a scientific laboratory. She had eventually abandoned the job but always did her own grocery shopping, dropping her favorite cake mixes into her shopping cart.

As we readied ourselves to visit families for Eid ul-Adha, or Bukreid, as we call it in India, I decided to cloak myself in a *burqa*. I wanted to know the existence that my mother had once lived. Now it was Arina's turn, her wide eyes and angular face always hidden from public viewing. I allowed my eyes to be exposed to the world.

We slipped from house to house, through dusty alleys and narrow doorways, eating the traditional sweets of Bukreid. Our long dark shadows stretched anonymously out on the street in front of us. What I discovered was that the cloak didn't disguise my true nature. I still had my curiosity and intellect. But it was true that cloaked I had to ask myself who I was on the inside when the outside no longer defined me.

We were joined in our excursions to the homes of relatives by the daughter that Nasheed Apa had had after settling in India. There was talk that Zafar Bhai had wanted to marry a second wife upon his return to India—to help, the argument went, a poor Muslim woman. Nasheed Apa, to her credit, didn't buy it. When her daughter was born, they gave her the name Ayesha, after the young wife who became the Prophet Muhammad's last wife and supposedly his favorite. Whenever we climbed into a rickshaw, her mother instructed her to recite a *dua*, or prayer, to protect us during our travel. Ayesha did so promptly. It struck me as no different from the mantras that Hindus chanted for protection, dismissed by many Muslims as superstitious.

I learned the secrets of Aligarh as we wandered. Lesbianism, homosexuality, love triangles, second wives, illegitimate children. When a friend of Arina's got a Kinetic Honda scooter, so did the daughter of her father's second wife. He made sure he was always fair, as Islam said a man had to be when he married more than one wife. Even the young women in *burqas* lived surreptitious lives of romance, one of them keeping a list of the several dozen young men who had made overtures to her or her family. A boy who left cards was "Mail Man." He'd left a poem in which he said he never thought he'd know love until he saw her. She had cut out the boy's name lest her father should find it.

My days in Aligarh among my devotional relatives made me wonder about the way I wanted to practice religion. The rituals weren't as important to me as they were vital to Zafar Bhai, for example. For him, missing a prayer was unthinkable. For me, it was usual. It wasn't my place to judge, but I couldn't help but wonder if the strict code meant the loss of free thinking and even compassion. I left for Delhi, and when I returned to Aligarh a second time, I called to see if someone would pick me up from the train station. Zafar Bhai told me that the call for prayer, *azan,* had rung through the air. He assumed I was carrying the few bags of my first trip. He told me, "Get a rickshaw and come home."

Four strangers, who I could tell by their names were Hindu, helped me pile my baggage onto the rickshaw. When we arrived, I waited for the rickshaw *walla* to pull my bags off the seat. He took this opportunity to brush his hand between my legs and finger me. "Did he mean to do that?" I wondered, shocked. I was too flustered to even refuse to pay him. I handed him his ten rupees. This was the confusion of these men called "Eve teasers."

I had arrived for Arina's birthday, but certain Muslim interpretations said that birthdays shouldn't be celebrated, so we couldn't even acknowledge the occasion. Instead, over dinner, Zafar Bhai talked about the soul. In Islam, I learned the soul was called *ruh*. He said that a person's *ruh* disappears after death. To me, it was just like the *atama,* or Hindu concept of soul, I'd learned departs at the time of cremation.

He read from a book about how the Sufis considered it the most auspicious time to recite *zikr,* or remembrances of Allah, after the morning *fajr* prayer and after the sunset *maghrib* prayer. I was intrigued by this concept of *zikr.* I remembered the recitations Ishrat Aunty had taught me during my summer vacation as a child in Hyderabad, showing me how to count using my fingers. It dawned on me that *zikr* wasn't that different from the mantras that Hindus recited for the same purposes of concentration and remembrances of divinity.

Zafar Bhai continued to read, about a state of existence that was like a union with God. I asked him if he had reached that state of existence. He said that the recitations of Qur'anic verses in *salat,* or the Arabic word for prayer, took him close. "I become a ray of light. I see light. I am one with Allah."

"Are you a Sufi?" I asked. "Have you reached a higher state of existence with God?"

He responded, "I am nobody. I'm just dirt."

Although I hated to admit it, because my views were so divergent from Zafar Bhai's dogmatism, his was the answer of the truly spiritual.

In this household, everyone but Ayesha prayed the five daily prayers. She was still too young to be required to fulfill this requirement of Muslims.

"What happened to your prayers?" Zafar Bhai asked me one day.

How could I tell him that I was turned off by the hypocrisy of Muslims who prayed five times a day but mistreated their wives, sisters, and daughter or acted unkindly toward close relatives? I wasn't convinced that prayers made for a good human being. Every time I bowed my head, I confronted the realities of Muslim culture that clashed with my vision of a compassionate society. Zafar Bhai was always dashing off to the mosque a stone's throw from our front yard, but he seemed to preach with so much loathing toward America for its foreign policy and social values and toward Jews for their wealth and power.

I asked him, "Are you tolerant?" I thought I knew the answer.

He responded, "That's a predictable question." I didn't tell him I found his nonanswer also predictable because dogmatism meant to me an absence of honest self-criticism.

Because I'd begun to think so much about the concept of goddesses in Hinduism, I started wondering about the divine feminine within Islam.

Arina was a good window. She was a young woman who lived amid the modern furniture, slipping adult novels under her mattress. She borrowed a novel about a Japanese-American woman who solves a murder outside Tokyo. The love scenes didn't impress her. "They don't say enough."

She was protected from the outside world. Not a man outside the house had seen her face. Yet she told me tales of intrigue in which boys left cards at her doorstep and pursued her clandestinely, one even sending his mother to follow Arina around campus for just a glimpse of her. Her father grilled prospective suitors to see if they were interested in Arina's U.S. citizenship as a ticket to the United States. He refused any proposal if the suitor might be interested in taking his daughter to the U.S. Word was that he would only entertain meetings with *dahree wallas,* men with beards, which symbolized their piety.

One afternoon, a boy came with his family to explore a match with Arina. Arina's brother, Haseeb, ran into her room, laughing, "Nerd! Nerd!" The boy wore glasses. He was short. His father wore a baseball cap on his head, above his beard. Arina hid in her room, her dark blue *dupatta* framing her beaming eyes. Beckoned by the prospective in-laws, Arina emerged from hiding. The mother had hennaed hair, and she studied Arina, who was her uninhibited self. The mother said not a word. Her black chador hung around her shoulders. We heard the *azan* for *magrib namaz.* The mother asked for a chair because her stiff joints made it too difficult for her to prostrate from a standing position. Arina didn't connect with the mother.

Later, we sat on her childhood bed, and Arina wrote a matrimonial ad for me to run in the *Times of India* newspaper. "I am a 34-year-old Sunni Muslim attractive and outgoing journalist working around the world and based in U.S. Seeking a companion who's caring and remembers the last time he saw the full moon."

We crossed out a part I dictated about wanting a companion who played volleyball. We also crossed out a part Arina wrote, seeking a "religious" companion. I told Arina the qualities that I wanted in a man. Inspiring. Visionary. Compassionate. The ad left out all my confusion.

Meanwhile, I saw the extraordinary in the seemingly mundane. Ants raced beside me. A dog ventured through the yard. Nasheed Apa's flowers were blooming. I read *The Children's Stories of the Sufi Saints* to Ayesha, who always seemed to have a tuft of bed hair. I wanted her to know something about the accomplishments of women in Islam. I read her the tale of Rabia of Basra, one of the few women Sufi saints who rose to wide recognition in a circle of men. It was said she was a slave but she transcended her physical condition through an intense devotion to God that liberated her spirit. Her master freed her because he saw she could not be a captive.

Rabia of Basra said that when she heard voices that rang out like a distraction in prayer, they were actually fruits falling from the sweet tree of paradise. I'd be satisfied with a little grape. I tried to meditate as I had in Aunty Chawla's *mandir.* Praying in Arina's room didn't give me that quiet. My eyes drooped. I felt a negative spirit here, a lack of acceptance unless I prayed five times a day. I wanted to phone home for comfort. But Rabia's story explained there was the path of comfort and then there was the path of enlightenment. I had chosen enlightenment, and it was most certainly not a path of comfort.

I saw here expressions of the religious practice that I didn't find convincing. One day Arina ventured by and looked disapprovingly at her little sister, who was feeling ill. "You've got *nazar,*" she said, using the Urdu word for the Arabic concept of the evil eye cast sometimes by admirers but also by enemies. "You didn't wear your *ta'weez* for protection." The *ta'weez,* which means "the act of taking refuge" in Arabic, is a charm hung around the neck as a symbol of protection, usually with a surah from the Qur'an tucked inside.

I asked, "Do you really believe she got sick from *nazar?*"

Arina said, "Yes. Yes." I was surprised. She was a scholar of the sciences, awarded three gold medals at Aligarh Muslim University for her accomplishments in her studies, but she believed in what amounted to superstition to me. Even the devoted Muslim believes in *nazar* because the Qur'an offers numerous references to the effect of "the eye," distilling various protections in verses. But I couldn't be judgemental. I ran away from people I thought gave me "bad energy."

I then noticed their brother Haseeb standing in Arina's room, a door away. A few days earlier he had seen me praying and had come with a hand outstretched to congratulate me. "You're so pious," he'd told me with a beaming smile. I'd refused to accept the handshake. I didn't consider prayer an act to be congratulated.

Now, as I sat beside her, Ayesha vomited. Haseeb stood by watching. "You congratulate me for being pious," I said. "Piety means standing in the other room as your little sister vomits?"

It was a family of strict religious worship, yet the children were captivated by Western symbols of materialism. Ayesha wrote a poem in my notebook:

> *Nothing refreshes like Coca Cola*
> *Except for Pure Magic*

I like my Birthday
Especially when it has Coca Cola and Pure Magic

During my visit, Haseeb, Sumi, their other brother, Arina, and I sipped Pepsi and ate biscuits called Pure Magic with delight. They all jumped up in alarm when they heard their father's voice. Pepsi was one of the forbidden fruits.

A man arrived. I'd never met him before. He was Nasheed Apa's older brother, Azfar Bhai. He didn't ask me about the project that brought me to India. At the dining table, covered with clear plastic, he sat across from me and lectured me. "You should go to see your dadi immediately," he told me, urging me to go see my paternal grandmother in Pakistan. It wasn't for sentimental reasons or for my research. "She will find you a husband."

Zafar Bhai sat to my left and agreed. "You have to get married," he declared to me.

Nasheed Apa concurred. "You should listen to me. I'm older than you."

I protested that I was receptive to being married but hadn't found a good match yet. "You only have worldly wisdom," Arina said. Me? The one thing I thought I lacked, flying in the clouds, was wisdom about how to live on this earth, but I certainly didn't think people who had just been reintroduced to me after so many years apart, and one who didn't know me at all, would judge me so freely. I was clearly offended they didn't bother to first engage me in conversation about that which coursed through my soul, my *ruh*.

They told me tales of the dangers that lurked on the roads if I continued to travel alone. Azfar Bhai offered to escort me to Benares and the other places of my journey. Zafar Bhai chimed in with horror stories of murders and robberies.

At that moment, the phone rang. It was my mother.

"I don't know who this guy is, Mummy," I wailed, "but he's bugging me about getting married."

"Who is he?" she asked.

"Azfar Bhai," I answered.

"Stay away from him," my mother commanded.

Her advice affirmed what I wanted to do. I left the table, clearly upset.

I talked to my mother again. She told me Azfar Bhai was a faculty member at Shibli College in the city of Azamgarh, a place I'd never visited but the conservative Muslim city of my maternal and paternal ancestors. She also told me how he had scolded my brother when he arrived in Azamgarh with long hair and a wild spirit that few, including Azfar Bhai, could understand were symptoms of an illness.

I sat with Arina in a room away from her parents and Azfar Bhai. "Of course I would like to be married, to be united in love, but I do not want to be married for the sake of marriage. Why does everyone have to be judgmental and negative?" I rhetorically asked Arina.

"Ignore it," Arina told me with a wince on her face.

Arina confided to me the scheming going on outside our room. Zafar Bhai and Azfar Bhai had this idea in their heads to arrange my marriage to a cousin, a wildlife specialist at Aligarh Muslim University. He had been married in something called a *badal,* or exchange, marriage. He married a woman, and his sister married her brother. It was a sacrifice brothers sometimes made, marrying ineligible women so their sisters, also ineligible because of age, looks, or other biases, could at least be wed. But these marriages had fallen apart quickly. The family rumor was something about the new mother-in-law refusing to allow her son to leave Azamgarh. I'd last heard the divorces hadn't been finalized.

"He's still married!" I exclaimed.

"But he's getting a divorce," Arina argued.

Great. This man, still wed but soon to be divorced, would be perfect for this aging divorcee.

Finally, the next morning, I pulled away from Aligarh on the train to Lucknow.

I felt as if I was making my escape. A child with a bare bottom and a red string around his protruding belly swaggered by not far from the train tracks. A rush of rice fields swept by me. I was happy to be sitting on the train. It was so much better that I hadn't kept my New York home. I preferred this life of detachment. I still hadn't graduated to nonattachment.

A child galloped along the wheat field. Acres unfolded before me dotted with trees shading a piece of farmland. This was the first moment of solitary stillness I had felt since I arrived in India. It relieved me. I had found religion in Aligarh. I had even found belief in the spiritual. But I did not find spirituality. I looked out the window as I daydreamed. A clump of women in bright saris stood outside, some shielding their faces with their sari fabrics pulled over their eyes. A tarred road lay in front of me, and I dreamed of riding a bicycle along its stretch of flat land.

The train would have lulled me to sleep if I hadn't had to think about protecting my luggage from theft. I didn't like the effect that this oppression cast upon me. Thank God, my family warned me to stay away from Azamgarh. I wasn't strong enough in my sense of self. I understood now why my brother had cursed Azamgarh. It made me sad to think of my brother in the grips of illness in this land. As if explaining my brother's peculiarities, Azfar Bhai had told me, "He wanted to go into *mandirs.*"

How could I tell him that I had gone into the *mandirs* of Hindus and that I planned to go into more of them? My brother and I were more like the Sufis of our ancestry, free spirits. We felt different from our family. Zafar Bhai had relayed tales of the kindness of Hindus on his train rides with surprise in his voice. Arina and I had walked through the bazaar my last night in Aligarh, passed a Hindu temple, and Arina had said, "When a cow goes to the bathroom in the morning they pray to the manure." One of her best friends was a Hindu named Vibha, and Zafar Bhai proudly relayed how Vibha's father considered purdah a good thing.

I awakened from a slumber. My eyes batted open to be soothed to sleep again by the presence of my North Face bag. No thievery inside the train. No urban congestion outside. Stacks of manure so perfectly piled upon each other. India felt so foreign yet resonated so deeply within me. I thought of Lucy in this country. I had judged my cousin as others judged me. I hadn't had her accompany me partly because of her pale skin and English features. Plus, she wore pants in India rather than *shalwars,* baggy pants, and she didn't speak Urdu. I had wanted to see what it was like to experience this country by going native. But Lucy understood something deeper than I did. You couldn't be something you weren't. Now that I knew, I wished for her presence more than any other. I was also drawn to be with Dadi, to learn from her. The truth was that I had to forgive her for transgressions against my mother in order to fully embrace her, but I loved her for the mysterious parts of me that I knew spawned from her spirit.

As I sat in my train seat, legs flew in front of me as a man climbed down from the upper bunk, his feet clad in black socks, patting his thighs contentedly once his feet were fully tucked into slippers. The smell of food in the air was delightful. The taste of an orange Arina had given me lingered deliciously in my mouth.

CHAPTER 8
Implosion

T HE HONEYSUCKLE BLOSSOMS captured my imagination. They draped over a roof sheltering the stairs leading up to my family alcove in a place called Jahingarabad Palace. They were like flowers handed to us by angels.

They were white tinged with a pink not worn by the honeysuckle climbing the wall outside my bedroom at 208 Bevier Road in New Jersey. But their beauty was universal, and like a chord ringing through time it brought my childhood into my present. I was excited to be here in Lucknow. It was a town of great culture where Muslim nawabs once lived in palaces with the finest in art, music, and consorts. The nawabs in Islam were the rajahs of Hinduism. Lucy, Esther, and my mother advised me to make Lucknow my base because of an aunt, Rashida Khala, who ruled the roost here. I didn't know her, but I was here to give their suggestion a try. I planned to stay only a few days and then travel back to Kathmandu, just across the border, or venture to the many Hindu holy cities just a few hours' drive away. I came to Lucknow awakened to the boundaries between Hinduism and Islam.

I didn't even remember, until I saw photographs later, that I had been here before. That was long before the rajah of the palace rented a wing out to Baskin-Robbins so that its familiar pink-and-white sign was the first thing I noticed when I crossed the gate into the palace. In another space sat a breast enlargement center.

Long before, my uncle Iftikhar Mamoo had lived here for years and named the terrace apartment Markaz-e-Adab, meaning "Center of Learning" with *adab* meaning "learning." The palace sat at the foot of a neighborhood in a wide avenue of shops in a neighborhood called Hazratganj, where merchants today sold Ray-Ban sunglasses and Swiss Army knives. In his day, it was a bustling but quiet street. Two rooms sat off the top of the stairs. Pastel-colored fabrics filled the one on the right, and a man by the open door sat at a sewing machine, stitching yet another piece in the *Lucknowi chikan* business of intricately embroidered *kurtas* that my cousin Rehan Bhai and his older brother ran out of the apartment. To the left, a door led into the room where Rehan Bhai slept with his wife, my cousin-sister Baby Apa, and their son, Shaan. Here, on this bed, Mamoo's friends—poets, philosophers, academics, ruffians—had gathered and debated into the night. This was where Rachel Kennedy came as a porcelain-faced twenty-year-old from the hamlet of Maidenhead on the Thames River. She was in Lucknow to study about the Avadhs, the rich Muslims, called nawabs, who financed a high society of poetry, prose, and dance. Two sisters came with her. One of them took a liking to Mamoo. The other didn't take a liking to that. Mamoo took a liking to neither. He fell in love with the young woman with a gentle smile and big brown eyes. He had already been married, but his wife, a scholar of Arabic, had moved to Pakistan. He didn't want to leave his India. He had done the unthinkable and they were getting a divorce.

Mamoo took this British girl to his village, Jaigahan, and there they were married in raw simplicity that captivated the hearts of the villagers.

As I reached the top of the stairs at our home in Jahingarabad Palace, Rashida Khala approached me with a slow shuffle of a walk.

In Urdu, *khala* means "sister of mother." Rashida Khala was my mother's eldest sister. She was slender and smaller than I, immaculate in a white *shalwar kameez,* her gray hair tied neatly into a braid. She sat me down immediately to eat and then sent me off to take a bath to cleanse myself from my travels. She didn't know her age because they never recorded it back then, but she was thought to be born in 1922, making her an estimated eighteen years older than my mother, who was the youngest child. She always dressed in immaculately washed and ironed white *shalwar kameezes.* She braided her silver hair over her right shoulder and tied the thin ends with the bow of a white ribbon like the kind schoolgirls wore in their hair. Her face was lined and weathered and beautiful. Unlike the roar with which Zafar Bhai and his sons stormed through the house to get to the mosque before sunset, she awakened for the predawn *fajr namaz* without me hearing her, though I lay asleep right beside her.

She was married as a young teenager, like most women of her time. Her husband died tragically after the birth of their daughter, Zareena. In the custom still practiced today, her in-laws arranged for her to marry her husband's younger brother. With him, she had three more daughters. She was happy with him. But when I asked her to talk about this part of her life she always said, *"Chordo."* Let it go.

She taught me lessons without uttering a word of lecture or advice. All day, she stayed busy. When I awakened she was chopping onions or shelling peas for breakfast. She chased after Rehan Bhai's son, Shaan, to make him drink milk. Throughout the afternoon, she guided Anis and Parvez, the young men she had raised from boyhood, through chores. They were called servants, but she treated them like family. At night, they slept on mats even though Khala bought them mattresses. We slept on cots pulled outside on the veranda. It was a magical space with the stars above in this place where royalty once slept. The moon ascended before me and moved over my right shoulder in the wee hours of the night when I opened my eyes for just a moment to see it above me. I could feel Iftikhar Mamoo gazing down upon me.

One afternoon, Rehan Bhai sat against the bed mats and told me he had turned to religion a few months before, the result of conversations with Thabligi Jamaat men who attended his mosque. They belonged to a conservative Muslim organization. Followers grew their beards, as Rehan Bhai had, and men went to the mosque for their five daily prayers, easily influenced by the imam, or religious leader, of the mosque who lectured them about how to practice Islam.

I wanted to explore Lucknow, but Rehan Bhai set out warnings. I felt imprisoned on the grounds of the palace, and I didn't know how to break free. I was getting frustrated. The newspaper was filled with horror stories that reinforced his fears. The *Hindustan Times* wrote about a fifteen-year-old Dalit girl, the new politically correct term for the lowest "untouchable" class, whose gang-rape charge against men in her village went uninvestigated.

I didn't even know how to call home. The phone at the house didn't make international phone calls. Too much illegal splicing of telephone wiring, so neighbors charged their international calls to your phone. I piled onto Rehan Bhai's Enfield motorcycle. I rode Western in Kathmandu. Now, I rode sidesaddle as the women did here, and we set out just around the corner for a business setup with phone booths inside for local and international calls. I had to wait a few minutes for the connection. I wandered outside. Rehan Bhai waved to me from the *masjid* veranda across the street. He gestured for me to go back inside. He might have been worried about the sun overheating me, but it was just another signal of the repression I felt here.

When I finally got through, Bhabi answered. "Hello?"

My frustration silenced me.

"Hello? Hello?"

I started to sob, the tears ensnaring my words. Finally, I stuttered through my sobs, "It's so hard."

In her gentle way, Bhabi said, "Asra *baji,* you're so brave. You're so strong. Asra *baji,* everything will be fine."

My mother rushed to the phone. "What happened?"

I wanted to assure her I hadn't been raped, stabbed, or murdered. I could barely get the words out for my sobs. "Nuh-thing. Nuh-thing." I gulped. "It's just so hard." I sobbed hard. I complained about how I didn't feel as if I could leave the house. I wasn't free. A proposed marriage to a man already married. The lectures. The hatred for Hindus. The supremacy of Islam. My mother wanted me to give the phone to Rehan Bhai, to explain to him to give me freedom.

"No, I'll deal with it," I insisted.

My father got on the phone. *"Bayti,"* he said, using the endearment of all moments of trouble, "dear daughter, you learn lessons everywhere."

I told my father I had learned that being religious meant a devotion to God over humanity. My mother got back on the phone. "Come home," she pleaded with me. "You can always go back."

"I don't know," I told her. Would I have failed if I returned?

This was the long, dark night, as I succumbed to the tensions pressing in on me. I was here with *saaf neeath,* meaning "clear intentions" in Urdu, to explore worlds foreign to me. But I was dragged down by expectations others had for me as a thirty-something single woman. My parents had broken free of those expectations and had released me from them. But the

Indian culture around me had clipped my wings, and I was allowing it to ground me.

Ghosts haunted me. Rashida Khala sat on the *charpai,* cot, across from me on the veranda and told me about a night much like the clear one in which we were wrapped. My mother had come to Lucknow from Hyderabad to Jahingarabad Palace to give birth to her first child. Little could she have imagined then the demons that would rise in this city for her son, newly born, and daughter yet unborn.

She sat on the same veranda where I now sat. Rashida Khala sat beside her with Anwar Mamoo. My mother admitted to them that it wasn't easy for her with her *susral,* her in-laws.

Her brother dropped his chin. It was a shame.

As she told me the story, Khala remembered what she said back then about my mother: "She cried in her childhood. She cried after her marriage."

Another night, I lay on my back staring at the stars. My head burst as I felt the illness that gripped my brother here. Overhead, electric wires crisscrossed with the clothesline under the stars. The white light of a bare bulb shone in the other room. I felt naked like that bulb, as if India had stripped me of my resources of intellect and independence.

The next day, I retreated to the Fast Business Centre to find some sanity in the cyber world, not to mention quiet time in their private booths. Over the Internet, Lucy sent me encouragement. She asked if I'd avoided the snare of relatives. I hadn't. "Stay fresh because . . . holy eyes will quiver when you pass by, and skies will shiver in wondrous thought." I tried to call her but missed her. She wrote again assuring me, "India is oppressive sometimes, well most of the time, but it is like that in the most innocent of ways. It just wants to discover all about you. Be courageous. You have truly been touched by the soul of India, entrenched in the past, present, and the future of each of us. I know your turmoil."

I wondered if I had made a mistake in enveloping myself in family relations. Or did I just not know how to handle such relatives? Should I go home to America and regroup? Gather my strength? Renew who I was? Should I call home to get advice? Rehan Bhai watered the plants.

The sound of a saw filled the air. I awakened thinking of princesses who might have walked where I walked. I needed to go home to regroup. Make order of all these stories and impressions. Create my budget. Establish my itinerary. Get things under control. This investigation had stirred up too much emotion. I needed to center my *muladhara* chakra. And then return with a plan for the future.

I'd go home, but first I'd weave explorations of Hindu culture into my remaining days in the Muslim world of Markaz-e-Adab.

I was beginning to despair of ever finding the Tantric truths. Before Lucknow, the closest I'd come was a whiskey-soaked Vishnu Uncle and the apparently bored son of a Tantric guru. In Lucknow, the closest I got to Tantra was a carpet salesman I met in a bank. The carpet salesman said he practiced Tantra. He had had a Tantric lover. He had set her up in an apartment in Bombay. She got married and moved to Madagascar where she sold the business of Tantric black magic.

Wasn't he married?

"Yes, but the Tantric texts are clear. You can't practice with your wife."

That was convenient for a philanderer. I made the point that Tantra can and should be practiced with a spouse. Over the next days, I wasted my time, wandering around Lucknow as he tried to impress me with the important people he knew, police officers and government officials, some of whom he told me he was giving bribes. I didn't learn a thing about Tantra. When I finally met his wife, he tried to joke: "I'm trying to convince her that it's because I love her that I want to bring home a second wife to help her around the house."

I didn't laugh. I was beginning to feel everyone was nuts. I read in the newspaper about a young man who had supposedly chopped off his tongue after being possessed by Kali. So, I went to the temple with Akhtarul Mulk, a veteran Lucknow journalist and friend of my uncle during the days of Markaz-e-Adab. I wanted to prove to the Hindu worshipers that I respected their religion and bowed my head to Kali. When I met the young man, I asked him to pull out his tongue. I could tell that he hadn't chopped it off as he claimed. I could see from the stitches that it had been barely sliced.

Even the neighborhood police inspector laughed at this man's mockery of religion. "Everyone figures out a way to make money," he said with a laugh.

One practice I learned from a supposed Tantric I met with Akhtarul Uncle in his neighborhood convinced me I hadn't yet found any secrets. That man confided a ritual to me in which I was supposed to bathe and then yell curses at the sun. Yeah, right.

Before I left, my cousin Rakhshi brought me to her jeweler. She was the daughter of one of Rashida Khala's daughters, and I took a special liking to her because of her open-mindedness and vision. An assistant librarian at the British Library in Hazratganj, she dreamed of opening a coffeehouse bookstore in Lucknow, an ambitious dream for anyone, let alone a woman.

I sat in front of the glass showcase and explained to the jeweler that I'd come to India to learn about Tantra. There were charms with OM, the explain written upon them and swastikas, the marking of Hinduism before it was altered and captured by the Nazis as their symbol. The shop, Apurra Jewellers, was tucked in a long and narrow storefront in Hazratganj. The jeweler's name was Girish Narayan Gupta, a devoted Hindu.

"You were put on this earth as a Mohammedan," he told me, "because you committed a sin in a past life. This assignment came to you for a reason. It is an examination. If you go into the *mandir* and feel a connection, you have passed."

I feared I was going to lose my mind, torn sick by the divide between Hindus and Muslims. I was confronted by the tug of two societies who hated each other. Hadn't Hindus gotten the memo? Muslims weren't Mohammedans. They didn't worship the Prophet Muhammad. We prayed to Allah. Could they be any more ignorant? And Muslims could at least celebrate the fact that Hinduism teaches a spiritual discipline even if it was expressed through worship of brightly painted deities.

"Did you know today is Ram's birthday?" he continued, peering over the counter. I did, but I didn't know much about its significance. "It was ordained for us to meet on this day."

His family arrived to go to the temple with him. As we stood outside his shop, he looked at me and said convincingly, "You will become a spiritual healer. People will come to you and you will help them. You are on the right path to find your salvation."

As we parted, he inflated my spiritual ego. "You will be a saint." On my way home, I just hoped none of the juvenile young men of Lucknow would attempt a cheap grope.

At home, I sat with Rehan Bhai amid piles of *kurtas*. He wore his trademark *sherwani,* the long suit coat of formal Muslim culture, and *topi,* his hat. There was a lion, he told me, that hung out with *bukras,* or goats. The goats bleated. The lion roared. "A lion can hang out with goats, but he can't become a goat," he told me. "This is the same with Hindus and Muslims."

I was tired of stories with absurd morals about the divide with which some people wanted us to exist. "Just because you're a lion hanging out with goats doesn't mean you want to be a goat," I responded, thinking about the time I had gone to visit neighbors of Akhtarul Uncle. He had looked at me then told the girls there, "She doesn't speak Urdu."

"Yes, I do," I'd exclaimed.

"Do you pray five times a day?" asked one of the girls, using a classic Muslim barometer of gauging piety.

I wondered what she would think if I said I actually yelled curses at the sun.

Just before I left Lucknow, a familiar man ascended the stairs to our home in Jahingarabad Palace. I was filled with comfort.

He was my mother's youngest brother, Anwar Ansari. He had persevered in a life marked by the need to grow up early, and then a tragedy. After his father died, Anwar Mamoo raised chickens in the mango orchard that filled Latif Manzil's backyard. When Iftikhar Mamoo proved to be more a poet than a salary earner, Anwar Mamoo abandoned his passion for writing and sports and started the business of *Lucknowi chikan.* He built a Bombay export empire shipping intricately embroidered *Lucknowi Chikarikurtas* to America and the West. His second-oldest daughter, nicknamed Bubli, was on her way to his factory in Bombay when she died in a gruesome car accident, her crushed body, the word went, left for some time unceremoniously in a morgue. She was in her early twenties and beautiful.

Anwar Mamoo was always a philosopher-athlete wrapped in a business coat. In that room in which his elder brother captivated his audiences and, ultimately, his English bride, I spilled to him my frustrations with the divide and negativity in India. He shared with me his philosophies. They were the first ones I'd heard in days similar to my own. "I believe in universalism," he said, as Khala slipped in and out of the room, making certain he was eating his lunch. "Those who awaken for *puja* get up at the same time as those who awaken for *namaz*. What is the difference?"

To conquer India, he said, "You have to take the bull by the horns." It was a mantra I would repeat to myself often.

The next day, I planned to break free from the palace and accompany Mamoo on a business trip to Benares, the City of Lights. I had to take the bull by the horns. I sped to Benares with Mamoo and Rehan Bhai, a business supplier named Raju driving us on this one-day jaunt.

We rode on long stretches of highway past trees with red and white stripes painted at the bottom of the trunks like candy canes. A goat sat on bended knee. Strands of black thread were knotted and tied to the middle of the grill of a passing car. Shards of glass lined a boundary wall, like the walls in Aligarh, meant to keep intruders out. Mamoo told me that a strong will was the most important element in personal achievement. He didn't believe in the powers of Tantric black magic. "I once said to a sadhu, 'You can go ahead with your mantras and put a curse on me, but I have enough willpower that it won't have any effect on me.'"

Someone in the car quipped, "But give the sadhu some *cheras,*" the mixture of hashish and tobacco that sadhus in Kathmandu were smoking at Shivarathri, "and a spell will be put on them."

We slipped into the showroom of a Benarsi silk manufacturer, a silver-haired man with silver stubble on his face and buckteeth reddened from chewing betel in a leaf *paan*. We stood at his counter as he talked quietly to me, so Rehan Bhai and Mamoo couldn't hear. They were examining silk pillows made for Mamoo's daughter, nicknamed Cookie, who had started a business designing Western fashions with fabrics from India for chic Soho boutiques in Manhattan.

"I don't want you to write this because you will become Salman Rushdie, but Islam came after Hinduism. It received much from Hinduism." I agreed with him that, from what I'd seen, the parallels between the religions were many. He gave me a name, Sita Ram Kaviraj, as someone who would be a contact for my Tantra research and identified him as the VHP president of Benares, the VHP being a Hindu fundamentalist party.

Meanwhile, I was here to try to find an Italian scholar of Tantra recommended to me by someone in Delhi, a man named Mark Dyczkowski. I marked a spot on my *Lonely Planet* guide where I'd agreed to meet my uncle in a few hours. I slipped alone into a taxi and headed toward the Ganga River.

A boatman, Kailash, named for a mountain in Tibet where Shiva lived, rowed me down the Ganga. This was supposedly a place overcrowded with pilgrims, but that afternoon it was still and calm. It was the most sedate and peaceful place I had yet found in India. I didn't have clear directions to the scholar's house. "There is a *yantra* in the front." I didn't even know what *yantra* meant. Kailash landed me at a ghat on the Ganga where steps led up, in fact, to a giant symbol on a stone floor. Only a few people were doing their laundry on the steps. An old bearded sadhu lay in front of the door where I knocked.

A bear of a man with a thick beard and a hole in his right sleeve opened the door and welcomed me inside, ushering me into a room to the left. He left his slippers by the door and sat down with his back to the Ganga, so I could see the still river over his shoulder through the open window. There were stacks of books and papers piled in the room. I was to learn they were something called *shastras*. Mark was a window into intellectual Tantra. Tantra, he explained, was a substructure of yoga. It was based on an oral tradition and a written tradition of sixty-four *shastras*. Mark, it turned out, was a scholar of the *shastras*. A computer sat in the corner.

"Do you think Tantra is magic?" he asked me.

"I don't think it has to be," I told him.

"It isn't," he answered definitively, citing the *shastras* that he studied.

He flailed his arms. "What is Tantra? Is it the Tantrics who take away bad spells? It isn't. Tantra is the people who study Tantra *shastras.*"

"Do you practice Tantra?" I asked him.

He smiled. "There are many paths in Tantra. I'm a householder."

It was a term I hadn't heard much, but "householder" was a way of describing a man or a woman who practiced Tantra but still married and had families. It sounded like a path that appealed to me, to stay engaged in this life but aspire to a higher level of existence than mortgages, mini-vans, and Mickey Mouse vacations.

What had brought him to Benares? "I came here thirty years ago to find a guru, like everyone else." He no longer searched, yet he didn't leave.

In a symbol of how no space is protected in India, there were blouses and sari petticoats on the boat when I approached it to leave.

Finally, it was time to leave India. As I slipped out of Jahingarabad Palace, sorry to leave Rashida Khala, a half moon hung over my shoulder. The Muslim call for prayer broke through the air, as Hindu *mandir* bells clanged. Darkness sat in the morning air.

It was a moment of quiet contemplation for me on the train ride to Delhi for my connection to Bangkok, my first layover. What a journey upon which I'd embarked! I'd learned about the place of souls, Allah, goddesses, prayer, and spirits in Islam and Hinduism. Before leaving Lucknow, I had sat upon the raw wood *takht* whose base Khala had forti-fied with bricks and strips of white packaging fabric. I had heard her voice near the kitchen. It had reminded me of the gentle singsong voice of my nani, my maternal grandmother. I'd learned Khala's wisdom. I'd asked her the day before what she did to get *sukoon,* peace of mind, when there is much *gurbur,* or tension, in her mind. Her answer: *dua,* prayer. Five times a day she prayed quietly on the *janamaz* upon the bed.

On the train, a young student started to quietly tell me his story. "You look so peaceful," he said. Dazed could certainly pass for peaceful.

He'd started an affair awhile back with a married woman liberated, ironically, through her marriage to mix more freely with single men. Before he left to take an exam in Delhi, she told him she would kill her-self if he didn't return. He knew there was no future with this woman, but he was frustrated in a society where his future was dark in a sea of corruption, bias, favoritism, and prejudice. "India is bankrupt," he said sadly.

I stared out the window at the blur of fields. He echoed my feelings.

CHAPTER 9

Finding Freedom Again

W HEN I ARRIVED HOME from my travels, I hated India. I relished the beauty of Morgantown. Flowers were in bloom in North Hills. I breathed in the fresh air and knew deep within me why West Virginia's license plates read, "Almost Heaven."

As I pulled the Jeep out of the driveway one rainy morning to zip to North Elementary to volunteer for Safiyyah's third-grade phys ed class with Mrs. Garten, I stopped. There was Jaz, the wild calico cat who ate the food we put out for her but hissed and never came close. She stood with her legs wide apart with a black creature that resembled a rat underneath her belly. I stepped out of the Jeep to look closely. Jaz was using her body as an umbrella to protect a creature from the rain. "Why would Jaz be protecting a rat?"

I followed Jaz's path to the neighbor's driveway. I shimmied on my belly to look below a pile of logs where Jaz had gone. Kittens. There were kittens here. Jaz ran away. I scooped the kittens into a box and put them in our garage.

The kittens were the celebrity guests at Safiyyah's birthday slumber party. It was like the weekend from the Tantra workshop in Canada without the foot washes and explicit material. Al and Pala had told us that play was an important part of Tantra. Through the gift of my niece and nephew, my return to Morgantown was very much about play. Tantra is about being a child well. We dressed up. We threw a dance party. Stella, Bhabi's friend from Ghana, danced a traditional African dance. The girls were riveted by her mesmerizing swaying. Safiyyah's friend Breanna glided to "Genie in a Bottle." It was a *kirtan* à la Britney Spears and Christina Aguilera.

Late into the night, the girls lay belly down, and I lifted the heels of their feet to the sky and swung their legs together. "You're flying," I told them, just as I had learned to do at an R-rated *dakini* workshop in Los Angeles in which I learned the fine art of Tantric massage, only the intention here was strictly G-rated.

On Safiyyah's actual birthday on May 30, I enforced my rule that we never worked on our birthdays, and Safiyyah's mother let her stay home from school. We heard a mew that came from under our neighbor's deck. We crawled under it to inspect further. Indeed, it was another kitten. He teetered out to a bowl of milk we had. He couldn't be from Jaz's litter. He couldn't have survived all these days without her.

"What shall we call him?" I asked Safiyyah.

"'Special' because we found him on my birthday."

We dropped Special into Jaz's litter and stepped back to watch our wild, stray mother cat. Safiyyah and I looked at each other in amazement as Jaz started licking Special as if he were her own. She let him suckle freely at her nipples. Jaz was a lesson in unconditional maternal love, an untamed creature who accepted a stray as if her own. To me, she was my first Tantrika, free from labels, showing this love and compassion whether she was his mother or not. The kittens became Tantric teachers, showing me nonjudgmental love, playfulness, and innocence.

A few days later, I returned to Manhattan, one of four single women in a VW Bug headed to a wedding shower. From them, I heard about the six-minute date, the theme of an Upper West Side bar that hosted a night where men and women mingled for six-minute interviews with each other before moving onto another six-minute interview.

The girl in the front seat said, "I just want some Sunday morning sex."

What did that mean?

"Where you know each other well enough that you have sex on Sunday." Not quite the purity of the kittens.

Nothing had really changed in the singles culture of New York. I was relieved not to be a part of it. Sundays were claimed by a game I played in Morgantown with my family and Safiyyah and Samir, heading out for a drive where we took turns yelling "left," "right," or "straight" as our only directions for our day's travels. Somehow we always found our way home.

Another Sunday, I sat in the Morgantown High auditorium where a high school senior, Tim Maxey, had arrived with another girl after I'd enforced my no-dating rule when he asked me out and taught me one of my first lessons in dating.

I sat now in my lipstick red *kameez* with its golden *churidar*, tight pants that bunched at the ankles, part of the *jahayz*, or wedding gifts, I'd received from the family into which I had married. So what if the American parents showed up in shorts and T-shirts? We were from India and proud to wear our wedding finest at any special occasion. And this was a special occasion, Safiyyah's recital from Mindy's School of Dance. I was too uncool to ever be a student there. Safiyyah had a visa into a world I never knew.

These girls were a gyration of moves to songs that defied political correctness.

"Diamonds are a girl's best friend. . . ."

". . . it's raining men."

"Make way for Prince Ali. Show some respect."

A band of little girls threw themselves into handstands to the sound of a Minnie Mouse exercise song. One girl in pink remained lying down while the rest of her class moved through its routine. Her friend tapped her on the head. The girl wouldn't join them, remaining on the floor. She clapped for herself, to the delighted laughter of the audience. I laughed at this expression of her individuality. It was something I had missed among even the children I saw in my travels on the subcontinent.

Safiyyah's friend Breanna danced as the words "My boyfriend's back" filled the auditorium. Safiyyah took to the stage with her nimble body and flew through flips and somersaults with her friend Tali and the other girls from her gymnastics class.

Tears came to my eyes.

In the parched heat of India's travels and troubles, I had a dream of finding a respite for myself in the lush green mountains of West Virginia.

I told a friend of mine about this dream. She had been my friend for fourteen years since our orientation days at American University when we compared notes on the men from our new graduate school class. "Lou asked you, too, if you wanted a cup of coffee? And Larry flirted?

Me, too!" It kept both of us free from internecine romance, and we had remained great friends over the years. There was a part of her that I couldn't understand, however, in her spirituality and approach to life. It always seemed just slightly disconnected from my life. She watched my love life ride its roller-coaster with patience and guidance sprinkled just lightly. "I know it made you very sad, but you had to do it," she told me after my failed marriage. "You have to answer these questions about yourself."

Long before, she had told me about a Buddhist monastery she had been attending for years, tucked in the West Virginia hills with a lily pond beside it. She used to tell me about the calm she got at this retreat house started by a monk from Sri Lanka. I always admired my friend and politely heard what she said but had never really absorbed her positive experiences with Buddhism and meditation. But now, on this quiet day in June, I found myself enrolling for a weekend workshop at the monastery she talked about.

I felt as if I was walking on eggshells when I arrived. I didn't know how to act at a monastery.

The rules were spelled out. This would be a silent retreat. No talking except when absolutely necessary. A woman named Debra Jones greeted me with a beaming smile. She asked where I would like to stay. My friend had recommended the individual houses. "The *kuti?*" I suggested, hesitantly. The *kuti* was a peaceful one-room hut tucked into the woods with a single bed and a Buddha sitting on a table in a corner.

We gathered in a cavernous meditation hall where a golden Buddha stared back at us from an altar in the front of the room. Students sat on both sides of an aisle. I sat down on the left side, realizing only later that I was on the men's side. The monastery's monks sat in the front rows, clad in robes. Women sat on the other side of the aisle. It didn't surprise me that I had gravitated to the male energy. That's what I wanted to tap within myself. I sat cross-legged, mimicking those around me, my butt resting on the edge of a pillow. The senior monk from Sri Lanka sat in front of us below the Buddha.

"I am here," he told us, "to talk to you about mindfulness. It is about having control of our mind and our actions.

"You must develop insight. Look within. Each distracting thought is a cloud that passes you by. Control the mind. Think of yourselves as charioteers and the horses as your mind. You have the choice whether to be a charioteer or simply a person holding the reins on wild horses."

I felt stupid. So when I was depressed, I had to escape the quicksand of my negative thoughts. It was that simple. "Banish them," the senior monk said.

If he knew, he probably would have also told me to turn off Country Music Network after three songs, if not sooner. I felt so much lighter.

One afternoon, I experienced my first concentrated meditation. It felt wonderful. As part of the retreat, we had to do chores. I chose to pull weeds and couldn't help but observe the obvious symbolic value of digging my fingers deep into the soil to ease weeds out by their roots.

The Buddhism taught here was from a school of thought called Theravada, or Vipassana, meaning "insight." After the Buddha died, Buddhism seeped into other parts of Asia. In Sri Lanka and Southeast Asia, Theravadan Buddhism followed a more ascetic tradition with internal meditation at the center of the practice. Mahayana Buddhism spread through Nepal, Tibet, China, and Japan with a practice that incorporated meditation on deities.

The senior monk sat down with me so I could talk to him about my project. He listened carefully and spoke with certainty. "Research Tantra, but do not practice it. Have your own practice."

"Why?"

"That would be best for you. It is a dangerous practice."

A young woman named Kirsten helped feed us, a volunteer cook who had quit her job to live at the monastery in her own personal retreat.

In Buddhism, the *sangha* is a spiritual community from which we can learn lessons. I sat one night with Kirsten after evening meditation when we were supposed to be silent. She told me that she was a romantic, like me, but she had found a practice that helped her slay her romantic delusions. "Death meditation," she said.

"Meditate upon images of death," she said, "and you'll see the impermanence of life."

I'd heard about impermanence as a basic tenet of Buddhism but never quite understood what it meant. Could it free me from imagining honeymoons with men who didn't even call back? "It reminds you that death is inevitable and that it just isn't worth it to get caught up in obsessions."

Kirsten was using her practice to free herself from a crush she had developed on a monk at the monastery. She felt a deep love for him that was sincere and without expectation. Meanwhile, she was e-mailing a man in the outside world who had invited her to vacation with him and his family. She was trying to nurture a love without self-interest, a love that stemmed from only feelings of loving-kindness to the man. I knew that some of my friends would just say get on with it and jump in bed together, but I admired her aspirations. Maybe it was the romantic in me. Maybe she was kidding herself.

I asked another senior monk who lived here about this concept of meditating upon death. He was a former hippie from the States who had wandered the Indian subcontinent. In my mind, I nicknamed him Surfer Monk. In the monastery's small library, he pulled down a photo album from the shelves and showed me pictures of a cremation ceremony in India. Yes, death was a vehicle for liberation. "Recognizing the truth of death can free you in life," he told me.

"How did you choose the celibate path as a monk?" I asked him.

"Nothing I experienced sexually came close to the power of my meditations. There's nothing wrong with being alone. You don't have to be married."

I wondered that night about what he told me. It was true, I realized, despite all the pressures upon me to marry. I didn't have to marry. The bullfrog croaked in the pond, as if he agreed.

Over the next days, I meditated upon images of death and the potential for calm in this life. I saw the image of Iftikhar Mamoo lying before me, as he did, in a peaceful, dimly lit room at the hospital where he died from a heart attack. He was the only person I had ever seen dead. I wept hard when I saw him, but now his image didn't sadden me but rather simply showed me, yes, that concept of impermanence on earth. From the pits of darkness, I began to emerge liberated a bit from the shackles of illusory love. My loves had been filled with obsession, insecurity, and clinging. I wanted to strive toward the ideals I'd been told about, a love centered upon loving-kindness. I left the monastery with a meditation practice and a very clean minivan.

I was giving the monk that Kirsten liked plus an aspiring monk, Matt, a ride to Washington, D.C., and out of respect to them, I spent the afternoon before our departure cleaning chewing gum out of the drink cup holders, applying the concept of mindfulness. As we pulled away, I was nervous behind the wheel, not knowing how to relate to two men on the spiritual path. So what did I do? Told West Virginia jokes.

"What's the official state flower of West Virginia?"

They didn't know.

"The satellite dish!"

The cute monk smiled politely. When we stopped to let him duck into the post office, I swung around to appeal to Matt. "Help! I'm just blabbering, telling West Virginia jokes."

He looked at me through the gap in the front seats. "You know, he doesn't expect you to say anything."

Relief descended upon me, spilling over me as if I'd been freed from a burden that I'd carried of my own free will for so many years. I considered this idea. I didn't have to talk. I didn't have to talk? I didn't have to talk. I breathed with the relief that my breath didn't have to be a companion to spoken word. Matthew fell asleep quickly. I felt calm now with the monk. I wanted to ask him how he managed his sexuality on this path that required him to be celibate.

"How old are you?" I asked.

"Twenty-eight," he said.

"How do you handle the issues that most healthy twenty-eight-year-olds deal with?" He understood what I meant.

"I had a nightmare last night." In it, a beautiful woman had hovered over his body as he lay in his bed. He did in his dream what he did in reality. He broke her down into cells and blood and veins. She pulled her hand back. She slapped him hard against the face. He awoke from the slap. He felt a sting on his face, in reality. He admitted he has lived a nightmare since the day he was ordained. He thought his ordination would be a moment of transcendence, passing into a new life in which his spirit could soar. A magic transformation didn't happen. When we had to say good-bye, I was convinced he would leave the monastery during this vacation away. To my surprise, he didn't. But he did some time later.

Matthew slipped into the front seat. He was trying out the monastery to see if he would want to be ordained as a monk there. But he didn't like the energy at the monastery. The young monks exuded hostility, he felt, not calm, because of the way they had to handle their sexuality. It didn't feel right to me, either. I appreciated the Tantric principle of channeling our sexual energy into our entire being, not necessarily to consummate its existence, but at least to recognize it as a legitimate part of ourselves, using its powers for the creative and intellectual ambitions of our crown chakras, that soft spot in the head where our dreams and ambitions lived.

I made a pilgrimage to my bodhisattva friend's serene home, tucked into the woods in Virginia. There I smeared calamine lotion on my arms. I'd gotten poison ivy pulling the weeds at the monastery. "Your body is probably releasing toxins," my friend said, always one to see lessons in everything, even poison ivy.

At her house, I cocked my head to study the books on a shelf in her walk-in closet. She didn't have shelves upon shelves of reading, as I did at my home in Morgantown, many of the books unread and most of them beyond my understanding. My friend kept just a select few books she had studied carefully to know their teachings thoroughly. She told me we could all develop our powers of intuition through the purifying of our minds in meditation. "It doesn't mean clairvoyance. It's about intuition." I was more certain that I had chosen well in deciding to pursue the light, not the dark, side of Tantra.

In meditation that night, I saw the image of Iftikhar Mamoo when he lay dead in the hospital. I remembered the wrenching tears that seemed to swell up from my belly. Before the retreat, I had been writing daily to an old boyfriend, even though I never got a single reply from him. Now I no longer consumed myself with this obsession. I was free.

Safiyyah, my princess guru, helped me turn a tiny room under the stairs into a meditation room, much like the one Chawla Aunty had under her stairs in Delhi. I told Safiyyah, "Bring your favorite things." She brought chocolate chip cookies and a stuffed animal.

It was time to continue my search. The Dalai Lama was going to be leading an important Tantric Tibetan Buddhist ceremony called the Kalachakra initiation at a monastery soaring amid the clouds in northern India near its border with China. But floods had closed some of the roads to the monastery. Was it possible to get there? I searched the Internet and phoned travel agencies in India. They said it could be done. I meditated on the question of whether I should organize this trip with Lucy and Esther, who were booked to land in Bombay that week for a trip through India. Both would be on breaks from their studies in England, Lucy studying psychology and philosophy at the University of Leeds and Esther starting her studies at the prestigious Royal Academy of Art. The travel agent I'd picked up in Delhi during my first visit gave me the phone number of a man in Bombay who could buy train tickets for Lucy and Esther to Delhi. I made the arrangements from Morgantown. It didn't seem like much, but this act of independence felt huge. I didn't have to depend on anyone. I was self-reliant.

My reality check in America made me feel strong enough to avoid becoming ensnared in the expectations others had of me in India. If I lived in India as I lived in America, then I could chart my own course. My meditations on death released me from others' expectations of me. I wanted to be free in this lifetime, not shackled by being dishonest about myself to the world. For now, I recognized that I was a woman who wasn't intimidated by flying into a new city, renting a car, and hitting the road. Lucy wrote to tell me she agreed. "I feel that what is really important on this journey is us being in charge of our own destiny. The driving thing will give us that independence that you have to strive for in India."

Lucy sent her e-mail twice "as a chant." "It is I who am awestruck, gaping with inspiration. For even in the muted silence one can hear the echoes of the whispering souls, calling us to our own paths. Wisen our intentions and be bold in our deliberations. I'm on the path, always floating along beside you." That was a good thing. I knew I'd need her so that I wouldn't lose my mind.

CHAPTER 10

Pilgrimage to the Himalayas

LUCY, ESTHER, AND I were planning the absurd, something unheard of in our family, something never before dared by any in our shared Ansari ancestry.

The three of us were about to travel alone, unescorted, into the farthest reaches of India, the foothills of the Himalayas in the country's lush state of Himachal Pradesh. "Let demons run scared and courage be bold," Lucy wrote me before setting out for India. She and Esther, in their twenties, were more than a decade younger than I, but we were sisters in spirit, connected by our love of the mystical awakened in us by their father. We were going to have a male driver, but we planned to chart the course. We were going to stay in hotels alone. And, of all shames, we weren't going to call home, except once.

"I *can't* believe the Ahn-*sah*-ri girls are here together in India!" yelled Esther, pouncing on me when I greeted her and Lucy in Delhi at Nizamuddin Railway Station, named for a great Sufi mystic. Our train ticket agent came through in Bombay, and they had made it to Delhi without any trouble.

I already had the driver who was going to take us to a place called Ki, a village in the Himalayan foothills where the Dalai Lama was going to give special teachings to an estimated twenty thousand Buddhist faithful, many of whom had trekked for days through the mountains to illegally cross into India from Tibet. It was the closest the Dalai Lama had gotten to Tibet since he fled in the 1950s when China moved to stamp out Buddhism. Lucy and Esther knew even less than I did about the Kalachakra initiation.

The truth was that I wasn't quite sure what I'd get out of this Kalachakra initiation.

Legend goes that a Tibetan king, dealing with fears over his impending death, summoned a Tantric guru, Padmasambhava, to Tibet to teach him the ancient Tantric practices meant to help overcome fear of death. Padmasambhava ditched his beautiful consort, Princess Mandarava, with whom he'd been frolicking and of course meditating. She promptly died upon his departure. No worry for Padmasambhava. He made a big name for himself with the Tibetan king, wasting no time finding himself a new consort in a Tibetan deity, Yeshe Tsogyel, given to him by the happy king. Because of the Indian guru Padmasambhava, Tibetan Buddhism became Tantric Tibetan Buddhism, the path for which the Dalai Lama was now the spiritual head.

Esther and Lucy appreciated one simple fact: Princess Mandarava got a raw deal.

Buddhist Tantra is a branch of the Mahayana school. It teaches that with intense compassion, we can all reach Buddhahood quickly. It's critical not to be defined by the everyday ego with its infinite problems. We're supposed to visualize ourselves in the images of enlightened beings. It's not a crash course, though. First, you're supposed to be experienced in the principles of Buddhist thinking, such as the nature of suffering, the impermanence of existence, compassion for all beings, and the realization of selflessness. Then you're ready to practice Tantra. I, of course, hadn't yet unpacked my boxes in my parents' garage.

The official Dalai Lama Web site on the Kalachakra told me the word *kalachakra* meant "wheels of time." It was an entire cosmology and Buddhist system of exercises for developing awareness. The goal: enlightenment. They called it a spiritual state beyond all worries. It sounded like *sukoon* to me, the peace of mind I'd been seeking since my earliest childhood days.

The Kalachakra initiation is the largest of the Buddhist rituals, and the Dalai Lama presides over it every year. It's supposed to be about spreading peace and tolerance. It's a big deal to get initiated. It means you've been blessed to move forward on the Tantric Tibetan Buddhist path. Plus, you learn some of the practices of meditation that are supposed to make you a better person. Not everyone has to get initiated. But for

those who do, the ritual gives them a special blessing to promote peace
and harmony internally and in the world.

Buddha is said to have taught many ways to transform your consciousness and attain enlightenment. Tantra's techniques of meditation
and exercise are supposed to be one of the most effective. Or, at least,
that's what Tantrics say. Buddhism rests on the principles of Four Noble
Truths: suffering; the arising of suffering; the end of suffering; and the
path toward the end of suffering. Buddhism teaches that liberation of the
spirit, nirvana and the end of suffering, comes from freeing the spirit
from negative elements such as greed, envy, and anger.

I was starting to understand that the teachings in Canada and Santa
Cruz took students to the X, Y, and Z of Tantra in one weekend with
blissful sexual union with another as the reward, but I now saw there was
a lot of A, B, and C that had to come first. That's why the true Tantric
discipline had to be practiced alone first to overcome greed, envy, and
anger, the attaching emotions that make relationships miserable.

To get admitted into Tantra, you're supposed to get initiated. This
happens in a ritual blessing of body, speech, and spirit by a teacher who is
connected to the meditation Buddha. At the Kalachakra, that would be
none other than the Dalai Lama. The teacher initiates students into special
forms of meditation that are supposed to become a part of daily practice.

One thing I liked about the Dalai Lama's thoughts on this concept
was that he said we should study our possible gurus for twelve years
before deciding whether to go under their wings. My friendship with my
bodhisattva friend began in the summer of 1986, and I figured it took that
many years for me to watch her and recognize the wisdom in her guidance. Before I had departed for India a second time, my friend gave me a
nugget of wisdom that stuck with me whenever I doubted a decision I'd
made. "Don't question reality," she told me. To accept reality meant living in the present moment without flashbacks wondering why the past
had turned out the way it had.

Lucy and Esther and I drove on, hitting the Grand Trunk Road built
hundreds of years ago linking the Indian subcontinent over sixteen hundred miles, from Calcutta in India's east through Delhi to Amritsar in
northern India and into Pakistan and Afghanistan. I didn't know yet that

I would embark on this same route three times, each time with a different teacher, each time with different lessons.

Seventeenth-century European travelers used to call it the Long Walk. Sher Shah Suri, a sixteenth-century ruler of the Indian subcontinent, engineered the construction of this bold highway project to link trade and communication across his empire. In 1947, it was the path of escape for millions on both sides of the subcontinent's new dividing line. For us, it was a crowded highway with blaring lorries, the trucks of the subcontinent, painted bright colors. We passed the Parakeet Tourist Complex, a funny name that lodged in my mind. Lucy looked out the window and remarked, "Oh, there's an elephant." It was no surprise in India. We were following the trail of Rudyard Kipling, who set much of his novel *Kim* on the road, calling it "such a river of life as exists nowhere else in the world." Without fear, we told our driver to pull into a *dhaba,* as roadside restaurants were called, places where lorry drivers, not three Western women on a road trip with a Sikh driver, could rest. But we were modern Tantrikas, aspiring to be *dakinis,* with more than Swiss Army knives. Lucy pulled out a traveling Clinique soap dish whenever we stopped at a *dhaba* for our staple *chawal* and *dal,* rice and lentils. Esther carried a Scooby Doo soap holder.

It was a blur of new driving etiquette on the road, marked by signs that commanded, "Blow Horn." That was how drivers signaled they were about to pass, even though there were turn indicators in vehicles. "Use Dipper at Night." High beams were "dippers," and drivers were supposed to flash them before passing. Forget the turn indicators. As we passed through the city of Chandigarh, our driver pulled over so we could appreciate the Rose Garden. "The Rose Garden. Very nice." Our *Lonely Planet* told us it was Asia's largest rose garden, stretching over twenty-seven acres with more than seventeen thousand plants and sixteen hundred types of roses. We walked about a half acre, soaking in a long landscape of terrace, before it started to rain. We ducked under an awning next to a juice *walla.* Three portly middle-aged Indian women sat in the back, sipping their juice, also avoiding the rain. They could have been us, just born into different incarnations. One of the women studied my face as I talked to them about my inquiries into Tantra. She told her friends, "You can see the Kundalini in her eyes." The Kundalini was the serpent introduced to me in Canada that lay coiled in our sexual chakra, ready to unwind and unleash its energy throughout our systems. Of course, my eyes were probably just bloodshot from wearing my contact lenses too long. Our juice sister said she practiced breathing techniques to uncoil her Kundalini.

"What kind of shakti does it give you?"

"It gives me the power to run my family," she said.

Not so convinced about the Kundalini uncoiled within me, the driver let me drive barely ten minutes before taking the wheel again. I didn't like him much. We wound around curves as we climbed into the Himalayas. With the sunset a couple of hours behind us, the driver pulled into the parking lot of a place called the Hotel Hilltop outside the town of Bilaspur in District Swarghat. It was a government lodge run by the Himachal Pradesh Tourism Development Corporation Ltd., the type of two-star hotels my childhood friend Sumita had advised me to trust. My love affair with Indian government tourism lodges and their role in the liberation of the lone female traveler started here at the Hotel Hilltop.

In the parking lot, our driver told us he could keep driving if we wanted. "Whatever you wish," he said.

We conferred. "Yes, we'd like to drive through the night," I told him.

He started listing all the reasons he shouldn't drive through the night. There wouldn't be another hotel for many miles. It was too dark and dangerous. So, in fact, we really didn't have a choice. Classic. I liked him even less. We then performed our huge act of liberation. We checked into a hotel. We were on the road in India without a male chaperone. In the mind-set of many a family on the subcontinent, the driver could have been a rapist. If not him, surely someone would turn out to be a rapist, because that was what happened to women who stayed alone in hotels.

Our Bible on this journey was a book, *Passionate Enlightenment,* by a University of Virginia academic, Miranda Shaw, who chronicled the philosophies of *dakinis,* the magical goddesses of Tantric Tibetan Buddhism, also known as sky dancers because they are free of the conventions and restrictions of worldly existence. Lucy and I looked at each other as I read. We hated to be conceited, but we acknowledged what we were both thinking. "That's us," I scribbled in the margins.

The next morning, not raped, we continued on, escaping an avalanche of rocks on the road in Mandi, at the junction of the Kullu and Kangra Valleys. I saw a beautiful India I'd hardly seen except for a glimpse on our rides to our family hill station house in Panchgani outside Bombay. We climbed into mountains whose lush green was occasionally broken by gushes of waterfalls spilling down as if from the heavens. A rope bridge crossed a river beside the road. I wanted to walk on this rope bridge, but we were three *dakinis* on a mission. It was a virtual entertainment show on the road. A truck, marked "Highly Inflammable," blew dark diesel smoke onto our Tata Sumo, something like a sport utility vehicle. A woman walked on the side of the road with her *dupatta* tied around her forehead.

"Rambo style," Lucy quipped, just before we passed a road safety sign that proclaimed: "Darling I want you but not so Fast."

We started passing the first of many storefronts marked English Wine Shop, a commodity we couldn't figure out, no matter how hard we tried. As we climbed into the mountains, it felt as if we were headed to a place where the clouds met the earth. It was fitting that, on this road trip, I learned the Urdu word for clouds, *badal.* A Holiday Inn in the tourist town of Manali fell along this journey to the heavens.

The terrain began to change as we entered a treacherous stretch of road called the Rohtang Pass. By winter, it was virtually impossible to travel through here. Boulders became the flowers. We saw a sign for "Rohtang Chinese fast food and veg chow mein." Road workers stacked rocks into beautiful square piles. This was a place that inspired reflections upon clouds. We stared out our windows at one formation.

"It's an elephant," I said.

"I think it might be a pig," said Esther. I deferred to the artist in Esther.

Somehow, we hadn't gotten an accurate sense of how long this trip would take. It was time for another layover when we found ourselves in a virtual ghost town of a village that could have been a scene out of the moonscape of Star Wars, only this one with businessmen who banged on the door guest house door we locked. *"Baji, baji,"* meaning "sister, sister," one of them pleaded, asking us to open the door. "No worry. We're Indian businessmen."

We were in Koksar, a tiny village at a height of eleven thousand feet. It was a gateway to Lahaul and Spiti, the largest district in Himachal Pradesh, an expanse of high mountains and slender valleys surrounded by Ladakh and Tibet to the north, the village of Kinnaur to the east, and the Kullu Valley, which we'd just left, to the south. Villagers used the frozen river, covered with snow, during winters for mule traffic. We were in awe of the alpine flowers and herds of sheep and goats grazing nearby. A pretty woman with a pretty baby in pink was beating clothes with a broom.

Lucy had taught me how to wrap my *dupatta* so that only my eyes would be visible, a symbol of a devout Muslim girl, but her trick wasn't for the sake of modesty but because of the dust storms that swirled around us as we continued our climb on razor's edge through the rocky mountain passes. It was a virtual geography and geology lesson on the road. There was Chandra Tal Lake before us, "the lake of the moon" in Hindi, the Himalayas towering over it from the north, a magical place created by the depression of a glacier probably at the end of the last ice age. We rode through treacherous mountain passes and rivers with names like Pagal Nali, "Crazy River."

From a distance we saw colorful Buddhist prayer flags fluttering like bursts of rainbow around a compound. They surrounded a *mandir* to the goddess Kali, known as Kunzum Devi. The son that Buddha left with his princess wife was named Rahul, and it was said the name Lahaul came from Rahul. Locals considered it bad luck for a journey if you didn't pull over, so the driver, a Sikh who didn't bow his head to Kali, also wanted to pay his respects. At a tent colony where the Dalai Lama supposedly stopped to eat, we had picked up a friendly Buddhist couple who said their car had died. The prayer flags flapped with a background of snow-topped peaks and clouds. We ducked under the fluttering flags to enter the *mandir.* White *dupattas* waved at us, tied upon a string. Devotees had stuck coins into the main shrine to the *mandir* in a way I couldn't even figure out.

The Buddhist wife told me, "If your heart is clean, then the coin stays."

I took a five-rupee coin and tucked it next to the dark Kali statue. It stuck. The wife patted my head approvingly.

Our Star Wars–like experience continued, appropriately since Princess Leia seemed to me the ultimate Tantrika, as we nosed into a town called Kaza. It seemed right off the set of the 1970s movie with its narrow alleys and edgy locals. It was the major transport hub of Lahaul and Spiti, the administrative center of the subdistrict of Spiti. Lucy wanted to use the toilet in a restaurant where we stopped to eat. The waiter didn't know we were eating there and talked rudely to her: "The toilet is only for guests."

Lucy didn't take the disrespect well. She would rather have starved than eat at the restaurant. She refused to eat, even though we sat down because it seemed to be the only decent place in town.

After seeing so little civilization, we found ourselves staring at acres upon acres of tent colonies that lined a valley below the mountain where our destination monastery of Ki sat, eight miles from Kaza. It was home to the Ki Gompa, a looming monastery built into the side of a mountain, towering above us. Ki Gompa was the largest and oldest *gompa* in the Spiti Valley. It was built by Ringchen Zangpo and belonged to an order of Tibetan Buddhism called Gelukpa. Ladakhis, Dogras, and Sikhs invaded the *gompa* three times in the nineteenth century. Fire damaged it, and an earthquake partially destroyed it in 1975. But it survived as a home to Buddhist monks who lived and studied there.

For the moment, we were just impressed by the candles we found in our tents.

We were tucked into a far corner of the thousands of tents strung beside each other in this expanse of rocky terrain at the foot of the mountain in which the Ki Gompa sat. Our neighbors were mostly Westerners, many of whom, like me, had found the Banjara Camp on the Internet. Our tent was spacious with luscious sleeping bags stretched over cots for our weary bodies. We bathed in a camp bathroom that came with heated water, a luxury. Our tents circled a main dining tent with afternoon chai and regular hot meals. We'd missed the first days of the initiation, but over the next several days we got into the pace of the hikes up a rocky trail to the monastery for the Dalai Lama's teachings. The trek began for

most around 7 A.M. At the top, we saw a reminder of the twenty-first century: metal detectors through which we had to pass.

Lucy, Esther, and I hunted for places to sit among the thousands
assembled in the monastery's rocky backyard, a part of the mountainside.
A boy with "Teddy Bear" written on his shirt pointed a toy gun at his
mother and shot into the air. Indian police frisked boy monks. The Dalai
Lama sat like royalty upon a terrace festooned with golden banners. The
truth was that it was difficult to understand the teachings. They were
translated into English from Tibetan and broadcast through the radio
into headsets we didn't have. Even when a young aspiring Western monk
gave me his radio and headset, many of the Dalai Lama's teachings about
mandalas and deities went right past me.

The parts I did catch reminded us of what made common sense. Some
of us were just too busy or too self-involved or dense to remember the
essentials. He told us that enlightenment was a mind full of confidence
and clarity. He called it "the middle path." I closed my eyes. I saw a light
radiating within me. Rays shone down upon me. He was talking about
three critical elements of the Tantric path: bliss, emptiness, and compassion. Strong compassion, or *bodhichitta,* had to stay with us throughout,
along with bliss and emptiness. Bliss meant living with the teachings of
Buddha and not the temptations and distractions of samsara, attachment.
It had to be melded with compassion so that it wasn't selfish or self-
indulgent. There was "conditional bliss" based on the senses and experiences, considered contaminated by attachment, greed, and, often,
selfishness. Then, there was "nonconditional bliss," which was based on
emptiness or the imagination. I felt a bliss in the solitude of this moment.
My *muladhara* chakra in my bottom pressed firmly against the ground.

Plenty of folks in the camp seemed plenty freaky. An Indian police
officer appeared more interested in selling his coffee table photo book on
the Spiti Valley and impressing foreigners—"It's *yog,* not *yoga*"—than in
doing police work. A Western woman in our camp scolded Esther one
night at dinner for her definition of emptiness. "That's *not* how the
Buddhists define it," she said with a huff.

An Italian from the city of Assisi rescued us from the woman. His
name was Ram Alexander—quite impossible, of course, that his mother

gave him the name of a Hindu god to go with the reference to the Greek conqueror. In fact, with his tuft of white hair and thick white beard, he was a long-ago disciple of a Hindu woman who became known as a spiritual master in ashrams around India. That's how he got the name Ram. Now he was turning toward Buddhism. He was a virtual encyclopedia on modern-day Tantra, actually believing in *dakinis* as realities, not just the wild fantasies of three oxygen-depleted women journeying through the Himalayan foothills. He even knew of a Tantric Tibetan Buddhist woman, Khandro Rinpoche, who had been accredited as an incarnation of a *dakini,* who had settled not far from Delhi in a place called Clementown and was lecturing in the West. We talked about ritual bathing in a nearby lake he said was frequented by *dakini* spirits.

As we parted, twinkling stars filling the sky, he said to me, "You're either going to be a great sinner or a saint." It was a bit extreme, but his point didn't escape me. I could go down the dark path in this journey, or I could move toward light.

We found ourselves a new friend in the last days of the teachings.

In my wanderings through the monastery, I met a young monk who seemed to be a cross between the cook and personal valet to another incarnate, a young Rinpoche. First, I met the Rinpoche in his room, quite by accident when I was looking for the wife of the spiritual leader of the monastery. He and his wife seemed the perfect answer to my questions about how to practice spiritual Tantra as a couple. She was sitting with a nephew in the small room where the young Rinpoche was living. The Rinpoche had some chocolate tucked behind him. I tried but failed miserably to communicate my line of inquiry to her. She laughed a lot. Maybe that was my lesson on being a Tantrika. Be happy. Laugh.

This young monk invited me into the small kitchen as I was stepping through the Rinpoche's door to leave. A Polo toiletry kit sat on one shelf. Empty egg cartons on another. I had to share this find with my fellow *dakinis.* Lucy and Esther returned with me to meet him. He had studied in the western Indian state of Karnataka, thousands of miles from here, but he was from a village called Kibber, just seven miles from Ki. Part of the overland salt trade centuries ago, Kibber is considered the highest inhabited village in the world, at thirteen thousand feet, although a nearby village is a rival to that title. Our monk friend taught me another word: *dukh,* meaning "suffering." His mother, he told us, died when he was twelve years old. He was so consumed in *dukh* he became a monk, confirming my theory that many of us turn to the spiritual path because we're really sad. That last morning, we didn't see our young monk's face in the sea of maroon robes as we settled into a space beside a tree.

The Dalai Lama guided us through a meditation in which he talked about a mandala that monks had been creating since the start of the initiation, delicately using colored sand to create intricate designs with images of deities and other symbols of Tantric Tibetan Buddhism.

"Imagine now entering the mandala," the Dalai Lama said. At that moment, heads turned upward for the sweep of a rainbow over the *gompa* and the drift of a cloud through the rainbow.

The Dalai Lama continued. "Enter from the eastern door. Repeat mantra. Circumambulate three times.

"You see the many deities. Imagine yourself as Kalachakra by going to the principal deity. Fold your hands. Then, say the mantra." I didn't know the mantra. "Imagine giving the deity flowers." He joked that once when he guided students through a secret mantra, "I saw the curtain open, so I said, 'One of you should stand up and close the curtain.' All repeated what I said." He laughed hard at his own joke. In fact, he giggled.

The Dalai Lama invited us to enter the secret mandala created by the monks. Witnessing it would be a step toward liberating ourselves from negative feelings. "Make your life meaningful." His words echoed my father's guidance to me over the years. "You should develop the wonderful view of *bodhichitta,*" the Dalai Lama told us. "You will be able to help others and fulfill your goals even if you are a nonbeliever. Try to benefit others. Especially try to help others who are weak and suffering.

"You have come to such a remote place, so after receiving this Kalachakra initiation you will have to make the effort to continue the practice of *bodhichitta* and the meditation on emptiness.

"Buddha has said, 'I have shown you the path to nirvana, and it is up to you to follow it.'" Birds swooned overhead in a blue cloudless sky above the monastery. The hum of the monks filled the air. My mind wandered to the places where I found calm. The West Virginia forest

monastery. The meditation room with Safiyyah. Nurturing Jaz and her babies.

I was sitting with Esther and Lucy on the grassy lawn that had become our home many of these days. Before we knew it, the Dalai Lama was gone. A voice over the loudspeaker told us we could form a line to see the mandala handmade by monks using colored sand. The monks went first. Before we knew it, they shoved and pushed and scrambled up the steps that led to the room with the mandala inside. The scene quickly disintegrated into insanity. Indian police officers in street clothes hit long sticks into the air above the monks' heads. One smiled as he thrashed into the air to wave the monks back.

Tibetans then tumbled forward. The stampede turned into a virtual riot. Mothers tossed wailing babies into the air for the Indian police officers at the base of the stairs to pass to the officers up the stairs. Nothing in the air felt sacred.

I stood on our small lawn of grass and watched the stampede in amazement. A familiar face slipped toward me, Barbara Sansone, a spiritual tour guide from Mill Valley, California, outside San Francisco, whom I had met before departing for Kathmandu at the very start of my journey. She was the first person who spoke the word *Kalachakra* to me. She wasn't enjoying this chaotic scene. She disappeared.

I pulled a large women in Tibetan dress up a stone wall to the safety of the grassy lawn. I looked behind me. A thin old Nepali man with a weathered face was lying on the grass behind me, his head in the lap of a foreign woman who was plaintively throwing her wide eyes into the air searching for help. "Water! Get water! This man is dying!"

No one came forward to help. Everyone seemed more interested in seeing this blessed mandala. I crouched by the man's feet to wait for her instructions. "Rub his feet!" she told me.

I rubbed his feet. I felt him contract his toes in the palms of my hands. I told the woman, as she rubbed water on his forehead, "He responded!"

His eyes were glassy. His face was calm. There was a shine to his skin. He was still. A moment passed. The woman looked over at me. "He is dead."

We said nothing, but we both felt as if we were poles of female energy guiding the man into death. As I thought about it, I knew my reflections

were something I probably would have mocked a year earlier had I heard someone else expressing them. But this was the first time death had literally slipped through my fingers. The woman's left hand was on the man's silvery head. She extended her right hand toward me. I extended my left hand toward her. My right hand was on his feet. We clasped hands, creating a circuit between the man and us.

I studied the man now. His face was thin and leathered. He had wrapped mala beads around his left wrist next to a watch. He wore bright sweatpants below his trousers. We searched for an ID and found a hidden wad of 500-rupee notes inside a secret pant pocket. He wore a long-sleeved blue sweater with a ski pattern of zigzags and dots across the chest. We slowly eased his arms out of the sweater so a doctor could check his heart rate. We unbuttoned a shirt he wore with a white tank top underneath. The woman introduced herself to me as Isabelle.

I continued looking for ID cards. I found only a red ribbon from the initiation and a nut. Isabelle asked two Buddhist nuns to do a *puja* for the man. They told her they didn't know what to do. We suggested to a Buddhist monk who finally came by, after Isabelle's requests for help, that maybe the man should be taken somewhere calm for his body to lie in rest. The monk returned to tell us that all the rooms in the *gompa* were taken by *Lamaji,* the Dalai Lama. Isabelle and I looked at each other in disbelief.

The monks had found a friend of the man's son. "He is a Sherpa," the man told us. Some men arrived to carry the body. Isabelle and I walked with them. We were stunned to see them take the Sherpa's body into a dusty storeroom below the balcony on which the Dalai Lama had preached. Indian tea crates were scattered about. Some orange rope had been thrown idly on the ground. The room was littered with old butter cans and was filled with the smell of *ghee,* butter fat used for cooking. The Sherpa's son appeared. He was a young man in a pinstriped jacket and pants. Though the pinstripes didn't match, he had dressed up for this important last day of the initiation. I told him, "Your father died with Shanti." *Shanti* means "peace" in Sanskrit.

The Sherpa's son knelt next to his father and wept. From the storeroom, they carried the body of the Sherpa on a *chador,* a sheet, up to the

balcony on which the press had jammed to watch the Dalai Lama and moved his body into a room at the end. They passed a now-orderly line of people waiting to see the mandala. Thin maroon cushions and chadors lay strewn in the courtyard. Monks trickled inside the Sherpa's room to chant prayers. His son walked in. Isabelle's and my job was done.

I came downstairs. The masses had left. A boy lay on the dusty floor. A man in an open-collar shirt leaned over him with a stethoscope while a bushy-haired, bearded man watched. The man with the stethoscope was Dr. Tsetan Dorji Sadutshang, the chief medical officer at the Tibetan Delek Hospital outside Dharamsala, and part of the Dalai Lama's entourage. The boy had just had his second seizure of the day. Still, the boy's uncle, the bushy-haired man, wanted to carry him to the mandala.

"Maybe it will cure him," he said hopefully.

The doctor knew about the Sherpa who'd just died. The doctor said Buddhists leave bodies alone after death to lie peacefully so that consciousness can escape from all areas. "Westerners want to move so quickly. In Buddhism, we believe you leave the body to rest, to give time for *namshe,* consciousness, to leave the body."

I wondered if Isabelle and I shouldn't have pushed to have a respectful place for the Sherpa, considering the room of *ghee* where the monks took his body. The sky as a ceiling certainly would have been a better place for his son to find his father. The Sherpa's death gave me my greatest lessons at the Kalachakra. I saw little compassion expressed as monks and Tibetans literally ran over each other in their rush to see the supposedly magical mandala.

"Only 40 percent of the people know why they are here," the doctor told me. "The others are here for trade.

"Do they come to eat or because of devotion?" he asked.

To me, the stampede to the mandala was just another reflection of folks chasing superstition. The Tibetan doctor stood over the boy's curled body and reflected on the Kalachakra ceremony. "So many come just to see the mandala. They think they are going to get enlightenment from the mandala. That is why Lamaji said that deity worship is not important. You must live compassionately."

The doctor didn't shrug off the importance of the boy seeing the mandala. "By seeing the mandala he may gain some merits. It's a very auspicious mandala."

The gray-haired uncle bundled the boy into a red shawl. The boy's pants were dusty from the day's two seizures. Dust and noise were all around us. Thin mattresses lay adrift, cluttering the courtyard. Monks on the way to the mandala passed out nuts and yelled, "C'mon. C'mon. Move quickly."

They nudged the uncle with his nephew on his back to move quickly. I looked at the boy to see if he was moved by the spiritual powers of the mandala.

He was fast asleep.

CHAPTER II

From the Bay of Bengal to a Train Berth

DARKNESS DESCENDED upon us on a remote island in the Bay of Bengal, hundreds of miles off India's southeastern shoreline.

Lucy, Esther, and I had traveled from one of India's highest peaks to its farthest island outpost, so far from India we were just a skip away from Thailand. We were searching for a personal abandonment that we hadn't found in the daily teaching schedule and initiation rituals in the Himalayas. Esther and Lucy were discussing eggs with the hotel manager at the government lodge where we were resting for the night in the city of Port Blair, capital of the Andaman Nicobar chain of three hundred richly forested tropical islands. We were going to take the sunrise ferry thirty miles northeast of Port Blair to a tiny spot called Havelock Island. On an airport shuttle bus ride in Chennai, an Australian businessman had pointed us to the island. "Beach Number 7. Nothing like it."

"We'd like three boiled eggs please for breakfast to take with us," Esther told the manager.

"That's not possible. You'll have to have four boiled eggs."

"Why? I don't understand."

"That's the rule."

"Why?"

He finally said, "It's government. Eggs can only be made in pairs."

Lucy stared at him. "So basically the government is saying that we have to have four eggs?"

"Yes."

"I know. You make four eggs. We take three eggs and you keep one egg."

"No."

We boarded our ferry with four hard-boiled eggs, a reminder of the rigidity of culture here. The native people were all indigenous tribals not ethnically part of India. Marco Polo was one of the first Western visitors here. A Maratha admiral, Kanhoji Angre, fought the British off these islands until his death in 1729. After that, the islands became known as *kala pani* in India, or black water, because those who came here hardly ever returned. The British annexed them in the nineteenth century and turned them into a prison colony for the freedom fighters who were battling for India's independence from the British. They began construction of a circular jail in the last decade of the nineteenth century on Port Blair and finally finished construction in 1908. Many of the inmates were executed, only sometimes after a trial. Lucy, Esther, and I passed the jail in a drive across Port Blair, but these two cousin-sisters, born of a British mother, carrying British passports and peppering their conversations with British vernacular, had no interest in seeing this vestige of colonial power. We didn't have any plan except to find Beach Number 7. I fancied Lucy, Esther, and me as modern-day female Marco Polos, venturing into a place where few Indians even went.

Our fourth egg went to a ravenous litter of puppies that whimpered outside our door at Dolphin Yatri Niwas Complex, cottages by the sea on Havelock Island.

Havelock Island covers sixty-two square miles with bullfrogs that were the melody of the night. Bengali settlers inhabited the northern third of the island, since the rest was filled with tropical forest. Each village had a number. The boat docked at the jetty at Number 1. We spent our first night at a government lodge. A bus could have taken us to Beach Number 7, but we set out on foot, the bus bouncing past us with newly-wed Indian couples inside. We discovered on this island an ease in walking not found in the urban centers, where we had to deflect stares and Eve teasing. The three of us together were a shakti force emboldened by our fearlessness and our free spirits.

Children whose names I couldn't distinguish because they were so long bounded out of their houses and yelled to us with the little English they'd picked up from travelers before us. "Hellow! What is your name?" Women with teeth missing smiled at us. We walked past coconut groves and sparkling fluorescent green fields sunk in water. Two water buffalo submerged in water allowed me to understand why these animals earned their names. We passed chai shops, turning right to go to Beach Number 7. The back of my left knee ached from this six-mile walk, but my breath went deep into my belly from the sheer purity of the moment.

Lucy strode with an efficiency and silence that gave her an aura. I asked her, "What do you get from India?"

"The answer would be quite a monologue."

"We have the time before we find Beach Number 7."

"To me, India is grounding. The person I'm with is important, not the place. It isn't a special spirituality or sentimentality about India that affects me. I don't like to believe in sentimentality. But India is like the mother earth. In India, it is just about being. It is about existence."

A warm wind kissed our cheeks. We slowed to share the road with a passing bus labeled "Shivashakthi," with locals inside who were jostled whenever the bus hit one of the many potholes of muddy water dotting the tarred road. It swept by on its rounds many times during our walk. Mopeds whizzed by.

Locals called Beach Number 7 "Radhanagar." Radha was the favored consort to Lord Krishna, the god I grew. I grew up thinking of him as the playboy of Hindu gods. He cavorted with *gopis*, goatherders, stealing their clothes while they bathed along riverbanks, loving each one of them passionately but lavishing his greatest attention on a goddess named Radha. We approached the beach that bears her name and saw a stunning sight: the waves of the Bay of Bengal crashing against the sands.

Lucy and I looked at each other. "Let's go!"

We skipped into the waters, drenching our clothes but relishing the coolness against our skin, a pure expression of Tantric sensuality. I felt a lack of inhibition I'd never felt in India. These waters, once known as symbols of imprisonment, were a healing experience of freedom for me. Off the beach sat a tropical forest of trees. Like three fearless *dakinis*, we slipped into the forest at dusk. The trees towered over us. Darkness descended. Anything could happen. We saw a light.

"Hello! Hello!"

"Hello!" The answer came.

A beaming man greeted us and guided us into a large kitchen where a wood stove blazed. We were at the Jungle Resort at Beach Number 7 with posh huts and tree houses. The cook pulled a delicious impossibility of a birthday cake out of a mud stove for the owner's sister. Kittens tumbled over each other. It was a beautiful place in spirit and in nature.

We retraced our steps, a flashlight our spotlight upon our new world. Bullfrogs along the side of the road sang like a choir of tenors. The Jungle Resort manager drove by on a scooter and offered us a ride, along with a friend, also on a scooter. Lucy and I jumped on the back of the friend's Bajaj Classic. Esther jumped onto the manager's bike. The leaves above cast occasional shadows in the moonlight. The headlight captured the monsoon raindrops, but to me they were diamonds showering from the heavens upon us. "That's your father sending those to us," I yelled to Lucy, over the sound of the engine. "He is telling us that we're doing the right thing. He supports us."

"That's beautiful," she whispered, behind me.

"This is why we came here," I said to Lucy. "This is India. You keep going and going for one beautiful moment."

Beach Number 7 and Havelock Island gave us a freedom I didn't know could be enjoyed in the land of my birth. Maybe it was the spirit of an island people free in a place that used to shackle prisoners. Residents said Hindus, Muslims, and Sikhs lived here without the divide found on the subcontinent, intermarrying and worshiping together at the shrines of saints. We moved to the Jungle Resort, throwing ourselves every day into the Bay of Bengal's waters, the beach ours alone except for occasional local fishermen who walked by without disturbing us. A female dog with a limp kept us company. Lucy and Esther plunged fearlessly into the waves. I followed them a little more cautiously, my fear of water still holding me back, in a brown Lily of France bra and Gap underwear made see-through by the warm waters. We were like Radhas without need of any Krishna.

One evening I sat with Lucy and Esther on the porch off our hut, my white robe half open to my silky bra and bare skin, a candle flickering in a seashell we had plucked off the beach. Inside, our home was beautiful, with turquoise saris as curtains, bells jingling at the bottom. The ceiling towered like a cone, wood beams gathering in the middle. On the porch, we talked about sex, sensuality, power, love. I remembered an Indian man we had seen the day before with his arm around his wife's shoulder. He told us he was reading *Jonathan Livingston Seagull* for the second time. It made me wonder about the day when a man would have his arm around me like that.

In this adventure, we also became Durga, the fierce powerful goddess who rides a tiger. Our tiger happened to be TVS scooters we rented on the island, and I hadn't yet learned about Durga's power.

Lucy couldn't get her scooter started. A boy came over to help her. He showed her that she hadn't turned the ignition key on. She was edgy with him. She realized later that, unlike many others in India, he was in fact just coming over to help her. We skirted past fields of rice paddies. I felt powerful and independent.

As we sat on the dock, Esther befriended a drunken man who invited us to his house to visit his wife, Maya, and their children. Our Jungle Resort host told us the man had three young daughters and a son. He spent his money on alcohol, while his wife kept the family together. We rode our scooters to road's edge and walked through overgrown grass to reach the house made with a special mix of cow dung, mud, and water. It had a smooth, well-swept look, beautiful in its simplicity.

Maya was a beautiful woman, slim and smooth skinned with a sari wrapped elegantly around her. She crouched over a stove, making dinner in the house's main room. A doorway to the right led to the house's only other room, where the two eldest girls studied by the light of a kerosene lantern. I sat beside them to help them with their homework. All the clothes the children owned hung from a string stretched over the bed and family *mandir,* sitting in the corner. The youngest girl scampered about the rooms dressed only in underwear like bloomers and a smile.

Maya confirmed Esther's instincts about her. "I knew she'd be remarkable," she said, gazing at her admiringly. Much later, I discovered *maya* meant "illusion" in Hindi. In this Maya's life, it seemed, there was a clear reality to her existence. She showed us the singular strength of a woman poised against adversity.

On our porch, we imagined disappearing here to write, draw, and create, but our ancestral village was beckoning us. And for that, we had to return to the mainland.

We ventured to Pondicherry, a former French colony settled in the early eighteenth century, a bouncy car ride from Chennai across the border from into the state of Tamil Nadu. It proved that India could be run well. The streets were clean. Couples held hands. Women rode bikes. The Aurobindo Ashram was founded in 1926, named after a spiritual leader, Sri Aurobindo, who drew Westerners as well as Indians, including a woman who became his partner, Mother Meera. She ruled here until her death in 1973 at the age of ninety-seven. I wondered if Sri Aurobindo and Mother Meera shared the special union of Shiva and Shakti found in the god and goddess. He was a man. She was a woman. I could find no mention of a romance between them. Both were widely respected in India, and the idea would be blasphemous to some, but I came from the Jerry Springer talk show culture of America and wondered about that which was unsaid.

A sweet smell of jasmine lingered in the air at the Aurobindo Ashram on Marine Street. A woman bent down in front of a portrait of the Mother and showed her tall son how to pay homage to the Mother by touching the space below her feet. I loved watching belief in India. We were waiting for a relative of Nandi Uncle in Delhi. The relative's mother had done the unorthodox, leaving Delhi to settle in Pondicherry with her children as a disciple of Mother Meera. Her husband later joined her. Their daughter, Aster Patel, arrived and, looking at Esther, Lucy, and me as we stood before her in the reception area, said, "You have beautiful eyes. You are a Shakti fortress."

We knew what she meant because we knew the power we felt together. When we hit the road in England once, to land at a surfing beach town called Newquay, an Australian surfer traveling with his buddies watched us as we laughed and enjoyed ourselves along a bar. "I want some of whatever you girls are on," he said to us, thinking we were tripping on Ecstasy or some other mind-altering drug. We weren't on anything but the high of adventure.

This place carried the name of the man who inspired it, Sri Aurobindo, but it felt as if the Mother ruled it today. Her image was everywhere. One night at the ashram, I met a longhaired Indian who offered to teach me how to ride a motorcycle on his Enfield Bullet. We sat at a restaurant beside the sea, the waves crashing the rock as he sang a mantra dedicated to goddesses. I considered his offer. I remembered my friend Tom Petzinger who wrote a book about the airline industry. When I suggested working on the book with him, he said he preferred to do the work alone. "Amelia Earhart flew alone," he told me. She, of course, crashed, never to be seen again, but I thought he was right. And I thought of Durga on her tiger. "Durga didn't ride with anyone on her tiger," I told this weirdo, fleeing to make my 10:30 P.M. curfew at the ashram guest house where Lucy and Esther were tucked into bed behind room number 13, marked "Inspiration" on the door. I knew this was a path I ultimately had to travel alone.

On this trip, I was beginning to learn the stresses that men endure when they are economic shelters for others. I'd considered myself a host for Esther and Lucy on this trip, making train reservations, paying bills, making room reservations. I kept my thoughts to myself because I didn't want to taint our adventure with mundane problems, but I worried about money as I lay my head to rest at night.

It was their company that brought me to places like this experimental colony called Auroville. A stretch of land was dotted with homes of foreigners who had settled there, trying to live with the rules and philosophies laid out by Sri Aurobindo and Mother Meera. Esther was horrified at how most of the Indian faces belonged to the hired laborers.

We edged close to a looming building, Matrimandir. Scaffolding covered the outside of the dome. A tour guide told us the history of Auroville.

"The Mother sees a dream," he started. She worked with a French architect, Roger Anger, to create an experiment in international living. It opened on February 28, 1968, and included some seventy settlements now spread over about twelve miles with about twelve hundred residents.

"Mother says . . ." the tour guide started again, telling us the precise dimensions that Mother wanted the meditation room at the top of Matrimandir to be. We walked in circles around the mandir, "Silence" signs posted on the wall.

The way people worshiped Mother Meera made her seem more like a cult hero than a divine inspiration. It was a reflection of her power, though, that she stood out as a living saint in this country where the women revered by the citizenry were usually fictional.

Before we stepped inside the main meditation room under the dome, we were handed white socks. Inside the room, yards of white sheets spilled into each other, bathing the entire floor in a sea of white. A crystal hung from the epicenter below a sky window. A star was reflected upon the ceiling. Light danced. The crystal created a star with the shadows. We sat on white pillows. As I meditated, the energy bounced from the crystal to Lucy and Esther on the other side of the circle and then back to me.

We headed back to Chennai that night and stayed the night in a hotel across from the train station. We needed three towels. The clerk said that wasn't possible. He could only give me one towel.

"The *dhobi* not come," he said, referring to the man who washed clothes.

"Give me six sheets!" I figured we could dry ourselves with our sheets.

"Not possible. Not possible."

The next morning at the Chennai train station, a woman lay on a bench sleeping, wrapping her turquoise sari around her body to sleep with modesty. Our train had been canceled. We went into another building to get refunds, passing men as they urinated outside.

We stood at the counter trying to get our money back. I asked a man whose train was also canceled about the schedule to Lucknow. He answered briskly. I was about to fill out our refund forms. He looked at my pen, wanting to borrow it, and snarled, "Your pen!"

I thought maybe I'd repay his albeit small effort at helping us and gave him my pen despite his rudeness. When he left, Lucy laughed at his arrogance. "Your pen! Your pen! Your pen!" she repeated.

"Your pen!" became a symbol to us of a man's sense of entitlement.

We walked to the baggage hold. A dead body lay on the floor with a printed cotton sheet draped over it. I couldn't tell if the body was a man or woman. The only part of the body that peeked out was mangled toes at the end of worn, dirty feet. Flies fluttered around the toes.

We had a day to kill in Chennai. I got the address for the Enfield showroom. The store was too far away, but the dream of riding my own tiger continued to germinate in my mind.

We ducked into Jim Carrey's *Me, Myself, and Irene.* I understood now the popularity of Bollywood in India. Even if it was an afternoon with Hollywood that gave me the realization. We bought popcorn in cones. And we escaped from the traffic, the blaring horns, the Hulk Hogan billboards advertising large-sized men's suits. Men wolf-whistled when the Jim Carrey character went to kiss Renee what's-her-name. That was sexual repression in India. A young man named Krishnan left as we did, introducing himself to us. He asked Esther, "Would you like to go out tomorrow?"

The next two days we passed on the train back to Lucknow, listening to the train's catering manager tell us his Tantric meditation practice, which consisted of eschewing deity worship and embracing silent contemplation.

India. I loved it this time with Esther and Lucy. I didn't know what I'd do without them. It was a country that had such a public face of male energy. Sometimes I was angered by it. In fact, I hated it. Yet I felt like a powerful shakti force. How much I had learned.

Rail tie workers huddled on the track parallel to us. They carried metal rods in their arms. They wore scarves around their heads like crowns and *dhotis,* the fabric tied around a man's waist like pants. They rocked their bodies together against the ties to pull them up. A man with beautiful almond eyes had more cuts on the side of his torso than a workhorse. He wore baggy mustard-colored pants cuffed up to his calves. Together they chanted, led by a white-haired man in a pink-and-white-checkered shirt.

They threw their shoulders into the tie at the same time, like a serpent dancing.

We drifted away as they chanted, "Ooaaay."

I sat on the edge of the steps of the open door. A push from behind and I would have tumbled onto the tracks below. But I wasn't afraid. I was so enjoying the rush of the wind against my face. My hair flew so fast behind me. My toes peeked out from the sandals I propped against the edge of the stairs.

A herd of cattle grazed beside the track. The herder stood behind them with a checkered *dhoti* wrapped around his slender hips and a black Tommy Hilfiger T-shirt above it. He chased the cattle from track's edge. Slivers of silver shone through the green grass of rice. Shafts of white flower thrust above the carpet of green. Drizzle fell upon my ankles and feet. The train had a music of its own. Its whistle. Its rock. Its rhythm.

I had stepped off the train momentarily when it stopped at a station. The only other woman on the platform was wrapped in a sari and stood at the train door's edge. Otherwise, the platform was populated by the men from the AC compartment, including one with a khaki shirt and another with a golf shirt that said IBM.com. Cow dung sat piled nearby, covered with flies. It took the determination of my female energy to tuck my hands into my cargo pockets and walk from train door's edge to platform edge. Why in this land of goddesses were women so repressed?

Now, riding the rails, I breathed in India.

Brown rocks of earth lined the track's edge. Water sat in a field with a green grass edge. Colors blossomed everywhere. The silver lush of gravel. The bronze rush of track's edge. The red and white rush of the platform edge. A man stood thigh high in a blue *dhoti* in rice paddy waters. I sat perched at the door as the train approached a bridge. I felt the rush in my stomach. But I didn't stir. We crossed the bridge. My arm was taut against the silver handrail. The train door was painted dark blue. My feet sat on steps that had silver and black edges.

The caterer came by to visit. Later in the day I guided Lucy and Esther through the narrow corridor to the caterer's compartment. He didn't have enough supplies for the rest of the run. He had sent a telegram ahead for more ice, cups, and rice. Was Caterer Sahib worried? He wasn't. "All will be solved."

We were about to enter a town called Jhansi, and I read aloud to Lucy and Esther the tale of the Rani of Jhansi, a queen who dressed as a soldier to fight the British. In 1803 the British East India Company arrived here and took control of the state. The last of the rajahs died in 1853. Conveniently, the British had just passed a law letting them take over any princely state under their patronage if the ruler died without a male heir. They gave the rani, the queen, a pension and took full control of Jhansi.

The Rani of Jhansi wasn't happy about the British forcing her into retirement. When the Indian freedom movement exploded four years later, she led the rebellion at Jhansi. The Indian revolutionaries massacred the British soldiers stationed there. Then, the next year, when the rebel forces were embroiled in infighting, the British took control again.

The rani fled to a city called Gwalior and, in a brave last stand, rode out against the British disguised as a man. She was killed. Her stand, though, earned her status as the Joan of Arc of India and a role as the heroine of the Indian independence movement.

Her tale inspired us, and I was happy to find a model for a real Tantrika in Indian history, even if she had failed.

We arrived in Lucknow. Rashida Khala was as immaculate and caring as ever. Esther and Lucy, the two *dakinis,* argued with a men's tailor in Hazratganj who didn't believe they actually wanted their pants stitched at a men's tailor, something women here didn't do. "We do want our clothes tailored here," Lucy insisted.

I didn't know why I mentioned to Rehan Bhai my idea of riding a motorcycle. He was all against it. He told me about the highway bandits who made a motorcyclist pull over, stealing his motorcycle at gunpoint. I told Azfar Bhai and Rehan Bhai, "I don't want to talk about this anymore. I'm not interested in your negativity."

Azfar Bhai still wasn't ready to talk about ideas or vision. "Let me get you ice cream," he told Esther and me. We were grown women. I wasn't much younger than he was, but he still treated us like little girls. We dutifully walked down Hazratganj, the shopping corridor outside Jahingarabad Palace, with him always a few steps away from us. It was at least worth a good laugh.

For Lucy's birthday, we walked down Hazratganj, arms swinging, feeling powerful. A Shakti fortress. Most other women were escorted by men. It was so insane this town. During one of our walks, a man riding as a passenger on a motorcycle pushed me as Esther and I walked in front of our palace home. Another time in Haszratganj, a man tried to feel Esther's breasts. I caught up to him, gave him a swift shove, and screamed at him.

How could a town live with itself when its women lived in fear? Where were the parents? What were they teaching their boys? They were expecting to marry them into beautiful homes after a young adulthood of indecent behavior. It was warped. Sick.

Evening came. The motorcycle dealership was closing, but I had an appointment to learn how to ride one. I took a lesson on a Bajaj motorcycle with a Mohammad something sitting behind me. I drove, riding on the road beside the stadium where schoolgirls played volleyball. I felt the power of independence and possibility.

I enlisted Parvez in my quest. Parvez was Khala's handsome young servant whom she had raised from childhood with his brother, Anis. Parvez was a male not threatened by my ambitions.

One day at dawn I awakened Parvez and Anis to accompany me to the grounds to learn to ride the downstairs Hindu neighbor's Kawasaki single engine. At the grounds, girls sat on scooters, learning to steer. A brother sat behind one, a girl behind another. I started the engine of the Kawasaki and skirted cow dung and cows lounging in the open field. A beautiful energy coursed through me. A boy sat behind his mother. Another girl practiced alone. She fell over and picked up her scooter herself. Two *mowlana* types, orthodox Muslims with long beards, sat on an Enfield Bullet. It must be the chariot of Tablighi, men who belong to the conservative Tablighi Jamaat organization of my cousin from Aligarh; Rehan Bhai rode one.

I was the only woman on a motorcycle, not a scooter. I felt powerful. I did crazy eights sleeping cows, like the kind of crazy eights I used to run on the West Virginia University Medical Center hill when I was in high school cross-country.

I invited Akhtarul Mulk, Iftikhar Mamoo's friend, over to meet Esther and Lucy. They'd never spent time with him. He now carried a business card, "Chief Editor," *Area of Darkness,* an English weekly he had started. He gave me a card he had prepared with my name on it as a correspondent for *Area of Darkness,* marked PRESS in big red letters.

We were on a *takht,* the wooden platform, on the veranda. Akhtarul Uncle sat on a chair and leaned toward Esther and Lucy. "I knew your father. Your father was unhappy in England. He wasn't happy being away from India. He always had a longing for India."

Esther tried to speak up. Akhtarul Uncle tried to continue. Esther persisted: "No, let me finish. This is very important to me. Of course, my father missed India. But he was where he wanted to be. He was *in love,*" she screamed. "He and my mother were in love. They were deeply in love."

Esther and Lucy scolded this elderly friend of their father's. "Love isn't a place," they exclaimed.

I admired the way my cousin-sisters stayed true to their convictions. Trying to be polite, trying to absorb, trying to decipher, I seemed to get so distracted from my core beliefs. I turned to Rashida Khala and asked her how she dealt with the *bukwas,* or garbage, outside that makes us go *pagal,* or crazy. She told me the story about going to the crowded bazaar in an old part of Lucknow called Chowk. A relative complained afterward that she hadn't even noticed her as she had passed by.

"I just look forward," Khala said. I wondered if I could ever be so focused.

CHAPTER 12

The Village

KHALA DESCENDED with regal grace and threw an order over her shoulder to those remaining at Jahingarabad Palace from the household: "Be good."

She carried a small black leather bag as her only luggage. We climbed into a big white Ambassador car with a skinny driver named Ayub behind the steering wheel. Lucy, Esther, and Khala were my escorts for my first pilgrimage to our ancestral home in our village, Jaigahan. Esther and Lucy had spent their early years in the village, waddling into the fields with a Hindu gardener, Hardu Ram. During our adventures from the Himalayas to the Andaman and Nicobar Islands, I'd learned that I could be the master of my own destiny, even in this land so foreign to me. I looked forward now, and restrained myself from casting sideways glances to see what others were doing. That way I could create a reality different from the first oppressive trip I'd made to India. I saw the modern-day divide between Hindus and Muslims, the pursuit of real spiritualism versus spiritual opportunism, and the raw strength of women who ran households. Now, it was time to make a symbolic journey to my home in India. It was my maternal ancestral home, Latif Manzil, where I hoped to walk upon the land from which I came and know the ancestors whose voices rang within me.

It was early morning as we traversed a railroad crossing with the morning rush hour of bicycle traffic spinning past the eucalyptus trees that lined the highway. Khala wouldn't let me drive. I sat up front by the window with Khala's servant Anis between the driver and me. Khala sat in the back behind me, beside the window. Lucy and Esther shared the backseat with her. Khala said that Iftikhar Mamoo stopped going to Latif Manzil because of *sadma,* Urdu for "sadness."

Red Mahindra tractors, something like the Caterpillar tractors in America, passed us by. Khala wore glasses with a cream *dupatta* over her head. We rode behind a lorry that asked, "Horn palese," with the sort of incorrect spelling that was a common source of amusement in India.

Women here sat sidesaddle on bike racks as lanky men pedaled easily. Watching the spokes on the wheels turn slowly, I lost myself in the rhythm of village life. A woman in a bright yellow sari sat leisurely behind a man as he edged her past a gas station with a Bharat Petroleum sign. It was joked that women rode on the back of bikes and motorcycles as if they were sitting delicately on their living room sofas. We passed a woman doubled over with a bag on her back. Workers put grass over tar to fill potholes. Rows of bricks lay adjacent to road. A scarecrow stood in front of a bungalow. There were *tongas,* carts drawn by horses, just as my father had told me traveled on these roads. The signs were all in Hindi. I spotted a faded photo of the Hindu god Shiva on a wall.

Thatched roofs sat on bamboo legs. A sign for Nerolac Paints hung not far from a canopy of mango trees. Men's shirts billowed behind them as they pedaled in the cool air. A woman in a bright orange sari leaned on a stick, watching goats.

Dirty green Mahindra jeeps passed us with their window flaps bound close but their doors open. A man ran to make sure his goat didn't amble out in front of our blaring Ambassador. Rain snapped and crackled on our windshield. We passed a "Colgate Super Shakti" sign painted on the side of a brick building. We passed yet another sign declaring, "P.C.O. S.T.D.," the signage in front of stores with phones for the public. Men fished in a place called a *thalab,* throwing their netting into the water.

All of a sudden, our right bumper met a Mahindra tractor. It was a little after 11 A.M. We'd been on the road less than three hours, and already we were disabled. The driver pulled over to survey the damage. The hood could easily scrape and puncture the front right tire. The driver's side door wouldn't shut. I climbed out. I helped the driver and Anis move the car forward and backward, trying to jostle parts into place. Men stared. I didn't care. The driver slid into the mud.

The driver's side door wouldn't stay shut, so I whipped my sheer green *dupatta* from over my shoulders and handed it to Anis to tie the door closed. "Another entry in our 101 uses for a *dupatta,*" I told Esther and Lucy. The *dupatta* was a symbol of modesty, but to us it had also become a practical accessory, wiping up spills and now securing our safety. Back on the road, we passed a pastel green vista around us with mossy waters at road's edge, wild purple flowers in the water. We took a left at a garbage dump and barreled over a road flooded with rain, past the New Shahganj Medecal Stor with its misspelling and over more flooded waters. I didn't know it, but Shahganj was the closest urban center to our village, a small town of maybe a thousand residents and a crowded bazaar along both sides of the main road. Schoolchildren ambled by with books under their arms. Outside town, I looked out at fishermen sitting on the edge of small pools of water with bamboo rods. We passed Eastern Montessori School.

We had entered a Muslim enclave of India with *786,* the Arabic numerals I used to write on the top of my childhood exams, stenciled onto the window of one of the many Mahindra jeeps that bounced by us. When we reached a smaller city called Khetasarai, we passed an *ikka,* a horse-drawn cart, filled with Muslim women in black *burqas.* We drove by a band of young Muslim girls in school uniforms of blue *kameezes,* white *shalwars,* and white *dupattas.* A safety pin secured the *dupatta* in the back.

Simple village life flowed around us. A herd of pigs with testicles bouncing below their haunches grunted by our car. On road's edge, a child screamed, kicking his legs into the cool air. A girl walked through the village with a walker, next to a paraplegic boy spinning the wheel on a homemade wheelchair made from bicycle parts. We made a left at a bright fruit cart with red apples hanging on a string of red thread. We stopped beyond the cart to buy Esther's and Lucy's staple of fruits. A man with a mouthful of tobacco confirmed Khala's directions to the village. Water dripped from the tits of pigs emerging out of a muddy watering hole. A water buffalo chased another water buffalo.

"Look, they're playing tag!" I imagined.

Our car rattled, giving us little reassurance we'd actually make it the short leg remaining to the village. I was excited, but I didn't know what to anticipate. We took a right after a vegetable cart at a faded Union Bank of India sign. More purple flowers floated in a pond. We braked for a baby water buffalo and took an important right turn at a pile of rocks.

Through a narrow alley tucked between ancient-looking houses, we drove in front of our home called Latif Manzil. It was like a white phoenix rising from the rice paddy fields. I was in awe.

I felt as if I was in a magical place. It was beyond my wildest imagination. My mother played here. She ran through the doors. She climbed these stairs. It was a place where a lychee tree grew in the courtyard. She'd told of the jinn that lived in a storage space upstairs. I wanted to befriend this one who had haunted my mother for so long in her childhood. One of my mother's uncles, her father's sister's husband, used to tell her and the other children at Latif Manzil that they could see jinns if they put *kajal,* the black kohl of eyeliners, on their thumb. She tried but never saw a jinn.

Two boys worked a water pump in the courtyard so the driver and Anis could wash their hands. These first cousins held each other's hands and loved each other like brothers. Here was where my Khala had lived in her girlhood when her father and his three brothers created this home.

Our first night, Khala awakened and fidgeted with the mosquito coil. Her body was a silhouette of her white *dupatta* and white flowered *shalwar kameez,* all in cotton.

As I lay on my *charpai,* my woven bed, beside her, it was as if the walls talked to me.

The incarnations of so many lives stirred through me. The lives of my ancestors. The lives of my parents. The lives I'd lived within this one *junam,* or birth, that was mine. Not just the stuff of my memory coursed through me but also the memory of others. Tales told by deep eyes that stared back at me from black-and-white photos so old they stuck to the glass of picture frames. The psychic memory of a mother's lullaby. The karma of past lives—my own, my ancestors', and others'—paying me a visit. We inherit not only the color of our eyes and the color of our skin from our ancestors but also their legacy. To know our *atman,* our true self, we have to know these people whose breath echoes within us. I had learned so much, but I still didn't know how I fit into the legacy of Ansari women.

The tales began for me with the voice of a wife whose husband was not supposed to die so young. She was my mother's mother. I called her nani.

Her name was Zohra, Arabic for Venus, the Roman goddess of love
and beauty. She was the teenage daughter of a landowner when her marriage was arranged to a svelte, handsome, and gentle man from the same
village of Padghodia where she grew up in District Azamgarh in Uttar
Pradesh. She wasn't supposed to go to her husband's house until she grew
a little older.

Then cholera swept through Padghodia, seizing the lives of her young
sisters. To save the young bride's life, she was sent to her husband's second
home in the neighboring village of Jaigahan. Her husband became a well-
respected lawyer, rising in the political circles of District Azamgarh. The
British still ruled India. There was still a system of *zamindars,* or
landowners, who owned the country's vast rural farmlands. His family
was one of those *zamindars* with acres of fertile land of wheat and rice.

Her husband's name was Abdul Ali Ansari, my nana.

He was one of four brothers whose names began with Abdul. Their
father was Abdul Latif. He was my *per* nana, my maternal great-
grandfather. Latif is one of the ninety-nine names of God in Arabic,
meaning "the exceedingly benevolent," protecting for suffering. He
would treat his sons with great congeniality, referring to them as *ap,* the
respectful way of saying "you" in Urdu.

My per nana had a vision to build a house in the village where his four
sons' families could live as extended families under one roof. And so Latif
Manzil rose from the earth. The villagers knew of it simply as the *kothi,*
the "big house." Architecturally, it was designed as a *haveli,* a grand
house, in the finest tradition of homes designed by Hindu Rajput kings
and Muslim Mogul emperors. Latif Manzil and the Jaigahan culture
were testimonies to the harems that spread in India with the conquests of
invading Moguls. They had nothing to do with the Western concept of
harems—sultans in palaces with their concubines, slaves, eunuchs, and
countless wives in billowing silks. These were vestiges of domestic
harems, an Arabic word that meant the seclusion of women behind
boundaries. My dear friend Vasia had introduced me to a Muslim scholar
in Morocco, Fatima Mernissi, when I visited her in Rabat one winter. It
was Ramadan, and we had dinner together. The scholar said she wasn't
fast. "Too much work to do," she said. She was a Muslim woman to

whom I could relate. And the life she chronicled of the domestic harem into which she had been born was the same as the one my mother was born into. She, like my mother, had to break the *hudud,* the boundaries, that traditional Islam imposed upon women. It was the *hudud* of our culture that also settled like a noose around my neck. In India, the domestic harem translated into purdah or *zenana.* This was how my nani lived, behind a boundary that kept her from her husband's side even in death, and this was the rule into which my mother was born. But it was a boundary that Esther, Lucy, and I didn't accept.

The crickets and frogs of Jaigahan inspired my mother's eldest brother, Iftikhar, to pen the Sufi poetry he would one day read on the BBC. The family often returned to Padghodia. One day, Nani gathered with Nana and their children for a rare photo in the doorway of their home caked with the smooth mix of mud and cow dung. She looked down like the demure woman of India that she was raised to be. Nana told his children, *"Hasi mazaaq ke saath rahoe."* It meant: "Live with fun and laughter."

It was a pure and innocent image of a family before its world turned upside down. Nana came home one afternoon just as he did on so many afternoons. He ate his afternoon meal like usual. Then he fell sick.

Nani stayed by his side but then slipped out of the room like a ghost whenever men would come to visit him, bowing to the rules of her religion and custom to do purdah and not show her face to men who weren't relatives. He died after one of those times when she left his side. She lived with this quiet regret.

Nani also lived with a family secret. The doctor said her husband died of a heart attack. Descendants would say he died after coming home with a stomachache. Iftikhar Mamoo once confided to my mother that the cook told Nani a different story, that someone, jealous of Nana, told the cook to poison the food. The cook didn't know for whom it was intended. He did as he was told. And Nani lost her husband.

For years, his daughters remembered the *kajal* he always kept in his pocket to line the eyes of his children in black to ward off *nazar,* the evil eye. It was as if he died with *kajal* in his pocket, for it seemed that the evil eye lingered upon his widow and her children.

The family mostly left the village. We were fortunate in one regard to have a descendant living at Latif Manzil, protecting it. He was Zaki, a pocked-faced man who acted like the lord of Latif Manzil. Lucy, Esther, and I soon start calling him Bluebeard because he exuded so much terror, even in the company of his wife and younger son. He hadn't committed the horrible deeds of the mythical Bluebeard, but he ruled his grand home in the same way.

"Ammmma!"

My mother's voice and footsteps echoed on the stone steps that led upstairs to where I sat on Latif Manzil's top floor.

She was a young girl and had skipped school again, as she was prone to do. She was calling out to her mother who was downstairs, tending one of her children or cooking or doing one of the many things a woman running a household in the village does. My mother raced up and down these stairs all day long, playing with the *chamar* children of the village, born of a Hindu caste considered untouchables because their parents cleaned the toilets and cesspools.

But today Nani couldn't answer. Nani had tried to keep her family together but hadn't succeeded. She sometimes wondered why she hadn't died in the cholera epidemic along with her sisters. But Nani didn't weep about her lot in life. That wasn't her way. She was a model of *sabr,* an Urdu word of Arabic origin that meant more than the "patience" it usually described. It was wisdom. Compassion. Steadfastness.

My mother's shouts filled the village air. The day had turned into darkness. She had been piled onto an *ikka,* a horse-drawn cart. She saw only darkness and more darkness. Her mother was sending her to live with another relative where she could get a proper education. All she wanted was her mother.

She was taken, instead, eastward to Bombay, now Mumbai. She refused to live with a relative she didn't like. She was then sent to a hill station called Panchgani. A British officer had tried to convert Panchgani into a European health resort decades before. It was now home to some of India's finest boarding schools. She lived in a sweeping house, Buena Vista, where two older married cousins shepherded the education of their younger cousins.

One day at school, the nuns handed out Cadbury chocolate and roasted rice treats called *liee ke ladoo,* sweets that looked like today's Rice Krispies treats only they were white. It was 1947. India had just won independence from the British, and my mother was lined up in a hallway at her convent school, collecting her treats. The country was liberated. A new Muslim nation called Pakistan was carved out of India's northernmost region. Murder, rape, and pillage followed the migration of Hindus to India from Pakistan and Muslims to Pakistan from India. It mattered little to this girl. Her heart hadn't yet been liberated. Every night, she sat on a rocking chair and wept for her mother who still lived in the village.

"Amma!" the cries continued when she returned to the village. There, she didn't cry. But she asked her mother, "Why did you leave me?"

She grew into a young woman with a face as smooth as porcelain. Her eyes were a deep pool of brown light. Her cheekbones were high and her face narrow. She had a soft voice that called to her best friend with the lilt of birds. At each other's urging the two of them ripped off the black *burqas* that cloaked them on the way to their girls' college, Nirmala Niketan Home Economics College.

"We're not going to wear our *burqas!*" they yelled to each other.

It was the servant who told on them. He told her elder cousins that she and her friend took off their *burqas* when they got on campus. For this infraction, they pulled her from school. It was time, anyway, that she got married.

Her eldest sister, Rashida, and another sister, Shahida, had found a prospective groom at a wedding. What the two sisters liked about him the most was the way he bounced around the wedding, snapping photographs with boundless energy. His name was Zafar.

Khala told me more about our family. A snake bit her dadi. The wife of her father's eldest brother, her bari ammi, made a *masjid,* a mosque, in front of our village home in Jaigahan with the money she received as her wedding gift. A relative tore the *masjid* down and replaced it with a new construction, thinking he had done a great thing, not realizing he had dismantled family history. One night, Khala told me, she dreamed long ago of seeing a tree with an orange hanging from it. The orange fell into the water. She was pregnant and lost her baby that night. She said she felt sad at coming to Latif Manzil. "There are many regrets that surface here," she said.

She guided us through the alleys of the big house into doorways I wouldn't have known to enter. Zaki had told her about porcupines that had raided. Latif Manzil and Khala captivated our relatives with the tale as we sat in the courtyards of their neighboring houses. Khala unknotted a corner of her *dupatta* into which she had tucked a porcupine needle to pull out as evidence of these creatures. They had chomped through doors throughout the house. She had never heard of such a thing happening here before.

Lucy, Esther, and I ventured out alone into the farm fields, as the village men did every day but rarely the Muslim women. As we walked through the fields, Lucy warned me, "Watch out for the shit." It was an appropriate warning to keep us from soiling our spirits as Tantrikas as we traversed through life. A cow skull lay in the fields. We crossed into Khadnapur, the name of the village land that bordered Jaigahan.

Here we could feel the squish of the earth on our feet. A yellow butterfly danced in front of us, near white flowers. A rugged and handsome cousin of ours, Gama Bhai, led us over the land. He lived in the shadow of Latif Manzil with his wife, daughters, and son in a humble two-room house with a courtyard and open-air kitchen. His slow gait, measured speech, and the gray lining his trim hair gave him a dignified air beyond his forty-something age and his status as a small farmer in these parts. He was not a landowner, a *zamindar* in the tradition of our family, but plowed the land to support his family and eke out a small living. He impressed me as a stark contrast to Bluebeard.

"This is all of yours," he said, sweeping his hands over the land.

What a thought—to have a lineage that tied us to the land. It bound my heart even deeper to this magical place. Lucy swung a blue plastic bag filled with eggplant. Esther carried a bag of tomatoes and lemons. We went to Gama Bhai's house, where his mother, Bilkees Khala, sat in front of us. She was one of the elders of the village, a cousin to Rashida Khala, Iftikhar Mamoo, and my mother, so she became an aunt to Esther, Lucy, and me. She had lost most of her teeth so her cheeks were sunken, but, like Khala, she carried herself with grace, and beauty was chiseled into her face through a lifetime of village life. She reminded us of the essential: "This is your home."

Esther and Lucy did consider Jaigahan and Latif Manzil their home. But there was Zaki to reckon with. He was always the black sheep of the family, leaving a string of failed business ventures in his wake and such troubled relationships with family members. Esther and Lucy remembered how our cousin-sisters called him "Yucky Zaki" when they were growing up.

Now Zaki's wife, Shubnam, had joined him here after about two decades of living with her parents in Calcutta. They were running a school named after my great-grandfather, Latif Convent Academy. It was "English-medium," which meant that school was taught in the English language. But it was rote just like my young cousin Shaan learned in Lucknow. The young schoolchildren lined up in their uniforms in a room off the courtyard. It should have been an inspiring scene. But it was tortured. Shubnam Momani and Zaki Mamoo barked at the children all day. Zaki carried a ruler, a "scale" in India, which he used to rap the children's hands when he wanted to discipline them.

At 8:20 one morning, Zaki stood over the line with a ruler. At 9:08 A.M. I heard the smacking sound of the ruler hitting a child. Bluebeard was such a dark force.

Teenage girls slipped into the house in black *burqas* in the afternoon for "private tuition" with Shubnam Momani. She spoke an inspiring message about wanting to educate the girls so that they could be somewhat literate.

But the spirit of the house was oppressive with Zaki in it. Bilkees Khala sent food over for Khala. It was a ritual of respect accorded to Khala for her years. Zaki went crazy. "It's a sign of disrespect to me! Isn't my wife's cooking good enough for you?"

Khala was horrified. She slipped out of the house.

Esther and Lucy were shocked when they went upstairs to the two rooms in which their parents had slept. Clothes their mother had carefully folded spilled out of trunks, and the rooms were in disarray. "My mother packed everything so neatly," Esther said wistfully. "We left everything so tidy." Her mother had also given Zaki the keys to the rooms. His family seemed to have taken over. The rooms were now a mess.

I had read from one of my books about purification in Tantra. The room where a Tantric ritual was to take place had to be cleaned. Incense should burn there all the time. The room should be decorated with flowers. A meal would be laid out, consisting of four different ingredients, and wine decanted. Candles would burn or, better still, an oil lamp with oil that creates a special red light. Then the room and the house could be cleansed, sprinkling water and using mantras. Normally long verses of mantras were used. It was to go on so long and so thoroughly that you became completely absorbed, giving yourself seriously and without reservation to the purification.

We had no food of our own. We had no flowers. We certainly didn't have wine. But we had to cleanse these two rooms upstairs that Lucy and Esther's parents had called their bedroom. We cleaned like fanatics. I burned incense. I said my protection verse from the Qur'an. I twirled the incense sticks in circular motions around the room to clear it.

All the while, I learned lessons from Khala. She told me that if I had a nightmare, I should turn over on my right side to sleep and then give money to somebody poor in the morning.

Khala told me that in Islam it was said that if a husband looked at his wife with a smile then he would see the gate of heaven. Zaki Mamoo spoke loudly to his wife with not a smile to be found. His voice was full of so much anger. She and her husband had hardly lived together over the decades of years they had been married. Khala said, "The best thing is for the husband to be with the wife."

We lived in the village as we wanted to live. I even went behind the wheel of a Mahindra jeep. On the way to Khetasari, I gave an elderly man a ride. Our usual driver, a handsome young man named Abu Saad, told me later the man was Dr. Amanula Hakim, a doctor of Eastern medicine. He had probably never had a woman drive him around before. In Khetasari, we ventured unescorted to buy steel trunks. Esther bought new locks for the doors on her parents' rooms upstairs.

A runaway cow roamed the village. A woman stopped me in the street. I didn't know who she was, cloaked in a black *burqa*. She pulled the flap up to reveal her weathered face and a smile missing many teeth. She was our driver Abu Saad's mother. "You drove!" she said.

"What do you think of that?"

"It's a good thing."

To me, her affirmation far outweighed the haughtiest condemnation by the status quo.

It was the morning of September 11, 2000. How could we know how the world would be transformed a year from that day? For now, I was in this village where homes didn't have refrigerators because there were frequent electrical shutdowns, girls went behind the veil by the time they were teenagers, and there was no such thing as an Internet connection. It was 7:41 A.M. Khala emerged with a flowered *kurta* with embroidery on it and a white *dupatta* over her head. Khala and I sat on the *charpai*. Khala told me porcupines were called *shahee* in Urdu, information no more important than the fact that it came from Khala and made me one word closer to the pulse of my ancestors.

Esther came to tell us she had discovered one of her artist brushes missing. She wasn't angry about the brush, but its absence was symbolic of the violation she felt Zaki had made into the sacred space of her parents' rooms. She yelled at Zaki about the missing brush. He was adamant. "None of the children would steal."

Esther used the opportunity to tell him she didn't like the intrusion of the school into the space of Latif Manzil as a family house. Zaki started getting rude. "I have half of this house. We will split the house in half, then." As one of the descendants of the four brothers who shared Latif Manzil, his side of the family had a one-fourth share of the house, and he had gotten control over another quarter share by a side of the family made closer by marriage.

I joined the conversation. Zaki rudely tried to cut me off. "I will only talk to her." I didn't let his ego ensnare me. He tried to tell Esther that he considered himself like a father to her. When Khala talked to Esther later, privately, Khala told her to be strong against darkness. "Don't cry."

CHAPTER 13

The Sick Man

A STORY GOES THAT Buddha's decision to seek an end to suffering was inspired by his first deep comprehension of suffering through meeting a sick man, a beggar, a dying man, and a monk. His journey began on that day. On the streets of Lucknow, my *dakini* spirits Esther and Lucy transported back to their lives as students in England, I met my sick man, and he made me think, "There but for the grace of God go my brother, me, all of us."

I saw him first in front of the Clark Hotel, a naked man standing in the middle of traffic as if he wanted to be hit. I saw him again at Hazratganj, the street of businesses with Ray-Bans and Nike. I tried to feed him water from my Bislera bottle. He lunged at me. I was not scared. I looked him straight in the eye, as if I was disciplining my cat Billlie, and said, "No!"

The shoe *walla* threw water on him to make him leave his storefront. Then he locked the door with us inside. As he gazed out the locked door, this seller of shoes told me he had gone to a Tantric to try to get back his wife who left him. About the naked man getting water thrown upon him, he said, "In India, if you are falling people will only push you down harder."

I stood for an hour to watch the man as he crossed back and forth over the busy lanes of Hazratganj.

He was actually concerned about a scooter that hit a car. He went to the traffic cop to make sure he knew. The traffic cop hit him with a switch meant for horses. Was he mad or were we mad?

There was a psychiatric hospital nearby. It was Nur Manzil Psychiatric Centre in Lalbagh, a short rickshaw ride from Hazratganj, *nur* meaning "light," *manzil* meaning "resting place." I asked to see the director, a man named Dr. Arun Thacore. After waiting awhile, I was beckoned in to see a serious man behind a desk. He shook his head. He said the psychiatric hospital wouldn't take the poor man. "He is an indigent. Try the Sisters of Charity, and return tomorrow morning for an appointment at 9 A.M."

I headed back to Hazratganj to walk to the Sisters of Charity. I asked two women who dressed like nuns for directions. "Walk with us," they told me.

I waited in a corridor facing a courtyard. Images of Mother Teresa were everywhere with quotes about the light that shines within us. I thought about Mother Teresa as I never had before. It was true. For her to accomplish what she did, building a charity for the poor, this force of virginal female energy in this land, she had to be Shakti incarnate. I had never seen her that way before. The sisters said, "We can't take him because he's *pagal,*" mentally ill.

I visited a tailor that night. Rishi Puri, the tailor's son, hung around in the back of the store where his aunt took my measurements for new *shalwar kameez* outfits. He was a first-year commerce student. That meant he would have been a college freshman in America. He had driven by the naked man that day. He was so saddened he made himself look the other way.

His aunt had been working in the store for the last thirty years with the encouragement of her *bhaya,* her older brother. Her young nephew admired her. "She is very strong."

She wore the golden image of a goddess on a tiger on her chest. It dangled on the end of a slender gold chain.

I didn't recognize the image. "Who is that?"

"Durga." Ah, Durga. I was still getting to know her.

In the morning, I returned to Nur Manzil.

As I waited in the reception, a young man approached me. "Are you a nurse?" he asked with a voice that matched his gentle brown eyes and smooth skin. His dark hair had silken threads of golden brown spun into it. I laughed. I was the furthest thing from a nurse, though trying to find help for one naked man. He was Lokendra Subedi from Birendranagar in the Surkhet District of Nepal, a traveler far from home, at the hospital because he had been suffering from depression.

We started talking to another man in the waiting room, Lalee Takur, an engineer with the Survey Branch Office in the city of Dhangahi in

Nepal, who had also come from across the border to find help for his son, Kisore Sharma, who had epilepsy. His family had told him to take his son to a village Tantric to cure him. He got him medicine instead. But the rational mind at the hospital provided them little compassion. Both these patients had been waiting to see the hospital director, yet I was beckoned inside first. The psychiatrist was immediately interested in my position as a reporter for the *Wall Street Journal*. He was one of India's few subscribers, he told me. Now I knew why he wanted to meet me.

I told him about my project. He told me that parents came to Nur Manzil after failing to find success with Tantrics who claimed they could cure their children of mental illnesses by ridding them of spirits and spells that had supposedly seized their minds and souls. One set of parents brought their daughter in after she was tied to a rock, beaten, and starved to remove an evil spirit from her body. It showed me the horrors of Tantra being abused in the name of healing, another reminder that I didn't want to go down the path of learning secrets of black magic or spiritual power. I would rather be motivated by simple kindness. Despite all my intentions, however, I ended up as successful in helping the naked man as the tailor's son who drove by and did nothing. The inclination for compassion and empathy was low in this land of so much suffering.

I returned home to Jahingarabad Palace, where Khala shook her head, listening to the story of how I'd spent my day.

CHAPTER 14

Finding New Shakti

I OFTEN RETREATED to the (not so) Fast Business Centre seeking solitude. One day, I met a physical trainer named Michael Cowasji. We started talking motorcycles.

No sparks flew, so it was easy to go with him when he offered to show me motorcycles. I sat sidesaddle behind him on his LML scooter as we wove through Lucknow traffic to the Suzuki, LML, and Honda dealerships. On the ride, he told me that some years back in Delhi he had married a Hindu woman although her family didn't approve because he was Christian. They had lived together peacefully, but then she started visiting her family without him because he wasn't welcome in their house. She would return from every visit disheartened by him. She finally left him to stay with her family.

In Delhi the year before, he had gone to a Hindu Tantric who told him to feed a black dog a *roti,* a type of bread, with the wife's name tucked inside on a piece of paper. He searched through the night until he found a black dog. The dog wouldn't eat the *roti.* He chased after him until finally he ate the *roti.* Then he had to slaughter a certain-sized lamb. He realized that the Tantric had a scam going when he became displeased that Michael had brought his own lamb and didn't spend three thousand rupees on the lamb the Tantric wanted to sell him. Even though the dog ate the *roti,* Michael's wife never returned.

At the Suzuki dealership, I learned about a team of Indian army doctors set to start an expedition through the Himalayan foothills to Kargil in Kashmir on a new Suzuki launch, the Fiero. The sales and marketing men for TVS-Suzuki Limited encouraged me to sit on it. They took me seriously. They didn't ask why I wanted to ride a motorcycle. They just wanted to know which one I wanted. The bike felt sleek and powerful and sweet. Would this be my tiger? It was symbolically right. The banner showed a man in a leather jacket hunched low upon the Fiero, a blaze of fire behind him. Except for a sales consultant, Runita, I was the only woman in the showroom. She, too, encouraged me. A singer, she told me she sang to Shiva in front of an image of a lingam. "It keeps me calm."

On this trip, I somehow stumbled upon a real estate agent I had met once before. He ran into me as I scurried down Hazratganj. He told me he needed help. He hadn't been able to have an erection since a girlfriend left him ten years before. "What was your relationship like with your mother?" I asked, trying to test my theory of psychological male castration by overbearing mothers. I, obviously, still didn't appreciate the difficult task of raising a child, let alone a son. His mother gave his brother presents on his birthday when he was growing up, an explanation he gave for his impotence. I was dodging shoulders as I listened to him. "You have to unblock your chakras."

"Help me."

I looked over at him to see if he was serious.

"I'm impotent. I won't be a danger." We stopped at a building down the alley from the Fast Business Centre. He suggested I give him a lesson in his apartment upstairs. "Don't worry. We won't be alone. My servant will be there."

I remembered my promise to two friends in San Francisco before I left for the first leg of my journey, never to meet a man alone to talk about Tantra. I told him to masturbate pressing his heart chakra. I headed home—as fast as I could.

Over the phone, I talked to Dadi, my grandmother, visiting a daughter in Bombay, and she told me that she was headed back to Pakistan on a bus from Delhi.

I was wondering whether I should join her when I wandered into Ram Advani Bookstore on Hazratganj, a quiet and sophisticated enterprise with the latest in titles. Ram Advani was a gentleman scholar with a full-headed tuft of white hair and a silver beard to match. When I first came here, I had tried to speak to him in Hindi. He had responded to me in English. I wondered aloud to him whether to go to Pakistan with my dadi. He helped me make my decision by telling me his story. Before India's independence, his family had a bookstore empire in what was now

Pakistan. A well-read British officer told Ram's family that they could have a warehouse in Lahore if they used it for only one purpose—to sell books. They took the warehouse and turned it into a sprawling bookstore. In Lahore, he fell in love with a Muslim girl, Sara, pronounced the Indian way, "Sah-rhuh." Then, the partition happened. The Hindus were fleeing Pakistan. His family sold the bookstore to a Muslim family, who renamed it Feroze Sons. He fled, too, leaving Sara behind. He settled in Lucknow and fell in love with an academic researcher with a PhD. He showed me a book his son, a former editor at Oxford Press, had just published, *The Indus Civilization*. The heart of the Indus civilization was in Pakistan, not far west from Lahore, where Dadi was headed.

He confirmed my thoughts. "Go to Pakistan with your dadi."

My father's family had come from the village Bindwal in the same Azamgarh District where my mother's father took his last breath. My dada, my father's father, settled his large family in the city of Hyderabad, supporting them with his law practice. My grandmother, Dadi, sold her twenty-four-karat gold wedding jewelry to pay to register my grandfather's practice in the state's high court system.

Born in the summer of 1935, my father as a child climbed a tree to watch Mahatma Gandhi during his noncooperation movement when Indians defied their British rulers. During his college days, my father studied with the image of the Buddha before him. He was handsome, educated, and ambitious. He graduated in the class of 1955 from Osmania University's Agriculture College in Hyderabad with a first division rank that it was said no other student had earned in seven years. Panthers roamed the grounds of the rural experimental station in the village Rudrur where my father researched ways to stop the damage of the insect *Schoenobs incertelus* burrowing into the stem of rice crop, destroying the harvest. He slept on the farm to the roar of tigers outside the village. His top graduation ranking earned him a government appointment as an assistant professor at Osmania University's Agriculture College. His marriage was quickly arranged.

Her large eyes stared out so hollow and yet so deep on her wedding day. She was a virgin bride leaving her home to enter a new home of strangers, including her husband. She was too naive even to be frightened.

Her sisters clipped a gold chain in the part of her hair. A gold star hung from the end of the chain, slightly askew between her delicate brows, a ruby glittering in the middle. Her sisters lined her eyes with *kajal,* so the black lines met in the corner as they did centuries before on Cleopatra in a far-off kingdom on the Nile. They draped a sheer peach-colored *dupatta* over her head so only wisps of her hair peeked out from beneath the gold lace stitched on the edge. Her deep eyes were haunting not only because she dared to look into a camera, but also because they betrayed the promise not to reveal unspoken sadness.

She was filled with hope for a new life with security and a sense of home. She had spent her young life in the homes of relatives. Marriage gave her a home of her own, security, happiness. That's what she thought.

It was a small wedding in Bombay at a guest house. She was led forward with a gentle touch to a future she couldn't imagine. She pursed her lips tight and only kept her eyes downcast. My mother went to her family's house. My father stayed at the guest house with his family. The next day, she journeyed with her new husband and his family to Hyderabad. It was a city rich with the history of Muslim nawabs who ruled over the people. When they descended at the train station, her new mother-in-law, my grandmother, stared at the black *burqa* in which my mother was enshrouded.

"What is this?" my grandmother said, staring at the *burqa*. "Take it off!" she yelled, ripping the *burqa* off, shocking the new bride.

My father wasn't surprised by the move. Dadi had caused quite a stir in 1942 in Azamgarh when she'd pioneered her own woman's movement, removing her *burqa* and shopping freely in the bazaar. But the liberation movement hadn't yet touched my mother's family. My mother felt as if she was standing naked on the railroad platform, the *burqa* that cloaked her now just a bundle of black fabric in her hands. Certainly, my mother had gotten into trouble for taking off her *burqa* when she was younger, but it was in the safety of a girls' school. Here men—strangers—could see her. This was the first of so many shocks she endured quietly to adjust in this new home. The people were so different from her family. My grandmother spoke her mind forcefully. She ran her house with an iron fist. She cajoled all of her children, sons and daughters, to study and succeed.

She didn't listen to my mother's protests and made her finish the high school degree that she hadn't completed because of the *burqa* incident that got her pulled from school.

My mother's first day in Hyderabad, two of my father's aunts, his Mahjabeen Khali and Bilquis Momani, joked with him that he would consummate his wedding that night. He bet that he wouldn't. He lost.

On their wedding night, the third night after their actual marriage, my father couldn't contain his enthusiasm. He was a staunch Muslim, but he told his new wife about his philosophy of life, about his sympathy with the teachings of Buddha. He told her about his deep sense of spirituality and obligation to help humanity, how he wanted to alleviate suffering in the world. He saw her as his spiritual partner. She listened quietly. She just wanted to be loved. Her ideas about wedding nights came from the Barbara Cartland novels of her teen years, and Buddha was nowhere to be found.

In my mother's morning routine, she walked slowly to prepare chai for her husband and his parents. Her sisters-in-law scurried to school. She cleaned the dirty breakfast dishes under a hand pipe. She took a *jharu,* a broom made from the branches of a tree, and crouched to whisk the broom over the dirt floor of the courtyard in the center of the house. One day, one of her sisters-in-law compared her to the eldest brother's wife. "Raunaq did it better," she said.

It was probably true. She could admit she didn't play the part of Cinderella very well. It was harder when she was pregnant with her first child. As she swept, she coughed dirt into her lungs. The new bride felt under siege. She wondered how her husband could worry about saving humanity when his own wife was crying herself to sleep. That's when she made her husband put away the Buddha picture. A lingering sadness always remained with my mother, also, for she never saw her childhood home again in the village of Jaigahan, even though her mother-in-law visited there once, inspiring a story I heard of admiration about my grandmother's persevering energy.

I saw this energy explode in front of me in Delhi as my grandmother stepped down from the train from Bombay. She was older, but I could tell she still had fire in her belly.

The back of her hair had the orange-red of the henna with which she dyed it. The hair around her face framed her in silver. Her face was creased with a lifetime that had seen imperialism, revolution, war, famine, and the extension of her family to the far corners of the world. In Pakistan, she was part of the older immigrants from India who still wrapped yards of sari around her waist, throwing the *pallu* over her shoulder, instead of switching to the *shalwar kameezes,* the tunic *kurtas,* harem pants, and *dupattas* that were the style of Pakistan. She was certainly daring compared to the chadors that shrouded the conservative Muslim women of Saudi Arabia and Afghanistan in a sea of cloth. But she was an elderly woman and was allowed her fashion statement.

Since my earliest days, as my mother's daughter, I had had a conflicted relationship with my grandmother, probably because I had grown up more like her than not. When I was in Aligarh, my cousin from Azamgarh, Azfar Bhai, lounged on the bed and regaled me with the story of how my dadi traveled fearlessly even when religious divides split Hindus and Muslims after partition, crisscrossing into Muslim areas with a *dupatta* over her head and then into Hindu areas with a *bindhi* on her forehead. She was happy to get away with always pushing the envelope, something with which I was kind of familiar. She always loved India, but her sons convinced her to sell her house in Hyderabad and settle in Pakistan, where they could take care of her.

"Mataji, sit down here," the Indian police officers said respectfully to her the next morning before sunrise, using the Hindi term for mother, as we waited to have our luggage inspected before boarding the Peace Bus to Lahore. She chatted them up, as she chatted up just about anybody. They still confiscated my road map of Delhi, afraid it would be used against India in Pakistan, ignoring the fact that it was probably easily available online. But this bus ride was a political gamble.

The Peace Bus started as a stunt orchestrated by Pakistan's Prime Minister Nawaz Sharif and India's Prime Minister Atal Bihari Vajpayee to show friendlier relations between the two countries. The bus ran between the Pakistan city of Lahore and India's New Delhi on the historic Grand Trunk Road. From the densely populated paradox of Calcutta, the Grand Trunk Road cut through northern India, hitting the

Ganges at the holy city of Varanasi before charting a course to the capital, Delhi. It proceeded north on the road Lucy, Esther, and I had taken. Twenty-six kilometers, or sixteen miles, after the dusty city of Amritsar, the road crossed the Pakistan border and headed into Pakistan's grand center of art and culture, Lahore.

Despite ongoing tensions between the countries, the crossing usually wasn't a problem. The road followed an arc up through the capital, over the Indus River to Peshawar. Travelers could then head to the Afghanistan border at the famous Khyber Pass. It was an adventure, as were all outings with Dadi. Armed police sat in the front and the rear of the bus. I didn't know if they were guarding us from terrorists in India or guarding India from terrorists on the bus. Dadi didn't care. She went about her business. She tried to arrange the marriage of the Peace Bus official working on our bus.

When we arrived in Lahore, we spent our days in the house of my eldest paternal uncle, Baray Abu. Between meals and prayers and naps, Dadi told me about my ancestry and her life. My dada's father's name was Mohammad Isaq Nomani. His mother's name was Saboohath. They lived in Bindwal. Shibli Nomani was my dada's most renowned ancestor. I'd heard about him throughout my lifetime, but I'd gotten most interested in him as I tried to understand my ancestry. He was a scholar of Islam and the founder of Shibli College in Azamgarh. He was renowned for biographies he wrote of the Prophet Muhammad and Hazrat Omar, the second caliph, or leader, of Islam after the death of the Prophet Muhammad. I wondered more about him. I felt I was carrying on his legacy, as a researcher of religion and philosophy, even if it was, yes, with quite a different twist.

Dadi estimated she was eighty-seven, born into the rural town of Hinganghat in India when the British were still colonialists. Although not fluent in English, Dadi could spell her name, Zubaida, meaning "quintessence" in Arabic. She was married at fourteen to my grandfather, Mumtaz Ahmad Nomani, who became a successful defense attorney in the old city of Hyderabad. Before that, she traveled alone with her children in 1942 to the bustling Hindu holy city of Benares from Wardha, a city where Dada had moved the family in order to build his law practice. My father grew up there, affected by the nonviolent movement of

Gandhi, who himself had moved to Wardha, using it as a headquarters for his battle for India's liberation. Their family would picnic at Gandhi's ashram. It was a time when few women dreamed of doing such a daring thing as traveling unaccompanied by a man. But after the family moved to Hyderabad, Dadi even drove a car, learning on a racecourse, and driving until she hit a rickshaw. There were no power brakes back then. They paid off the rickshaw driver for maybe fifteen rupees, twenty rupees tops (between three and five dollars then).

"He was happy," she insisted.

Three sons and five daughters settled in Pakistan, uprooting themselves from their lives in India in the years after India won independence from the British in 1947. She did not shun the Hindu yogic traditions that ran through the culture but instead twisted her body into the yogic postures that I'd learned at the Eastern Athletic club in Brooklyn Heights when I signed up for my first yoga class years earlier. My father learned alternate nostril breathing from his mother, something she did proudly, inhaling deeply and exhaling with great force. Dadi pressed on the spots that I learned in the Canadian hinterland as the acupressure spots of our chakras. She pressed on the dip in the back of the neck below the nape of the neck. "It opens your blood."

One afternoon, I went with Dadi to a famous Sufi shrine in the middle of Lahore, Data Darbar, dedicated to an eleventh-century mystic, Syed Ali Hajveri, popularly known as Data Ganj Baksh. I didn't have a discipline that allowed me to have spiritual communion. I touched my forehead to the cool marble tile and felt a light connection to the mystical world.

Dadi took me by the elbow and made way for us in the men's section so I could take good pictures. She ignored the men who protested. To one, she said, "This is my granddaughter. She has come from America, and she wants to take a photo." This was Dadi in action. No fear. No rules. My cousin-brother, Sohail Bhai, an engineer, worked across from the shrine that we visited. It was the red-light district, alive and prospering in this Muslim nation. Criminals, he said, kidnapped girls from the Sufi shrine. His boy was with us today, his daughter at home, but he told his wife to watch their child closely.

We went to another shrine. Sohail Bhai's wife said, *"Tawba. Tawba."* seeking forgiveness in Arabic, slapping one side of her face gently and then the other for what she saw before her: Muslims bowing their head to the shrine. To her and other Muslims, it was a sin to bow your head to anyone but God.

My uncle, Baray Abu, and his wife, Bari Ammi, represented simple devotees to me. They punched a small handheld counter with their thumbs as they recited a *dua,* or prayer, over and over again to earn blessings for their son's impending marriage. Baray Abu rose before dawn to do *fajr namaz.* He wouldn't take me to the *masjid* with him because the subcontinent culture didn't allow women to enter anymore. When he returned home he unlocked the door from the outside. I hated this security system, because we were essentially locked inside the house when he went to do his prayer. I would wait for him to accompany him on his walk in the park as the sun rose.

He talked about selfless generosity to family. He made me think that I hadn't given enough to my own family. Living alone had made me selfish even if I had good intentions. Late into the night, I talked to Baray Abu. Somehow the subject turned to the Kama Sutra. He admitted that he read it. He didn't approve of its teachings. "It allows for immoral activity. It says it is okay to sleep with the wife of your enemy."

He had found religion again. He said it was a personal violation for him to hear anyone question the Qur'an. Faith amounted to belief in the sanctity of each word of the Qur'an, he said. He had a *mowlana,* or Muslim teacher, who came every day at 3 P.M. to teach him how to properly read the Qur'an in Arabic.

In her room, Dadi taught me that shakti can be expressed in many forms. In Hindu mythology, female energy manifests itself through the fierce Kali, the protective Durga, the knowledgeable Saraswati, and the monetarily successful Lakshmi. I wondered how to understand Dadi's special brand of shakti.

On the one hand, she was pioneering, aggressive, inspiring. After all, she drove a car and traveled alone in the 1950s when few women did. "I never had any problems. All men were my brothers."

On the other hand, she was aggressive and offensive. She made my innocent mother's life a living hell when my mother moved into my father's extended family house in Hyderabad. For a decade after she left for America, my mother had nightmares about my grandmother. I sat across the dining table from Dadi, and I was brazen enough to ask her that question that Rashida Khala had warned me would be impolite. "Do you like my mother?" I asked, trying to reconcile the shakti forces within my life.

She didn't bat an eye. She wasn't surprised by the question. She defended herself. Of course she liked my mother, but somehow my mother got the wrong idea because my grandmother asked her to help wash the clothes. "We all washed each other's clothes."

I was dumbfounded. How to continue this conversation after it turned to dirty laundry? Somehow that was a good way of understanding what we were talking about.

Ready to change the subject, too, Dadi told me the tale of our mystical Sufi ancestry.

She said her great-grandfather was a Sufi who isolated himself in a nearby jungle to pray. He married at his mother's request but returned to the jungle. When his mother asked him to bear children with his wife, he took a leaf and chewed it. He gave the chewed leaf to his wife to eat, and she became pregnant.

I knew this was controversial territory. Sufism was to Islam much like Tantra was to Hinduism. It was shunned and whispered about quietly as a fringe culture that deviated from the main religion. Many Sufi philosophies mirrored Tantra: the transcendental meditative oneness with the universe, the sense of divinity in all people, and the renunciation of things material.

Dadi told me about her devotion in Hyderabad to a Sufi *pir*, a healing saint. My brother accompanied her on those visits. She didn't call herself a Sufi, but she took up the practices of Sufis. She fell asleep reciting *zikr*, remembrances of God, on her *tuz'bi*, her prayer beads, after doing her *namaz*. She kept *duas*, prayers, by her pillow, waking up in the middle of the night to recite them. When Baray Abu got something in his eye, Dadi said a *dua*, pulled the eyelashes aggressively, blew into the eye, and cured him.

My uncle called a friend who belonged to a Sufi family. The man suggested I meet his sister. I talked to her and agreed to join her for a women's gathering to discuss the Qur'an.

She told me she hadn't missed a single of her five daily prayers in her entire lifetime. At our women's session, she told the story of helping even an ant by giving it sugar, at the same moment that I, not very absorbed in her lecture, happened to give an ant some sugar.

I met her brother. He was an elderly man, serious and pious. He told me he couldn't teach me unless I was a good Muslim, praying five times a day. "Do you pray five times a day?"

I knew this was no time to lie. I admitted that I didn't.

"I cannot teach you unless you pray five times a day."

We continued talking anyway. He told me he went to a camp for *mujahadeen* fighters in Kashmir. "They had a glow on their faces as if they were angels." His sister went, too. She was beaming, remembering the light that she said shone from these *jihadis,* fighting a "holy war" against India for Kashmir.

She brought out a receipt book for donations for the *mujahadeen.* I bought two coupons. I returned home and started praying five times a day, continuing to meet with him over the next two days. He read my *Wall Street Journal* Tantra article by our third visit. He took me upstairs. "I have a book I want to show you." He turned to the topic of my Tantra article.

"There are some things I didn't understand," he began.

"What?"

"G-spot? What is a G-spot?" I had mentioned the G-spot in the description of the sacred spot massage taught in Santa Cruz. I figured a lot of people would like to know. Delicately, I tried to explain its location and purpose.

He continued. "Where is the clitoris?" I didn't remember mentioning anything like that in the pages of the *Journal.*

I tried to remain clinically vague. He paused. I asked him if something was the matter. "What a shame. I was almost going to ask you to show me your clitoris."

I tried to be forgiving. "God will forgive you."

"And God will forgive you, if you show me—for just a moment."

I saw the man now as a man. He was no Sufi from whom I could learn higher levels of existence. He was still quite base. In case I wasn't certain, as I left he embraced me, planted a kiss on my cheek and forehead, and tried to kiss me on the lips. I turned my head quickly to make sure he missed. He tried again. Disgusting. When I returned home, I didn't tell Dadi.

CHAPTER 15

Durga on Her Tiger

I KNEW THAT I WAS more like Dadi than not. I had lived under her tutelage for the first four years of my life and inherited from her the strength and willpower that made us determined yet obstinate. Even at eighty-plus years old she wasn't restrained by convention.

Things hadn't changed much in Pakistan since I was eighteen and stopped in Lahore as part of my cross-country jaunt through Pakistan. That summer, I jumped on a bicycle to take a spin around the neighborhood. My cousin Aamir chased after me to get me to return home.

"Don't embarrass the family," he yelled at me. "Girls don't ride bikes here."

During this trip, we didn't leave my uncle's driveway—I was too afraid Dadi would fall and break a bone—but Dadi wasn't afraid to climb onto the back of another cousin-brother's motorcycle with me in front. She settled onto the back, sidesaddle in her sari. I gave her my shades and wrapped my *dupatta* around my face so only my eyes peeked out. We looked like two *dacoits,* the subcontinent term for a brand of criminals straight out of gangs like the one led by a poor Indian woman dubbed the Bandit Queen.

Later, my cousin Omar happily let me ride his Hero Honda CD-70 through the streets of Lahore. We visited Ferozsons, the bookstore that used to belong to the family of Lucknow bookseller Ram Advani. The bookshelf included *The Hite Report on Male Sexuality.*

When we pulled out of a McDonald's, a young woman did a double take and yelled, "*Ya Allah!*" meaning, "Oh, God!"

I returned to Delhi, this time knowing that I had to tap into the boldness I'd inherited from Dadi to overcome the fear that so inhibited freedom in India, freedom of movement. I wanted to go to the Dalai Lama's home-in-exile in the town of Dharamsala in the Himalayan foothills, but from the traffic I had seen on the Grand Trunk Road first with Lucy and Esther and then with Dadi on the Peace Bus, I didn't feel safe driving my own car. The roads were too narrow. I realized there was no better expression of my independence than a motorcycle.

The creature stood before me, sleek, powerful, and intimidating. I stared at him in the gentle evening breeze and wondered if I could tame him.

Quietly, I did what I needed to do to bring him to my temporary home in the posh Golf Links neighborhood of Delhi. I couldn't even drive him there myself. I had to ride—sidesaddle—behind an employee of Khanna Motors, as he nosed my new black Hero Honda Splendor into the parking space where I was staying. I'd done something I'd never even contemplated doing in America. I'd bought my own motorcycle. My bike was nothing more than the power of a scooter back home, a 100cc machine that wasn't even allowed on the interstates in America. But here the Hero Honda Splendor was the tough bike of tough young men. It was a big machine for me to control in the stop-and-go traffic of urban India, where being able to pick up a bike toppled to the ground by an errant bullock cart was as important as gunning the engine.

There was a reason I had gotten this bike. It expressed the independence and fearlessness with which I wanted to live. I'd be riding alone. No Shiva for this Shakti. My motorcycle was my tiger. It would rile the Shiva energy within me. Mastering my tiger would require concentrated meditation. I knew overcoming fears was an integral part of spiritual liberation. That's why the darkest of Tantric yogis meditated with corpses on their laps. In my case, I wanted to be free in this land of my birthplace from the stranglehold of others' fears. I wanted to travel India without the fear of rape or murder but rather in the spirit of adventure. I purchased two helmets with the company maker, Studds, emblazoned across them and strapped them on the back. Now, how would I get this tiger to purr?

For help, I turned to a British woman, Kate Lee, who happened to be staying in my guest house. Back in England, she taught people how to ride motorcycles. Now she sat in front as she took me around Golf Links, teaching me the gears. I sat Western style behind her. Then she sat behind me as I stopped and started, practicing with the gears. I braked too hard. I started too fast. I did everything wrong. But I was moving. And I hadn't fallen over yet.

I knew I had to jump-start my riding lessons if I ever wanted to get out of Golf Links. I called Hero Honda Motors Limited and talked to the marketing manager. He told me he would have an employee give me lessons. He assigned Amit Chopra, senior engineer in service.

When I talked to Amit, he asked, "Can you drive over here?"

How could I admit I couldn't? Easily. "I can't."

I got a ride to the Hero Honda corporate office. Amit looked like a sincere man in his late twenties, bespectacled and serious. "You have a motorcycle license back at home, right?"

It was one of my guiding principles never to lie. But this time I didn't think I could tell him the truth, although the obvious would soon become apparent. "Yeah, sure, license back at home. Yeah." Biggest two-wheeler I'd ridden at home was my Gary Fisher twenty-one-speed mountain bike. We rode back to my Splendor at Golf Links. Amit hopped on the front and took us to India Gate, a massive monument in the center of a strip of land made to resemble the Mall in Washington, with the Capitol, the phallic Washington Monument, and the Lincoln Memorial lined up in a row. The India Gate was a monument to India. There I learned how to ride the Hero Honda, even though I still braked too hard. I felt brilliantly powerful and free.

I continued riding circles around Golf Links. I used my turn signal for turns, a clear sign that I was a foreigner. I braked to see if I could stop without the engine dying. Sometimes I could, other times I couldn't. I restarted to see if I could start without the engine dying. I was moving slowly, but I felt great. So independent.

One afternoon I nosed my bike slowly around Golf Links, passing a band of *hijras,* or eunuchs, collecting money door to door. They were men who dressed as women. Many people were frightened of them, and the *hijras* used the fear to extort money. Some of them, it was said, were castrated. I remembered first seeing them as a child in Hyderabad. Dadi hurled money into their hands with a grunt. Parents tugged their children away, afraid they would kidnap their young ones, castrate the boys, and make them beg. I was never afraid of these colorful characters. Since

I broke gender boundaries with my motorcycle, I related to them. Finally, I emerged from my circles at Golf Links to ride through Delhi, following my map to the embassy enclave where the streets were wide, clean, and mostly free of traffic. I explored. I meandered. I found myself at Buddha Park, where I paid my respects to a giant statue of Buddha. Couples hid in quiet corners behind trees.

I rode to Khan Market and walked up a flight of stairs into a beauty salon called Shahnaz, intending to defy the traditional image of beauty in India. Cascading long hair was a trademark of a woman's femininity. My peers had already abandoned our mothers' style of parting their hair in the middle and tying it into single braids that stretched like ivy down their backs. Sometimes, if our mothers were feeling particularly sultry for a photograph, they swung their braids over their shoulders, like Bollywood heroines sometimes did. Today's women let their hair loose like a dark waterfall, an act of liberation. I usually wore my hair wavy and thick, free. Since I had been a child, I'd had it above my shoulders only once, when Nasheed Apa cut it into a bob.

I sat in my chair and told the manager, a woman named Sabeeha Shah, "Please cut it short, like a boy." Although women rode scooters in the urban centers, I hadn't yet seen a woman on a motorcycle. I wanted my hair short enough that none of it peeked out the back of my helmet. I wanted to avoid attention on the road. And harassment. My hair fell to the floor with each snip, and I watched myself rid my identity of more than my hair. In Tantra, cutting the hair also amounted to shearing our egos.

Sabeeha asked me my birth date.

"June 7."

"Seven. That's independent and unconventional."

To some, that would by synonymous with stupid. Around the corner, I stepped into a man's world in the auto market to get my license plates made. *Kajal* lined my eyes, my effort not only to ward off the evil eye but also to express something feminine. I wondered what it meant in India to have power outside the home as a woman. Did it mean becoming a man?

It didn't matter much to me, as I sat behind Amit as he rode through the streets of Delhi, my Studds helmet secure on my head.

Amit had come by after work to pick me up at Khan Market. I had straddled his CBZ—Western style—and we careened through the crowded bazaar lanes outside Connaught Place to exchange my Studds helmet for one that fit. We roared to the Nike store, and I bought myself a Nike windbreaker. I felt strong behind him.

Amit, an educated, modern man, lived with his parents in India, like most single men and women. He told me that he had a woman he liked whom he had met working in Chandigarh, the city where Lucy, Esther, and I got our Kundalini lesson in the Rose Garden. But he wouldn't marry her because she came from a different caste that wouldn't meet his parents' approval.

We rode now in the darkness, the streets mostly empty, headed to the shrine of a famous Sufi saint, Nizamuddin Auliya, renowned for his generosity and compassion, always feeding his guests while he sometimes fasted. I was on my bike. Amit was on his bike. We skirted broken glass. We parked in a narrow alley and quietly entered the shrine. *Dupattas* were draped on the lattice. Beggars stretched out on the shrine marble. I did my Muslim *namaz* as Amit sat quietly beside me in meditation. My helmet sat beside me. I was so happy in my independence.

I had no itinerary except a plan to ride out of Delhi onto the Grand Trunk Highway toward the place where the clouds met the roads. I planned to veer off and head a different direction than Lucy, Esther, and I had followed, moving instead through the foothills of the Himalayas into a hill station called Shimla made famous by Rudyard Kipling and then on to Dharamsala, home to not only the Dalai Lama but also thousands of Tibetan Buddhists. For me, this motorcycle journey was a new birth. My stomach was tight because of the fear people had expressed to me. A friend, Ravi, told me danger lurked on the Grand Trunk Highway. "There is a murder every two days. I wouldn't do it."

In my experience, to live in India was to live a lie. My mother taught me to change from my jeans and T-shirt to baggy *shalwar kameez* outfits while in flight to Bombay. From early on we hid the truths about ourselves to satisfy the quick judgments of relatives. I learned to be a chameleon so well my father told me I would make an excellent diplomat. But now I realized that as a Tantrika I had a choice to accept myself as I was. I simply had to be strong in the face of judgment.

I hadn't accepted who I was during my first trip to India. This trip, I had learned with Lucy and Esther to accept myself without looking over to see what the *sabzi walla,* the vegetable seller, thought. It wasn't the *sabzi walla* who intimidated me. It was my own relatives.

On the eve of my departure for Dharamsala, I gazed at my image reflected back to me in the mirror. My Nike windbreaker and Gap knock-off cargo pants was my night suit. My haircut. My cheekbones. My eyes. I felt beautiful. I felt my own power, and I loved it. Choice, strength of will, personal expression, following one's dream, self-knowledge. I felt free.

In the early morning, as the blazing sun rose above India Gate, it was just me on my tiger, circumambulating the monument in homage to this place where I found my liberation. A man waved his arms in circular motions, exercising them as he walked. It was a glorious moment as the sun rose into the sky, a blaze of orange.

In Tantra, the perfect human being is supposed to express the fusion of male energy and female energy with *ananda,* or eternal bliss. Tantra is the union and harmony between the polarities of masculine and feminine. In Morgantown, it hadn't been enough to call rough-and-tumble girls "tomboys," the nickname of my youth. Safiyyah had called them "he-shes." That was how I felt with my *kajal* and Studds helmet.

I pulled over after a few hours to sit down for chai. Two men, broth-ers who owned the chai stall, sat on a bench outside. When I sat down, one of the men admitted to me that when I pulled up his brother was bet-ting him two hundred rupees that I was a man. But before he could close the deal, I had taken off my helmet.

At the end of my first day on the road, I had watched pigs and water buffalo jog across the road and learned meditation tricks from a hotel manager as we sat in a boat made out to look like a white swan. I turned off the Grand Trunk Highway into the parking lot for a hotel called King Fisher in Ambala.

It wasn't the serene respite that I wanted. A rumble of cars blared by the hotel. But if I didn't stop, I'd collapse. It was past sunset. I'd broken my rule not to drive in the dark. I sat in my room and meditated again on the image of Durga on her tiger. What I'd learned was that the deities in Hinduism were a point of meditation through which we, as humble human beings, could aspire to some value each embodied. In the case of Durga and my motorcycle journey, I was trying to absorb some of the fearlessness of this goddess. The Buddhists, too, used this technique in their practice. In a meditation called *anusmrti,* they cultivated a vision of a deity. Using a practice called *atmotpatti,* they envisioned themselves as the deity. That's what I did as I sat on the soiled carpet in the King Fisher.

But what was I doing? Was I crazy? I had come near death with lorries passing by me, ready to crash into me with the slightest turn in their steering. A man pulled a horse-drawn cart right in front of me on the road to sit on the median and wait for the passing traffic. To understand India meant driving its roads. I saw a boy on the road today, blood spilling from his head. Near death there was no fear of death.

On my way to Shimla, I wanted to stop at a garden called Pinjore. I came to a turn in the road. Esther, Lucy, and I had turned to the left, to Chandigarh and the road to Manali, instead of to the right, to Pinjore Gardens and Shimla. It was supposedly from here that the losing warriors of the Mahabharata, the great Indian epic, disappeared into the Himalayas. That was what I felt I was about to do, even if I won the war. Somehow, I passed the gardens. As I did a U-turn to find the gardens, I heard two uniformed schoolboys, carrying their book bags, exclaim to each other about my gender.

The first boy: "Is that a madam?"

The second boy: "What else?"

My adventure in nonduality was a trip into the world of the he-she.

As I crossed from the state of Harayana to Himachal Pradesh to ascend into the Himalayas to Shimla, I warmed myself on the heat of exhaust fumes expelled by lorries. I stared at Durga as she came toward me, painted onto the front of oncoming lorries. I'd put 362 miles on my odometer. I thought to myself, "I am Durga."

To focus on the road and not the cold, I chanted another mantra, picked up from a billboard: "Food king. Homely food. Food king. Homely food. Food king. Homely food. Food king. Homely food." I learned later that there is a Tantric teaching called *nyasa,* in which we synchronize different parts of a mantra with the limbs and organs of the body. It sounded ridiculous, but it made sense as I rode up these narrow tarred roads, curling the fingers of my right hand around the accelerator and the fingers of my left hand on the clutch, synchronizing the changing of the gears with the gentle tap forward of my left foot to gear up and backward to gear down.

There are different levels of *nyasa* practice. In the first, the mantra is divided into six parts grounded in the thumbs, index fingers, middle fingers, ring fingers, little fingers, and palms through the power of concentration. This is called *kara nyasa,* synchronization of the mantra's power with the energies of the hands.

Next comes *anga nyasa.* That means synchronizing the six parts of the mantra with the energies of the heart, the head, the crown of the head, the chest and shoulders, the three eyes, and the space of the pranic body. This is what I did as I concentrated on the road, keeping a vigilant eye out for black dogs and piglets that might be jogging across the road.

As we climbed the mountain, my tiger stalled and fell in the middle of the road. I was in third gear when I should have been in second. The right-turn signal light cover shattered. Lorries could come around the bend straight at me. I chanted a Muslim *surah,* or Qur'anic chapter, that my mother had told me since childhood to recite for protection. An epiphany came to me. In this foxhole, I remembered God. She was not Durga. He was Allah. I didnt even know it, but that's just why the chapter was called, *alIklas,* meaning "The Purity of Faith." With an energy I didn't even know I had within me, I lifted my bike and hurled it upright, rolled it into the side in neutral, and somehow with a power regained, I started my tiger, and he roared gentlty to carry me forward.

I passed a sign for Tara Devi, a temple devoted to the goddess Tara. I should have stopped there to pay my respects. But surviving this climb would, I thought, be respect enough to feminine energy. It was dark now, and we were mostly alone on the road. There was nowhere to stop to rest my head for the night. I continued until I saw the sign telling me I'd made it to Shimla. I pulled over at a roundabout, where I spotted an STD booth, the phone booths of the subcontinent.

I found a room at the Himachal Pradesh Tourism hotel and turned it into my cocoon. My lower back was aching from lifting my bike. Rudyard Kipling had written a novel in Shimla. I watched MTV and HBO.

On MTV, I saw a bump-and-grind dance party under the Brooklyn Bridge. It was a place I used to retreat to, to feel the magic of the Manhattan skyline set behind the calm waters of the East River. It had been taken over by svelte young women in bikinis and young men with rippling muscles. I pressed my thumb to change the channel. The Palestinian intifada filled the screen on CNN. I wondered about this world in which we live between MTV's *The Grind* and Palestinian uprisings. Where did I fit in?

Over the next two days, I eased my sore body through yoga stretches on a wool checkered blanket I lay on my hotel room's ratty soiled carpet. I ventured into the hillside of lights that was Shimla, wandering through narrow stairwells that climb into the city's town square. A gaggle of Muslim girls wearing head scarves filled the square, jostling each other, waiting for chai. They were on a school trip. They reminded me of Arina, although I doubted she would ever have been allowed such a trip, even escorted. I thought about their lives, protected and clear, in contrast to my own. Their lives held a temptation for me because at least they had more security and stability. No matter the attraction, I knew I was on a much different path.

The story of Shiva and Shakti continued beyond the love story I already knew. Shakti, also known as Sati, vowed that she would kill herself if her husband were ever insulted. Sure enough, her father insulted Shiva one day, and Sati burned herself alive in a *yagna,* a fire ritual. Silly girl. Hadn't she learned to transcend ego? Shiva was devastated. He picked up her body and spun in the cosmic dance captured on statues now popular. He rampaged through the three worlds. The other gods were frightened. They asked Vishnu for help. Vishnu unleashed his chakra, or power, in the form of a volley of arrows that cut Sati's body into fifty-one pieces to save the earth from Shiva's anger. The fifty-one places where Sati's body fell are known as Shakti piths. A Himachal Pradesh tourism magazine told me the state was home to several of the fifty-one Shakti piths where parts of Sati's corpse fell. It was more than perfect for me to put at least one of them on my itinerary.

I set out again on the morning of Diwali, the Hindu festival of lights. I was nervous. My motorcycle seemed so daunting. When I had last sat on it, a few days earlier, I had been exhausted. I didn't know how I was going to be able to control it now. My doubts were confirmed. After successfully making it out of town, I veered to turn onto a back road. I found myself facing a climb. I didn't know what gear to put my bike into. I toppled in the middle of a village bazaar. Men I didn't even notice suddenly appeared. They picked my bike up from both sides and assured me that this was the last of the steep climbs.

"Drop down to first gear or second gear," one told me, "and all will be fine."

Another man offered to ride my bike up the hill. I accepted, although I wondered if I'd ever see my tiger again. I jogged up the hill behind him, my helmet still on. He sat waiting on a flat of land in the bazaar. I climbed on again, and I found myself in one of the most beautiful states of being I'd ever enjoyed. On this day when the mountains were mine to behold, the valleys mine in which to sink, and liberation mine to know, I felt like the caged bird who suddenly finds the flutter of the wind again under its wings. I pulled over to eat an apple. I took a photo of myself. I was so happy, calm woven with glee interspersed with awe.

A man in a tight Nike T-shirt stood in front of a shed that looked like it was set up for bicycle repairs. He confirmed that I was on the right road to a place called Naina Devi. It was a Shakti pith where Sati's eyes were said to have fallen. I really wanted to go only to the Shakti piths in a corner of India where her yoni supposedly fell. That was the one that Vishnu Uncle in Kathmandu had offered to show me, but I had chosen not to trust a guru and his Bagpiper Whiskey.

I turned off the back road onto a windy path that was National Highway Number 21. To my surprise, I saw the Hotel Hilltop sitting on a hillside at a bend in the lane. That was where I had stayed with my two *dakini* sisters on our first night on our own in India. Naina Devi sat not far away, tucked away in the many curves and hills of Himachal Pradesh on a hilltop in the state's Bilaspur District. The sun was setting. I found myself again on the road as darkness neared. I chose to take the gamble and continue forward. This narrow bumpy road wound up through a mountain. A jeep full of passengers passed me. Then I passed it when the driver pulled over to let off passengers. At least I had company. Only the faintest light remained. I could see the glitter of white lights far away, like a white glow upon the hill.

The word *Naina* is synonymous with Sati's eyes. I wondered if she could be watching over me. I found myself at a gate. The man there pointed me to a new *dharamsala,* or hotel, where he said I could spend the night at the foot of the hill on which the temple sat. This would be the first time I had ventured into a *mandir* alone. Fireworks shot into the sky for Diwali, the Hindu holiday of lights I'd celebrated only once before in my childhood with my friend Sumita. Would they be inviting here? A Sikh Punjabi looking after the ashram guest house checked me into a room and offered to go up to the *mandir* with me. He was supposed to meet the temple's pandit up there.

We climbed hundreds of stairs that ascended past stalls with shutters rolled down over the front of them. A giant pipal tree stood to the left after we crossed the main gate. It was a calm scene tonight. I took my shoes off at the foot of the stairs and climbed upward. We circled clock-wise, and I found myself in front of a dark goddess figure. She had a daunting black face with a gold *teeka* hanging from the part of her hair to the space between her eyebrows like my mother wore on her wedding day. I offered my *prasad,* my gift of food to the goddess. The pandit smeared a *teeka* on my forehead.

As I sat on the cool temple tile, another pandit told me the tale of how the gods were confounded by the terror of an evil monster. The legend said that only a woman would be able to destroy the demon. The gods created Durga to destroy the monster. The evil force tried to seduce the beautiful Durga. He could not entice her. She destroyed him. "From sky, fire fell. There was so much power. She used to kill with her *phoonk,*" the short breath that I knew in a different way from my childhood, my mother breathing upon me for protection after reciting a verse from the Qur'an.

"Look," he said, gesturing to the shrine, "this is Ma's power."

I settled in a corner of the small room in which Naina Devi's shrine sat. Christmas lights strung around the mother goddess image flickered red, yellow, and green. "Jingle Bells" wafted out of the lights. Then came "Santa Claus Is Coming to Town." Flowers were scattered around Naina Devi. Two men in robes fed her. The smoke from incense spiraled upward. A brass railing divided devotees from the goddess, and a padlocked silver-colored box sat in front of the railing, past which devotees trickled to pay their respects and drop coins and folded rupee notes.

As the story goes, Durga threw her *paseena,* or sweat, behind her at Naina Devi, leaving her presence behind. The Muslim in me couldn't relate to this devotion. Barbed wire surrounded the temple. A monkey squeaked. Hindi music filtered up the hill to the temple from down below. More fireworks popped. This was a temple like many where a pandit's family ruled.

Back at the ashram guest house, the pandit's children tumbled inside, fresh faced and eager. They were normal young boys with dreams. Aditya Gautam, thirteen, aspired to be a businessman. Abishek wanted to be an air force pilot. The eldest was headed to cricket camp the next morning with the dream of becoming a cricket star. They asked me to climb to the rooftop with them. Once, they had stood here, they said, and the power of the goddess, whom they called Mataji, or Mother, swept into their hands in the form of lightning that sprang through the sky.

"Mataji is power," said Aditya. Mother is power.

Their father wandered by the next morning, his hair twisted into a small ponytail. There was a smear of yellow on his forehead and on his earlobes. He wore a gold pendant of Durga on the end of a gold chain, a peek of the white cord that marked him as a Brahmin underneath a dirty shirt. He said he went to a degree college for one year but was unemployed. He wasn't warm or engaging like his sons. Still, I ventured to ask him to tell me about Tantra. He didn't want to talk about it. "It's secret."

I headed one last time up to the temple to see it by day. The stalls in the bazaar, now open, sold the coconuts and red ribbons of Hindu temple worship. They also had black plastic toy guns, another fixture at temple bazaars, just like the one a boy was shooting at the Kalachakra initiation in Ki. Durga was painted upon the white tile in the temple, supposedly at the top of 213 steps. I lost count at thirty-nine.

Cries of "*Jai* Mataji!" broke out every few minutes. "Victory to the Mother!"

I was told to go search near a *goofa,* a cave, for a baba. Someone yelled at me. I turned around. It was the baba, looking very much a sadhu with unruly hair and leathery skin. Only this one lived in a well-equipped room with a television in one corner beside a telephone. He sat in front of a fire in the middle of the room, tridents stuck in a cauldron, a symbol of Shiva's weapon against three evils that have to be destroyed in order to get to enlightenment: anger, lust, and pride. I sat down.

He said, "Shanti comes from being cool."

It soon became apparent that he got his peace of mind from something else. He talked to me between hacks of coughing, as he smoked what smelled like marijuana. He seemed a rather unhealthy person to be dispensing advice. Men trickled inside until the room was full of company. They passed his cigarette around. He flipped through a photo album and stopped at a photo of a Western woman. "She is my student." Every baba seemed to have a token Western disciple.

I hit the road again for a place called Chintpurni, weaving along a back road as I passed a glorious splash of lake. Darkness descended, but I kept riding.

Smoke from a fire in the fields filled the sky. It was heaven on earth. I slowed down for a lizard crossing the road. Piglets danced at street's edge. A train passed me. I was the motorcyclist that I saw from the train door on the journey from Chennai to Lucknow. I was what I wanted to become. I saw a woman in a *shalwar* riding a bike. She didn't know it, but she gave me silent moral support.

After I pulled in safely to Chintpurni, I stared at an image of Durga on her tiger at the STD/ISD/PCO, acronyms dear to this traveler's heart, Subscriber Trunk Dialing/International Subscriber Dialing/Public Call Office. She sat sidesaddle with eyeliner accenting her eyes. Her feet were laced with the artistry of *mehndi,* the temporary henna tattoo Madonna popularized in the West. I wondered if her back ached as mine did. Even my butt ached a little. I wondered if Durga's butt ever hurt, riding that tiger of hers into battle. Sati's feet supposedly fell here. Pilgrims flocked here because they believed that Ma Chintpurni cleared away the worries of any devotee who visited her.

I slipped into an STD booth. I hadn't called home until now because I hadn't wanted to admit to my mother that I was riding a motorcycle alone. She hadn't heard from me in so many days, she knew I was up to something.

"Be careful," she told me gently, but she said nothing to dissuade me. My parents always let me fly.

Two middle-aged men and a young man came inside and sat down at a table. After I got off the phone, the men invited me to join them and told me the story of how they had walked ten hours to get to Chintpurni. I had probably passed them on my ride here. One of the older men promised Shakti Ma sixteen years ago that he would walk to her if she gave him the strength to win a lawsuit at work. He won the lawsuit in 1984 but forgot the promise. He said, "Ma didn't forget."

He said she roused him awake while he slept two nights before and told him to fulfill his promise. He told his best friend, who agreed to set out with him on this pilgrimage. The devotee's grown son was with him. The next morning, he planned to travel the one and a half miles to the Shakti pith by doing prostrations. He said he'd allow me to join him.

"Jai Ma" rang outside on speakers in the early morn before the sun rose.

He wore maroon MacGregor shorts marked XXXXL. We set out just after 6 A.M., the father limping from his walk the day before. The sun rose as we passed a sign for NIT Computer Institute, a reminder of the modern day. The father slipped out of his *chappals,* sandals. He crouched and splayed his body out straight on the road, stretching his arms over his head, his bald spot staring at the sky. His friend used a small rock to mark a line in the road beside his outstretched fingers. He lifted himself up and stood up, stepping toward the line his friend had marked. He crouched and lay outstretched again. A man walked by and yelled encouragement. "*Hai,* Mataji!"

He panted before he replied. "*Hai,* Mataji!" He continued with his prostrations, over and over again. Sweat dripped from his forehead, sitting on the tip of his nose. He spoke to Mataji. "*Jai* Ma! Call me! Give me shakti!"

He took his shirt off, his bulging belly squeezed only under a white *bunyain,* a cotton undershirt.

His friend pointed out the glory of the rising sun to us. He turned to me. "Do you have the sun in America?"

Water splashed against his *bunyain* as our devotee lay in a puddle. He picked himself out of the puddle. A dog with a stubby tail drank from it. He walked past Neha Beauty Parlor with its advertisement as a "Treasue of Beauti treatments cum training centre." We went past stands selling the temple staple, including more black plastic guns. A sign over one stall made me smile. "Get a key ring with your lovely name."

His friend exhaled, "*Jai* Mataji!"

Wet dirt clung to the hair on our devotee's arms. We reached the steps leading up to the *mandir.* Our devotee told a sadhu reclining on the stairs his story about his unfulfilled promise to Shakti Ma. The guru listened and agreed, "She doesn't forget."

The devotee continued. The front of his *bunyain* was soaked through. A friend recognized him. He asked him if he fell. Not quite.

We bought *prasad,* an offering of flowers, at a stall in front of a sign for "Krishana Prashad Bhandar." His friend started marking his progress with just his foot. Our devotee smiled now, glowing from his sweat. We crossed the threshold into the *mandir.* He had fulfilled his promise. The *mandir* was under a tree. We slipped with the flow of the crowd in front of the shrine. Two eyes stared out from under colorful *dupattas.* That was supposed to be the Shakti Ma we came to see. A pandit standing inside the shrine explained to me, "Shakti Ma has the power of Shiva lingam." We offered our flowers. A man took them and guided us to step aside to let new devotees bask in Shakti Ma's aura. I sat down on cool tile, trying not to discount the power of this Shakti pith by the rushed moment in front of the deity. I hoped to absorb the energy of this site sacred to Hindus through quiet meditation. Just as I crossed my legs beneath me, a pandit found our small group. He muttered a prayer, handed us sweets as our *prasad,* our gift blessed by the goddess, and opened his hand, looking for a donation for his prayer. This place wasn't inspiring much in me. I felt conned.

I found out that cute girls who seemed to be venturing out for school were actually going up the hill to beg for money from pilgrims. One tagged after me as we descended the hill. She was beautiful with dark skin.

She glared at me. "If you don't give me money, Shakti Ma will curse you."

I laughed at her threat and suggested she didn't have to be so dark spirited in her begging. I gave her money with a smile. One of her young friends grabbed the money from her hand. She tagged after me for more. My pilgrim friends shooed them away, although I would rather have talked to these girls. All of us returned to our hotel the regular way, on our feet. Back at the hotel, the father admired my Nike windbreaker. Trying to learn to be selfless, I gave it to him. It was sunny as I headed out again, this time on to a temple called Jawalamukhi. Boulders and purple flowers lined the road, and I passed a storefront with a sign for Shakti Studio. She seemed to show up in the most unlikely places.

The temple sat in the south of the Kangra Valley. It was the temple to Jawalamukhi, the goddess of light. From the distance, I saw the golden spire that topped the temple. A wealthy devotee had built it.

This was where Sati's tongue supposedly fell. Legend said Jawala Ma took form in the perpetual flames called *jyotis* that sprang out of nine different rocks in the temple. This was the first *mandir* that I ventured to enter without an escort. No one stopped me. I went into a tiny square chamber where a pandit muttered a mantra and waved a flame. Natural gas was said to come out of a copper pipe that shot out a tiny blue flame. This flame was worshiped as the manifestation of Jawalamukhi. I walked around the pit and touched a corner of the temple from which a flame burst out. There was another flame in a pit in the center of the room. A man gave me white kernels for my donation. He put Hindi newspapers and green leaves over the fire. A chant broke out.

As I left the temple, I asked for the relatives of the pandit family whom I'd met at Naina Devi. I was guided to a narrow store that sold the symbols of *prasad*, bright red fabrics, goddess pictures, coconuts, and sweets. The pandit's son began talking with me. He practiced Tantra. A baba came by and told the young man, "You should be married."

"But you want to find your Shakti," I told him.

At that, he confided that he was a Shiva plotting the kidnapping of his Shakti. He was in love with a woman who came on pilgrimage from another town, but her parents had rejected his marriage proposal. He belonged to the highest caste, Brahmins, but he came from the wrong caste for them. They had arranged her marriage to someone else. A friend came from Delhi to help the pandit's son carry out a plan to whisk the woman away from home. She was party to the plot. But our Shiva had doubts in himself. "I am not strong."

This was modern-day romance in India, the assertion of choice through kidnappings. There was so little personal liberty here. I wished him well.

I hit the road again, cold from having given away my Nike jacket. The warmth during the day had felt so wonderful. Now, as day turned to night, I passed rocks and boulders, making a hairpin turn. I rode through a tunnel, so confining and so cool. My bike stalled when I stopped to read directions, and then it fell over. A cow with a full belly and dark eyes came up the hill. It was fall number 4, not that I was counting. The owner of the cow came running out to help me. The cow sniffed a yellow flag and a bush before walking away uninterested.

On the road to Dharamsala, I rode through Kangra, once the seat of the Chand Dynasty, which ruled over the princely state of Kangra. I went to find the famous temple of Bajreshwari Devi. Muslim visitors of the past had a different mission than me. The temple had so much legendary wealth that just about every Muslim invader took the effort to swing through here. A Turkish invader, Mahmud of Ghazni, supposedly stole a fortune in gold, silver, and jewels in 1009. Another ruler, Firoz Shah Tughlaq, ransacked it in 1360. It rebounded. By the time the Muslim emperor Jehangir's reign came, the temple was paved in plates of pure silver. *Lonely Planet* said the temple was in the bazaar at the end of a serpentine series of alleys flanked by stalls hawking *prasad.*

I ended up asking directions at a bus stop where an eager young student wanted to practice his English. He told me to forget the Shakti pith.

Come see his village's Shiva temple. Why not? I spent my day with a village baba and the disciples he protected from Tantric spells. He looked younger than his forty-three years, his uncombed hair framing his easy smile. Mortal women weren't allowed into his inner sanctum, plastered with images of gods and goddesses. He took ash from his *havan,* a fire pit, put it in the palm of his hand, and had a woman disciple drink the ashen water from his hand. As I headed out for Dharmasala, I followed his instructions and dipped the ring finger of my right hand into the ash and put a *teeka* on my forehead. He guided me, too, to drink ashen water that he poured into my right hand. It tasted wretched.

This motorcycle trip through the Shakti piths, ending with this taste of ash as a gesture of hospitality, was important not so much for the places I visited but for the simple fact that I made the journey safely and peacefully. Bandits didn't rob me on the Grand Trunk Highway. Pandits didn't drug and rape me in darkened corners of Hindu temples. On the contrary, I, a Muslim, was greeted with hospitality and enthusiasm for the curiosity I expressed about this Hindu culture foreign to me.

As I nosed my sleek Splendor away from my newest friends, I turned around one last time to wave good-bye to the half-dozen children who had led me through the narrow passageways between their houses to show me their village.

"Ta-ta!" they yelled at me.

"Ta-ta!" I yelled back, happy to adopt their colloquialism inherited from British colonialists.

CHAPTER 16

Dharamsala

I RODE PAST SUNSET, again breaking my rule not to ride in the dark. The road through Dharamsala was a cluttered bazaar. I pulled over but didn't even get off my motorcycle.

"A sweater, please, *bhai sahib,*" I said, referring to the sweater *walla* with a respectful honorific for brother. It was something that I had learned from Dadi. Always try to relate to men as either my brother or father to deflect any connection to me as a sexual being.

I continued on the road, winding around the mountain, wondering when I might reach this place called McLeod Ganj, up the mountain. Here, too, I didn't have a plan. I had a few names of both Buddhist representatives of the Dalai Lama and regular Tibetan citizens, but I hadn't called ahead to let anyone know I was coming. I wanted to leave with some lessons from Tantric Tibetan Buddhism, because it seemed to express itself in the modern day with more of the light of spirituality than the darkness of Hindu Tantra's black magic, but I was leaving my experiences and lessons to fate.

When I arrived, I rode past a garbage dump. It wasn't what I had imagined. I drove through town to the Himachal Pradesh guest house but decided to stay instead across the road at a guest house run by a Tibetan. I had taken a liking to the Dalai Lama. When I had returned to Delhi from Pakistan, I had gone to Buddha Park for a teaching by the Dalai Lama. It was a hot and sunny morning, the Dalai Lama sitting on a dais in front of thousands of disciples. Early in his talk, he spotted an elderly woman in the front, chin dropped to her chest and head slightly askew in a wheelchair. The sun was emerging from behind clouds, and the Dalai Lama gestured for an aide to go to the woman and stand with an umbrella over her to protect her from the sun. This act seemed to be the embodiment of the gentle compassion that we should show each other. When the Dalai Lama finished, he shook the hands of elderly women and monks who lined up to see him off, leaving each one of them laughing and smiling in his path. Later, as I sat for the evening session, I looked for a man whose name I had gotten from Mrs. Amy Wen, a dear family friend in Morgantown and the mother of my childhood friend Pauline. Mrs. Wen's niece had married a nephew of the Dalai Lama, and the nephew advised me in an e-mail exchange to find his eldest uncle. Somehow, I had ended up sitting beside him, a distinguished-looking man in a jacket. I'd told him about my project.

He had told me, "Read the sutras. Read *The Way of the Bodhisattva.*" I'd never heard of it, but I plucked it off the bookshelf at Khan Market and read in iambic pentameter this Tibetan Buddhist classic on how to be compassionate.

I didn't know what I'd learn in McLeod Ganj. Would I learn from the Dalai Lama? He was supposed to be in town. It was Halloween when I arrived. I daydreamed about passing out candy in one of the Tibetan schools. I felt as if I was living a masquerade party, pretending to be a great female spiritual seeker. A monkey walked by my veranda at the guest house, delighting me in the surprises of India.

In my walk through town, I noticed advertisements posted for Tantra teachings by Dudjom Tersar Ngondro, also known as Rigdzin Namkha Gyamtso Rinpoche, to be held on the rooftop of the Tenwang Hotel. He even had a Web address, www.flamingjewel.org. Flaming Jewel. Sounded dicey. He was born in a nomadic highland of Tibet and was supposed to be an incarnate of a hunter of treasures hidden by Padmasambhava and his Tibetan consort, Yeshe Tsogyel. I ventured up to the rooftop and stumbled onto a young man with long sleek black hair and a golden robe sitting on a veranda. I chatted with him, thinking he might be our teacher but not knowing. He asked, "Where are you from?"

I told him about my travels from America. "And you?" I asked, able to come up with little else in striking conversation.

"Tibet," he said, as if I should know.

I figured it was time to join the class. A young woman with a mane of dark hair made room for me beside her. She picked up the brochure I put on the ground beside me. It had the guru's photo on it. Turned out it wasn't a respectful gesture to put a guru's picture on the ground. She had gone to a cave where Princess Mandarava had supposedly meditated on the road from Delhi. I had stopped there with Lucy and Esther on our ride back to Delhi from the Kalachakra initiation. The daughter of a king, Mandarava refused the many offers of marriage that came her way, wanting instead to meditate and retreat in the forest. One day she met Padmasambhava when the yogi who came into her kingdom. They went into meditation together. The king was angry and had Padmasambhava burned in a fire. The yogi emerged unscathed and withdrew with Princess Mandarava to caves that surround a lake now called Rewalsar Lake. The king of Tibet, King Sron Btsan Sgampo, heard about the wisdom and marvels known to Padmasambhava and called him to Tibet to spread his dharma. He is said to have left for Tibet from Rewalsar. Some consider it the most sacred site of Buddhism in Himachal Pradesh. Legend says that the spirit of Guru Padmasambhava still lives on the islands floating in the lake.

Esther, Lucy, and I had passed the base of the mountain, where we had once dodged an avalanche and wound our way around the mountain to Rewalsar. The lake was now a collection of Pepsi banners and guest houses. We had circled the lake counterclockwise and gotten caught in a rainstorm when we saw a sign that said, "Princess Mandarava's Cave." An elderly woman with a shaved head waved us into a small alleyway to a doorway. I entered a small room and then through another doorway stepped into a room with cave walls. The woman was a nun at one of the *gompas* there, taking care of Princess Mandarava's cave. Her Hindi wasn't fluent. My Tibetan, nonexistent. She gestured to all of the photos of various lamas, it seemed to test to see if I knew their names. I knew not a one, though one looked like the incarnate I'd met at Ki from Karnataka. I fumbled an answer and was relieved she seemed pleased. I sat and meditated in Princess Mandarava's cave and imagined the presence of this spirit of yesteryear.

Back on our rooftop retreat, I asked the woman next to me, "Do you want to be a *dakini?*"

She looked at me. "Who wouldn't want to be a *dakini?*"

The man with whom I'd just had my uncomfortable chitchat stepped forward as our incarnated teacher. I felt like an idiot. We slipped into a lesson. "Visualize on the right your father, on the left, your mother. In front of you is your greatest enemy, worst enemy. The reason we visualize our worst enemy in front of us is that this is a path of patience. Our parents have been inconceivably kind to us. They cannot be objects for patience. They are people who are kind to us. They let us practice. If there is somebody in our life who harms us, and we are angry, then we have lost a great opportunity. Our own worst enemy is considered to be kind to us. Imagine all sentient beings at our side and behind us. We do this to benefit them."

I thought of an oppressive man that I loathed. I tried to send him the same affection I felt for my mother and father. It wasn't easy, but I made the effort.

A place called the Library of Tibetan Works and Archives was a magnet for the Westerners who come here to study Tantric Tibetan Buddhism because it hosted daily classes taught in English. I sat in a morning session. It was an earnest group of students asking long questions with many independent clauses. I wasn't sure I could stomach these teachings. But I found my way into the office of the Venerable Achok Rinpoche, director of the Library. He was a robust, bespectacled man, sitting behind a desk in a neat office. I wanted to know more about Padmasambhava, known to many as Guru Rinpoche, and his consort, Princess Mandarava.

Library Rinpoche was surprised to hear their names.

"You know about them?"

I nodded.

"Guru Rinpoche looked outrageous," he said. "I would say he was a crazy human being. She must have been a crazy human being, too."

I wanted to know if there were any Padmasambhava aspirants among the Buddhist adepts of the modern day, such as Library Rinpoche. At the Kalachakra initiation at the Ki *gompa,* the Dalai Lama had led us through such an intimate meditation with a consort sitting in a mandala, I wondered, as blasphemous as it may seem to think such things of a monk, if he had a consort. I hedged my curiosity with Library Rinpoche.

"Would you want a consort?" I asked him.

"If I have a consort, enjoyment is there, but I might have to live with squabbling, hate, and jealousy. It may not be easy for me, I would say. Padmasambhava, and also Tantric saints, had sexual practice. It didn't affect his emotions. He was still a free man. I'm afraid I'm scared. I have enough to go through. It is easy to strike me."

He had left his family at the age of three. The goal of the practice is a divine state of enlightenment. "I didn't know if it was attainable." He remembers his mother and father squabbled. "Relations between people have to be honest."

He continued, "Whether you have honesty or not, that question must be answered by yourself. The divine knows exactly how much you're honest." He reflected on the emotions that interrupt relationships. "If you can rationalize and concentrate, you can control hate and jealousy. These are the worst traits."

Padmasambhava and Princess Mandarava faced great humiliation and harassment from her father. "They just didn't care. You get most crazy."

Would he seek the Tantric path? "I don't practice Tantra. I have too much attachment to the privileges of my position."

It was true. To fully adhere to the Tantric path required a certain nonattachment to *samsara,* the worldly life that I symbolically left when I drove out of New York, even if it was with a moving van packed with belongings. "At least you are honest," I said.

He laughed. "I have a few good virtues."

I wondered aloud, "What does it take to learn Tantra?"

Across his desk, he answered, "You have to be a little crazy. Are you crazy?"

I nodded. Riding alone from Delhi to Dharamsala on a motorcycle certainly qualified me as a little bit crazy.

To me, Library Rinpoche was definitely a little crazy. He looked at me with his crooked smile as we talked about searching on the Tantric path. "Maybe you'll help me?"

I hoped he wasn't serious. He answered the question with another crooked smile, perhaps sensing my discomfort with such a proposition, and offered me an assurance he was content on the celibate path. "I'm not really looking."

The evening set in. He said, "Will you give a prayer for me?" That was a cue for the door. I said my surah from the Qur'an for protection and blew a *phoonk*, a breath of protection, in his direction.

Volleyball was my ultimate release, the play that had taught me so much behind the Lincoln Memorial after my divorce.

I was so happy to find volleyball on a blacktop court on the campus of the Library. I made a twenty-something friend, Kelsang Tsering, who worked in the Library. He was a classic new generation of Tibetan Buddhist born in India, singing Bollywood songs and practicing his English on Westerners. He joined me on the court, and I played with ten other young Tibetan Buddhist men. I loved the game even if this was the gentlest game of volleyball I'd ever played. The Tibetan boys only hit hard once. And even then they giggled. I went for a pass. I felt a rip in my right knee, followed by an excruciating pain. I hobbled to the side. My knee locked, and I couldn't put any pressure on it. I remembered something my friend Kent had told me. "Don't ever let them see you in pain," he'd said one afternoon when I stumbled as we left a New York Yankees baseball game.

In retrospect, maybe that was ego talking, an important element of competition, and maybe not appropriate to recreational play in the middle of the Himalayas. If I hadn't pretended to be so strong, I could have gone straight to the hospital. Instead, I was about to endure a painful dharma lesson. I sat on the side until all the men cleared out after the last game was over. Kelsang invited me over for dinner. His cousin was cooking. We hobbled together through the Library dormitories. I couldn't even contemplate going up the mountain to my guest house. I decided to take the risk with this stranger and spend the night in his dormitory room. I slept not one moment. Kelsang slept peacefully on the floor below. It reminded me of the nights I had lain awake in emotional anguish while the man I married slept calmly beside me. I tried to awaken my new friend but failed. I tried to meditate through my pain.

By morning, my knee had swollen into a balloon. I winced from the shooting pain that flew through me. Kelsang got a taxi to take me up the hill to McLeod Ganj. I resorted to my strategy to go into five-star hotels when I needed help. The road was so bumpy I wept from the pain. I limped into the Surya Resorts. Kelsang left me in the lobby to go to work. I crumbled into a chair, weeping from the pain. A Thai woman from a tour group studied me sympathetically and gently handed me Tiger Balm. Another taxi came. The manager told a dark-skinned, scrawny Indian man to accompany me to the hospital, and I went back down the hill again, tears to accompany me on this trip.

This stranger carried me into the Tibetan Delek Hospital. I knew this hospital. I had come here the day before to visit the doctor whom I had met at the Kalachakra, tending to the boy who had just had a seizure.

I had asked the doctor, "Do you practice Tantra?"

He had looked at me from behind his desk. "I don't practice Tantra," he said. "I am still not compassionate enough."

That was hard to fathom from a man who spent his days healing refugees, monks, and children, but his reflection made me contemplate the extent of personal growth I had to achieve before aiming for such noble pursuits as personal enlightenment and divine love.

I couldn't even bite my lip through my own pain.

As I entered the hospital again, I realized I didn't even know the name of the man who was helping me. He wrote his name, PAL SINGH, in capital letters on a Surya Resorts business card. He stayed with me, later bringing me an omelette for breakfast. To me, he was a lesson in compassion embodied. He was a stranger with such virtue, refusing any money in return for his kindness.

The nurses shot me up with the painkiller morphine. The pain drained from my body, and I felt light as a feather. "Now I *know* emptiness," I told the young doctor with dark hair over his ears and wire-rimmed glasses. "Is it wrong to cry from the pain?" I asked, my cheeks still wet from my tears.

He smiled. "Pain is a reminder that you are still in the birth and rebirth cycle." So much for pretending to be Princess Mandarava.

They moved me to a ward where I stayed for two nights, befriending the Tibetans who were the other patients. In one corner, three monks cared for an ailing monk. On the second afternoon, a woman with long wheatish-colored hair walked into the room with three men. She saw me, clearly not a Tibetan, and asked, "Why are you here?"

I told her my story, riding my motorcycle up from Delhi and landing in the hospital after tearing my cartilage playing volleyball. There was a pause. I asked her, "Why are you here?"

I didn't know who she was. The Tibetan patients didn't know who she was. The nurse told me later that she was Princess Diana's sister-in-law. That made her Fergie, the dethroned Duchess of York. She turned her head toward her male companions, looking slightly thrown off guard by my question, as if searching for the answer.

She answered, "Why *am* I here?"

Clearly, she was just another one of us.

CHAPTER 17

Morgantown

A N MRI SCAN of my knee in Delhi revealed that I had ripped my medial meniscus cartilage in my game of volleyball with the young Tantric Tibetan Buddhists.

I had parked my tiger for the winter at the Tibetan guest house and had taken an excruciating jeep ride down from Dharamsala. I went home to the States, straight onto the operating table in Morgantown, and was grounded for a month.

This is what I seemed to do, wear myself out on the road and come home to heal. Each trip back to Morgantown meant bringing home the lessons I'd learned in the world. This time, I felt as if I had conquered India on the merit of simply being true to myself, doing that which I wanted to do. I also carried back with me the magic of the village, figuratively and literally. When I arrived, I pulled out for my mother a stone piece of the veranda that had gotten dislodged from Latif Manzil. I wanted her to touch the home that she'd had to leave as a child. I was my mother's proxy in reclaiming our land. My home in Morgantown was where I was tested to the core of my being when my absentminded professor of a father said, *"Hahn?"* Urdu for "What?" when I talked to him. It was where I saw if I could distill in relation to my family, the people most important to me, the great wisdom I'd gathered on the road.

I tried to be of selfless service to my family. I redecorated my mother's store based on principles of feng shui, espoused by "the Black Hat Tantric" school, of all things, turning the love corner into Safiyyah's corner and the children and creativity section into Samir's responsibility. Samir painted a Buddha meditating in the corner where spirituality was supposed to be activated. "Ommmmm," Buddha said in the drawing. Together, my mother and I learned the differences between the Tibetan deities drawn on lampshades she sold. She called one day asking me to identify one. I thought it was the goddess Tara. We saw later a label that said he was Manjushri, Lord of Wisdom. Whoops. We thought he was a she.

Islam's pious month of Ramadan arrived, and my father awakened me every morning before sunset for a meal meant to shore up our reserves for the day of abstinence from food and drink.

It was a special time I shared with my father. I ate raisin bran cereal. My father ate salad with homemade hummus salad dressing for research he was doing into the merits of different diets for fasting during Ramadan. He had carved a niche in Ramadan fasting research as his specialty as a professor of nutrition, even starting a *International Journal of Ramadan Fasting Research* on the Internet. What I appreciated about his work was that he was looking at a world close to home, as I was doing. I read that a Kashmiri princess named Biksundi Lakshmi taught a Buddhist Tantric fasting practice, using the image of Avalokitesvara, a deity statue I had once coincidentally gotten during a trip to China, as a point of meditation.

The princess had taught that the fasting practice relied on abstaining from food and drink and including prostrations, prayers, and the recital of mantras in a discipline that usually ran from two days to four days but sometimes also stretched into a period of several months. Disciples also had to shave their heads, walk barefoot, and eschew leather, ending the fasting ritual with a feast.

The last morning of Ramadan, my father and I went to our local Morgantown mosque for the morning *fajr namaz*. I slipped behind a curtain drawn to make a women's section. My father was faculty adviser to the Muslim Students Association. For years, starting in 1981, they had prayed in the basement of a building with the Needle Barn, a knitting and needlework store, upstairs and the Monongalia County Jail across the street. The association had collected enough money to buy a house to use as a mosque. I told my father, "You can't have women slip into the *masjid* from the back. You have to give them a front entrance." And he did.

I stared at the fake wood planks on the wall, meditating. The light was out. A shelf of Qur'ans and Arabic books lined the wall to my left. I was the only woman. Men were reading parts of the Qur'an over the loudspeaker and getting corrected. Crackles of laughter interrupted the recitations with each correction. A voice broke through, trembling. "Please don't laugh." I recognized it as my father's voice. "Reading the Qur'an is like a prayer to God for me. Please don't laugh."

My father moved me.

I tried to decide whether to go to Lahore from Morgantown to attend a cousin's wedding. For months, his parents had been reciting prayers to extract extra blessings for the wedding.

The cousin was being wed in an arranged marriage to a woman he had met just a few times, but they were getting to know each other the new millennium way, on the Internet. Sexuality expressed itself differently in that culture. He told me he asked her over the Internet to go to her room and look at her own breasts. She did. To them, that was a big deal. He was a big talker, but, faced with his own wedding night, he was afraid he would have premature ejaculation, something that had happened to one of our other cousins. The advice he got was to masturbate before he was alone with his wife.

Safiyyah meditated with me on the dining table over this question of whether to go to Pakistan or not before heading back to India. I would have had to scramble, overnighting my visa application and passport to the Pakistani Embassy. Safiyyah stared and meditated so close to the candle she singed her bangs.

"Don't go," she concluded.

"Why?"

"You shouldn't do things that'll damage your head."

Spoken like a true child spiritual genius.

I ditched my North Face pack to get an army surplus knapsack that was discounted because its military green was faded from sitting in the window.

It was after 10 P.M., and I was going through the racks at Wal-Mart, hunting for white buttons. I had an idea for using buttons to help school-children connect to my travels and learn about the world. I was trying to learn how to be more giving, abandoning the self-centeredness of single life. I didn't have my own children to inspire. In my own work, maybe I could inspire a lot of children.

I sent notes to Safiyyah's fourth-grade teacher at North Elementary, Mrs. Virginia Hammock, and Samir's second-grade teacher, Mrs. Jeanne DeVincent. I told them I wanted to bring mascots to their classes who would go on my travels with me, sending photos and messages back to the children. I plucked a unicorn and a parrot out of the top bunk in Safiyyah and Samir's room.

In Safiyyah's class, I told the children, "Close your eyes. Fly away with me." And I took the kids on an imagination ride with their unicorn, including the minivan ride to Pittsburgh and the airplane connection in Chicago. But first the unicorn needed a name. "Murph" won. Wait. No, I'd heard wrong.

"Merve!" cried out Sam Walker, a little boy who had interviewed a classmate for other people's secrets when he was in Mrs. DeVincent's second grade with Safiyyah and I had taught the children about journalism.

I passed the Wal-Mart white buttons around and instructed the children to pick two buttons that they liked and to write their names on both of them. I'd sew one button on Merve. "A part of you will also be flying across the ocean with him." The other button they'd keep at home as their lucky wish button.

The winning vote in Samir's class for the name of the parrot was Blink 182, after a popular band. I figured we could settle the trademark infringement issues later. I had the traveling members of my *sangha,* my spiritual community, for my next adventure.

Samir took me to the Morgantown Mall. We meandered toward a kiosk in the middle of the mall where Samir pointed toward a Pokémon card tucked into the glass showcase. "That one, please."

The saleswoman pulled out a hologram Pokémon card protected with a plastic cover. It was Charzard, a fire-breathing dragon. It was thirty dollars. I converted the price in my mind into rupees. Thirty times fifty. That was fifteen hundred rupees. A night at the Residency, the guest house where I stayed in Delhi. A month's wages for a servant.

"Do you really want it?" I asked Samir.

"Yeah," he said, quietly but without shame. I had to give him credit for his tenacity.

"Okay, we'll take it," I told the saleswoman.

I wrote to Lucy about this disconnect between the worlds in which we traveled. She wrote back to me with her wisdom. "It's all relative. It's always relative. Wherever you are, and whatever you're doing, you have to take it in the context. Beauty and truth lie in the most hideous of forms. But taken in the sunsets and sunrises of life, the gray concrete of the pavement acts like shot silk basking in white light. That was the Pokémon doubt cast in the light of the all."

CHAPTER 18

Thirty Days in a Spiritual Prison Camp

T HE BARBED WIRE stared at me like a divide between the real world and the spiritual prison camp in which I found myself. I'd traveled a distance greater than miles from Morgantown.

Back in India, it was barely 4 A.M. and dark. I was supposed to meet a Tantric swami who told me the predawn hours were the most auspicious for meditation. But the gates to this tented ashram colony where I was staying were locked so that I was stuck behind the chain-link fence that surrounded us on all sides. Along with about three hundred other Westerners, I'd paid the Himalayan Institute some five thousand dollars to stay one month in the luxury of these tents colony on the banks of the holy Ganges River, a package that gave us ID tags and a regular newsletter. We were here during the Maha Kumbh a Mela, a celebrated pilgrimage that drew millions of devotees to bathe in the river waters. This pilgrimage was particularly special because the position of the stars and planets made it a holy alignment that was last seen 144 years before.

It was a last-minute decision that got me to jet back to India to experience the Maha Kumbh a Mela. The year before I had been at the Himalayan Institute in Honesdale, Pennsylvania, where I'd spent the weekend with my father learning to breathe. Its pandit, Rajmani Tigunaut, had set me on the path of identifying myself to my Rajput ancestor of thirteen generations ago. I thought maybe I could learn more about authentic Tantra from the pandit here where he was conducting the retreat. For now, I just tried to figure out one thing.

"How am I supposed to get out of here?" I whispered to myself.

Our registration fee amounted to about four years of salary for the guard who was supposed to wake up early to unlock the gate. Needless to say, he didn't wake up. I scanned the fence to see if there was a hole in the dirt through which I could shimmy to escape. I couldn't find any way out. I settled cross-legged in one of the thatched huts made with hay and gazed toward the slow-moving Ganga that flowed before me. On the narrow strip of beach a band of sadhus walked toward the main encampments of the Kumbh a Mela. They had a freedom we'd surrendered for the luxury of these Swiss Army tents, chai breaks, and a store with goods for sale from mala beads to *shalwar kameezes* and an Ayurvedic medicine called Elixir 29. The guards locked the gates between 6 P.M. and 6 A.M. The breakfast buffet included porridge every day, for which we created special recipes, adding sugar one day, bananas another, honey and peanut butter yet another. At dinner one night, we compared this camp to the prison camp in the World War II TV program *Hogan's Heroes.* We tried to remember the camp's name.

"Stalag something," I said.

Someone played off Elixir 29 for our new name for this camp: "Stalag 29."

Stalag 29 sat outside the city of Allahabad, a town my mother remembered from her girlhood train rides from Bombay to Lucknow. A thrill would buzz through her compartment as everyone awoke from slumber to throw coins into the Ganga for good luck.

On my father's side, my dada earned his law degree at Allahabad University before moving the family to Hyderabad. In Aryan times, Allahabad was called Prayag, and many Hindu nationalists still called it by that name rather than evoke mention of Allah through its Muslim name, meaning "the city of Allah." It's a sprawling city today with a train station where a cousin of my father's worked. He brought me to our campsite on his scooter, standing outside with me at a massive gate where the security guards wouldn't allow entry without proper authorization. As we drove through the tent colony on roads that workers swept with brooms, he shook his head at this place created for foreigners. "They're making a fool out of people." I happened to be one of them, the fools.

Every morning and every night, the pandit sat on a stage in a large open-air tent, holding lectures that were supposed to be a smart spiritualist's guide to the Vedic principles behind Hinduism. Several rows of

Americans sat cross-legged on mats in front of the stage, dozens of rows of folding chairs filled with more attendees behind them. At every lecture, a cameraman stood in the middle of the tent, filming the pandit to sell him on videotape later.

The Ganga and the Yamuna Rivers were real bodies of water, but the Saraswati was an imaginary river that was said to intersect with them in Allahabad, although it had run dry. Figuratively, it was the symbolic channel of wisdom within us. The three rivers were said to run, figuratively, through our seven chakras and, literally, through a place called the *sangam* here in Allahabad, a special area where pilgrims bathed by the millions. These bathing rites were a joke not only to my Muslim relations but many Hindus as well, who considered it the construction of pandits and other religious leaders trying to exact money from the faithful on the basis of ritual. Hindus hardly cornered the market in this regard. I'd already seen Muslims who backbit while praying five times a day and a Buddhist pilgrimage where a Sherpa died in a stampede to see a sand mandala.

My introduction to this tent world hadn't been inspiring. I had slipped into the tent assigned to me when a voice, clearly irritated, had sprung from the darkness. "Who are you?"

"My name is Asra. I've been assigned this tent."

The voice had answered, "This is *supposed* to be a *private* tent!"

Oh. I learned later that the woman behind the voice had been negotiating with the Himalayan Institute organizers for weeks to pay extra to get a private tent where she could hold her own personal retreat. I found myself, instead, in another tent with a Seattle couple and their young blond daughter, Shanti, meaning "peace." Instead of sharing the main tent space with the family, I made a bedroom for myself in a front area, laying hay in one corner and sleeping atop the pile with woolen blankets bundled on me for the cold nights. I walked to the *sangam* the first morning with the pandit's family, most of them settled, like him, in the U.S. One of his sisters married a very American Indian whose brother led our march in a North Face jacket and constant reminders to his niece and nephew to pull out their water bottles: "Drink more water!" The tents stretched for miles and miles and were packed with pilgrims and sadhus who had traveled from all over India to be here. The part of the *sangam* we found was a beachfront lined with the faithful watching each other's belongings as they dipped in the holy waters. I didn't go in, this time.

When we walked back, I gazed upon the rows of tents stretched along the banks of the Ganga, a glorious sunset silhouetting them in a haze of orange and red.

"What do you see?" I asked the pandit's brother-in-law.

"*Maya,*" he said.

"*Maya?*"

"You don't know *maya? Maya* is illusion."

I peered out at the sunset and tents again. After my retreat at the Buddhist monastery in West Virginia, I explored the illusion that was within me. Now, I looked outside myself and tried to examine the *maya* outside me. The pandit, with all his philosophical teachings, had turned the pilgrimage into quite a business operation. Excitedly, one night, he announced that we could invest in the future of this enterprise. "We will have timeshare on meditation retreat huts where you can stay in the blessed ambiance of what we have created here." For a $5,000 donation, I could be "a founding patron." I passed.

I finally got out the gate to join my Tantric, Swami Yogi Prakash, a man with a business card advertising his talents: "Astrologer, Yoga Expert, Tantrist, Counseller, Healer & Naturopath." I entrusted myself to him somewhat because he was the resident swami at a camp run by a respected author and journalist I'd met in Delhi by the name of Bhaskar Bhattacharyye. He was a bespectacled, bearded man who wrote a book, *The Mystic Lover,* about the Tantric songs of a nomadic people called the Bauls of Bengal.

When I first met him, the swami had hugged me, breathing deep into his gut so his potbelly rose on my flat stomach. "Feel something?" he had asked.

How could I not feel his big fat stomach? He had tried to kiss me. I had averted my face so he couldn't kiss my lips. I returned to his tent this time because I was still just a little bit curious. This time, he fed me by hand from his *thali,* a plate with an assortment of vegetarian dishes.

"You must surrender to your teacher," he told me, between bites. "I will be teaching you out of love."

"I don't even know you," I told him. But I did. He was a loser, Swami Slime, showing me, after my experience with Sufi Slime, that lechery crossed all boundaries.

The most attention at the Maha Kumbh a Mela went to the *naga babas.*

In search of these *naga babas,* a group of hashish-infused ascetics who renounced clothing, families and jobs—everything but their drug habits—I swept through the dusty Mela grounds with a band of new American friends from the Himalayan Institute camp. Jack was a big, barrel-chested scientist with a wry sense of humor. Anaya's real name was Deborah, a recently separated forty-something Jewish-American whose mother still hadn't forgiven her for not marrying a Jewish man. She came to India to meet a Hare Krishna boyfriend who ditched her at the last minute, stranding her with an airline ticket she decided to use anyway. Anaya now had a crush on Kevin, a doctor who joined us as we went in search of the *naga babas* on an auspicious bathing day. Jack's stature made him a magnet for curious Indians, and he became a mini-celebrity shaking hands with more good humor than I could ever muster for eager young Indian men who wanted to practice their English.

"Jack Smith from America! Jack Smith from America!" the young men repeated to themselves after Jack introduced himself.

I repeated to my friends something Lucy said during our Himalayas jaunt about the reception just about anyone gets in this country where the men especially aren't shy about stopping and staring. "In India, everyone becomes a movie star."

The *naga babas* sat around fires surrounded by entourages of disciples and curious hangers-on. Exploring one day, I had found a popular *naga baba* who had his leathery arm in the air, his fingernails so long they had curled around his fingertips. He supposedly hadn't dropped his arm for years. Somebody from his entourage had beckoned me over. I had sat down around the fire, honored.

"Do you want to take a photo?" they had asked me, eager to please. "Chai?"

I had been befuddled by their hospitality until one of the entourage members started negotiating. He had thought five hundred rupees was a fair gift for me to leave. Not to leave any confusion in my mind, he had said that would buy plenty of the *ganja* the sadhus around me were openly smoking. I hadn't brought any money.

"I'll come back," I had said, I don't know why.

"Okay, but remember if you don't come back in this lifetime, you will have to return in another lifetime to repay your debt."

Return to support a *naga baba*'s drug habit? That didn't sound right, but I had looked high and low for that campsite again with a five-hundred-rupee note ready to hand over in this act of blackmail. I searched again with Anaya, Jack, and Kevin, but I couldn't find the arm-in-air baba again.

We joined the parades of *naga babas* to the *sangam*. It was a peaceful procession considering the millions of pilgrims that were there. At the beachfront, the *naga babas* stormed down to the beach. They were a blur of dark skin in a cloud of dust. One *naga baba* wore a heavy wooden and brass chastity belt that locked around his waist, encasing his lingam. There was no worry this year about a stampede like the one that happened years ago. The *naga babas* got a special VIP bathing area.

Anaya and I ventured out on another auspicious bathing day to dip into the Ganga.

There were millions around us as we settled onto one spot of the beachhead. I went first. I stood in the water, my pants rolled up above my knees. I'd heard a lot about the diseases that could be gotten from these waters, where corpses often float. To die here was considered a blessing. I wondered if I would perform the ultimate act of faith and dip my face into these waters. The photos of Sonia Gandhi, the Italian daughter-in-law of India's only woman prime minister, Indira Gandhi, showed that she didn't when she came to the *sangam* just days earlier. I leaned forward and splashed water on my head. That was the most faith I could give this ritual.

It was a cacophony of experiences here. The pandit promised us a night with the saints. Everyone in our campsite dressed up. The stage filled with babas with entourages, mobile phones, and armed guards. They spent the evening lauding the pandit, who beamed throughout the night, a larger-than-life photo of Swami Rama on the stage. Night after night, he brought us the same baba, a bearded man called Tapasvi Baba, meaning "Meditation Baba."

Anaya and I went in search of this baba one morning when our camp was invited to his campsite. We'd made an appointment with a camel driver to ride his camel into the main Mela campgrounds. The camel and his owner showed up late. The camel driver explained the camel ate breakfast late. You couldn't rush a camel. We waddled happily to the Mela grounds on our camel and stopped for chai. I was questioning the pandit's earlier advice to hide my Muslim identity among Hindus. It hadn't mattered among the people of Himachal Pradesh. Sitting at the chai stall, a man with a thick mustache started talking to us. He described himself as an artist from the Rajput caste. I admitted to this Hindu that I was Muslim. No one banished me. No one stoned me.

I started to reconsider my entire experience at this tented colony. Was it the camp that was a prison, or was it my mind, like so many of our minds, that restricted me because it so quickly judged and dismissed? We judge so quickly in this world, based on cynicism affirmed by sitcoms such as *Seinfeld.* But when we dismiss people, places, ideas, or experiences, we close our minds to the possible. I got so distracted by the barbed wire, I didn't appreciate a secure place, far from the likes of potbelly swamis, where I could truly contemplate. I got so hung up on Panditji's warning not to identify myself as a Muslim to Hindu teachers, I was wary of a friendly Rajput artist. I was so turned off by the messenger, Swami Rama, I rejected his message. Restrictions and restrictive personalities often so irk independent spirits like mine that we became ensnared in the human dimension instead of just staying free and focused on our own personal mission.

On my last day, I met the woman whose private tent I had intruded upon. It was a bright sunny day. The waters of the Ganga, as the Ganges is called in India, sparkled. She was embarrassed she had kicked me out of the tent, but she appreciated the solitude that she'd enjoyed. I had wanted to spend my month like she had done, but instead got distracted by the outside world.

"I stayed here mostly," she said. "It was very good for me." Unlike me, she saw past the barbed wire and penetrated the place that was usually the spiritual prison, herself.

CHAPTER 19

Riding into the Village

M Y ANCESTORS called me.

I drove my motorcycle with Anaya behind me through the rain to Jaigahan. An Ambassador with another friend, Matthew, and our belongings followed behind us as we crossed the breakers that were speed bumps at railroad tracks. We now had Cheenie Bhai with us, our blossom-headed, ring-necked parakeet, rescued outside the city of Jhansi on a road trip through the sex temples of Khajuraho and the Tantric temples of remote cities with names like Dhatia and Chitraukaut. In Khajuraho, a tour guide we dubbed Swami Eloquence spun the mystical tales of the temples filled with sculptures showing the evolution of human beings from bestiality to human expression to sublime and then divine. In Dhatia, I meditated for the first time upon the power of the energy exuded from a lingam statue and listened to men sing prayers to the mother goddess who was the main deity there, touched by their devotion and wondering if they applied the same reverence to their wives at home. In Chitraukaut, a yogi at a special mountain shrine to the god Ram pretended to teach Anaya, Matthew, and me yoga but instead used the opportunity to cop a feel. He became Copafeel Swami. Along the way, I saw the beauty and grace of India in a small town called Orchha, which entranced me with the simple splendor of a sunset behind a slow trickle of a river. Translating for Anaya and Matthew, I realized that I had a gift that I had little appreciated as a bridge between the West and the East. Or at least one of those rope contraptions I'd seen stretched over rivers in Himachal Pradesh. I could speak to both worlds and didn't have to be claimed by just one.

Cheenie was loose in the Ambassador, sitting at times at the window, making me giggle as I passed him at the railroad breakers.

The rain felt glorious, and I drove slowly to make sure nothing stupid happened. Anaya rode well in the back. She didn't jostle much and dropped her feet when I needed her help to balance when we slowed for traffic in the towns we crossed. We were going about half as fast as usual, to be safe. It was late when we hit Shahganj. We found only one hotel. It was disgusting. I wanted to vomit when I went into the bathroom. One of the hotelier boys drove my motorcycle into the restaurant. In Shahganj, I went with the hotelier to buy a gas cylinder and stove, a true act of liberation. To have my own kitchen was almost equal to having my own home in India, a place where many women in an extended family shared the kitchen.

I figured a woman had never steered herself alone to the village, let alone on a motorcycle. The feminist manifesto from a village in India had now been declared. I felt triumphant, as if I had returned from a war. In a way, I felt as if I had won a battle to overcome the fears that paralyze us. The next morning, I guided the Ambassador from Khetasari. I knew the right turn at the Union Bank sign, past the long road of fertile fields and trees lining the road. It was a clear day, cool and bright.

I led us down the couple miles to the pile of rocks where we turned right at the chai *walla* stand. The road was rocky. The World Bank was apparently funding the tarring of this road as another route to Jaunpur. I veered to the right around a giant tree, kicking up dirt. The Ambassador followed. I watched carefully for the alley through which my mother was first taken away from Latif Manzil.

We eased our way through the still-teetering gate and over the cobble-stone circular driveway. I stopped in front of Latif Manzil. Bluebeard's son and his cousin-brother came running. I took off my helmet and felt as if I had been blessed and kissed by the divine touch of life. It was glorious to be back.

We embarked on a magical adventure of independence in the village house.

Anaya helped me make a home of the two rooms in which Iftikhar Mamoo and Rachel Momani had loved each other. She swept and cleaned with me. We pulled out old photos of my ancestors and hung them on the wall. I was pleased to find my paternal ancestor, Shibli Nomani, the Islamic scholar, among Mamoo's photos. We opened the trunks and unfurled cotton blankets onto the *takht,* a platform, to create a sitting area in the front room with pillows against the back.

In the room with the veranda, we lined a *charpai* near the balcony door so that at night I could gaze at the stars. It was romantic and inspiring. We had hardly settled into the house when a familiar face walked into the upstairs courtyard. It was Sean McLachlan, a journalist I'd met at the Maha Kumbh a Mela amid the *naga babas.* He had gotten an e-mail from me, giving him directions to Latif Manzil. A *mowlana* type who worked on the bus line in Jaunpur and lived in Khetasari escorted him here. When I saw Sean, I instantly embraced him in greeting, yelling, "Sean!" Zaki, who was standing nearby, later asked me incredulously, "You hugged a man who isn't your husband?

Every night, we cooked our own meals. I didn't want to get caught in Bluebeard's web and chose to live independently with my friends upstairs. We gazed at the stars. Sean taught me that the sun doesn't actually rise or set, but we rotate away from it. "We should call it earth move instead of sunset," I offered. We picnicked every night on the courtyard floor with the stars as our canopy and our lanterns as lighting. One day we plucked the most beautiful purple carrots from the *sabzi walla* in the bazaar. Anaya stirred the pot that night, stewing the carrots. Somehow, they burned, but we didn't know it because it was so dark. Sean bit into the carrots and, somehow, we started joking about them, not realizing we we were hurting Anaya's feelings.

To soothe feathers the next day, we played a game Safiyyah and Samir had taught me from their days at North Elementary. "Each one of us draws a name and writes a nice thing about the person whose name you've drawn," I suggested.

I scribbled our names. Matthew. Anaya. Sean. Asra. Sean drew my name and wrote:

Asra
    Warm, welcoming, spiritually aware,
    A firm base for any group
    The only person I know who can be sparkly and serious and silly
at the same time

How kind. Spiritually aware? Who would have thought a year ago?

My dream of living independently came true a few weeks later. After my friends left India, I returned to my village again, alone except for the companionship of Cheenie Bhai and Cheenie Apa.

The wind caressed my face. Crickets chirped. Song filled the night air with remembrances piped on loudspeakers to Hazrat Ali, the son-in-law of the Prophet Mohammad and the first imam, or leader, of the Shi'as, the minority sect of Islam. They believe the prophet Mohammad designated Ali to be his political and spiritual successor, while the Sunnis, the majority of Muslims and my family's sect, didn't accept this and instead elected Abu Bakr as the first caliph of Islam. In Jaigahan, the Shi'as lived for generations in a separate part of the village from Sunnis, but they always got along well. It was the holy month of Moharram for the Shi'as when they mourn the murder of Hazrat Ali's son Husain.

One night, the sound of a young girl lyrically reciting surahs from the Qur'an spilled through the air to me. I was lying on my bed below the gold embroidery of a sheer pink sari that meant happiness for me, the stars winking at me through the open veranda doors. How far I had come in claiming India as my own, even the ugly parts. I had come to my village to live alone, something women don't do, let alone with a laptop that made occasional sounds as if it were breathing. I was trying to make this my home, living and writing here. In the mornings, I went to our short strip of a market to buy eggs and provisions. I bought carrots. Orange ones. I bought glass for my lantern and knew, because Bluebeard told me, that the glass costs five rupees each. I hung a brass bell I bought in Khetasari from my balcony, a purple string hanging from it so visitors could tug at the string and get my attention with the gentle tingling. It was an unusual sight in a Muslim home because it was usually used in Hindu temples. Bluebeard yelled at his son and nephew for ringing my bell in play. I got the electrician *walla,* who was actually a boy, to come to the house on his bicycle to wire the light switch in my rooms. The gas *walla* came by, too, with three keys strung on a black cord around his neck. He told me, "Call your mother," thinking I was one of Rachel Momani's daughters. I told him I was alone.

One afternoon, I cut through the narrow alleys of Jaigahan with a woman in a big red *bindi* who lived next door to Najma Khala, my mother's kind and smiling cousin-sister. A woman with sagging breasts and a sole tooth hanging from the top of her mouth was visiting in Najma Khala's courtyard at the same time. She told me she was looking for a wife for her doctor grandson living in Australia. The woman threw her hand behind her hips, not far from her sagging breasts, and said she wanted a modern girl who walked the modern walk. "I know the perfect girl," I told her enthusiastically. I thought of one of Rashida Khala's granddaughters, whose parents were looking for a match, worried that she was getting too old although she was only in her twenties. The woman was excited about the prospect. When she left, gentle and kind Najma Khala made a face and reproached me that my cousin could never marry into the woman's family. "You are Sheikhs," she said, referring to the family name of my maternal grandmother, a revered name. "They're low-caste Muslims." So much for modern.

Esther had taught me how to take the long broom to water to sweep away *gurd,* the dirt that was always a fixture on the floors at Latif Manzil. Despite all the work and frustrations of a modern-day pioneer, I felt so happy to be in the village. I hired an errand *walla,* who didn't show up one morning by 8 A.M. as he said he would. The *lukree mistri,* the woodworker, didn't show up another morning as he said he would. He told me the next morning, "I forgot." Still, I felt a calm being in Latif Manzil. I felt joy in sitting alone, eating my plate of sliced red tomatoes and orange carrots under the night sky.

The most serious problem I was facing was, literally, finding energy in my village house.

Shakti had mostly been of symbolic importance for me as I traversed India. But, in the village, it was something that I needed so I could write on my laptop. We got electricity for only a few hours in the late afternoon and another few hours in the late night. When it came, it sometimes surged so powerfully it threatened to fry whatever was plugged into the socket. It was a fate I preferred not to see my laptop face. I asked around. I got confusing electrical advice from a brother of our neighbor, a college student who couldn't speak English even though he had read Shakespeare. It was so frustrating trying to make sense of his instructions that I started crying. I didn't know whom to trust, and I felt obliged to be nice to everyone. It seemed that I needed something called a voltage stabilizer that would cut off the electrical supply to my laptop if the current ran too high.

The biggest city close to us with a big market was Jaunpur. One morning, I climbed onto my Splendor to head to Jaunpur to buy my stabilizer. In Jaunpur, a stabilizer *walla* insisted he had just what I needed. He seemed trustworthy. Back home, I plugged my electrical fan into my stabilizer. I couldn't believe I was wired at Latif Manzil.

The joys in our village home were simple but plentiful.

I awoke most mornings before dawn with the sound of *azan,* the call for prayer. One day, the full moon sat over my left shoulder like a celestial fruit hung atop a magical tree. Cheenie Bhai and Cheenie Apa stirred awake. I found one of Cheenie Bhai's long green feathers and one of Cheenie Apa's short gray feathers.

My *mandir* bell rang. It was Anis, who worked for Rashida Khala in Lucknow, delivering, of all things, a Federal Express package my father had sent from Morgantown with an extra battery for my laptop. He walked straight out of a Fed Ex commercial. He wouldn't stay. He hated Bluebeard. One time, he recalled, he had rested on a *charpai* after a long day of work, and Zaki had yelled at him for sleeping on his *charpai.* "We all come into this life. We all go," said Anis. "Everyone is human whether you are poor or whether you are a *crorepati,"* a multimillionaire.

I went with Anis to visit our neighbor behind Latif Manzil. Khala's friend, an elderly cousin-aunt of mine, told me how her life had paralleled Khala's life. She had married twice, like Khala, and both of her husbands also had left her a widow. Tears came to her eyes. It was a lonely life.

I awakened with the sound of *azan* just after five. The kitchen bulb was lit. The electricity ran. I inserted the extra battery my father had sent in my laptop to recharge my source of shakti. It was ultimately in the parakeets that I found so much innocent joy. I prepared breakfast for them, carefully tucking half pieces of grape between the silver wires of the Cheenies' cage, the juicy middle a temptation they couldn't resist. The wild ones came like clockwork, that morning at 6:14 A.M. Five minutes later, a bee, big and loud, flew nearby. A squirrel darted onto the balcony railing, swiping a grape. This menagerie of parakeets and other creatures stayed active until the first hint arrived that the morning's cool weather would be consumed by the day's heat. Then they all fluttered away.

I had to hit the road to get cash. In Jaunpur, a young man at a chai shop climbed on a bike to show me the road to Benares. I followed him on my motorcycle, hypnotized by the ballooning of his shirt behind him, and I was heartened by the small gestures of kindness I found in my travels.

It was a day so hot I could feel the heat engulf me. I remembered the mornings at Stalag 29 when I had wished for warm air and knew that was now being realized. A young idiot on a scooter played rabbit with me, as I used to play in high school cross-country. He looked respectable in a white *kurta* and *pyjama,* but he passed me, slowed down, waited for me to pass him, and then passed me again. He tried to talk to me.

"Leave me alone!" I screamed. He zipped off.

As I rode into Varanasi, a lanky young man on a bicycle followed me. I screamed at him. He quickly turned down another road. At an intersection, one boy asked another boy on a motorcycle, "Girl?" They flustered me. I stalled.

In my drive back to Jaigahan, I turned into a motorcycle repair shop to replace rearview mirrors cracked when I took a frightening spill on railroad tracks so dangerously aligned with the road the workers told me the crossing claimed several lives a year. A crowd of boys and young men gathered to gawk at this woman who rode through their bazaar on a motorcycle. I knew they were a bored, aimless generation. Uttar Pradesh was one of the country's poorest states, battling high unemployment and low literacy. A hotel manager I'd met in Himachal Pradesh said that the culture of his state wasn't so oppressive as in states such as Uttar Pradesh because "We fear God."

I knew these boys needed to fear something. I threw my broken rearview mirror at one who kept staring at me. I was just sorry it didn't hit his head. Next time a crowd gathered around me, I daydreamed that I'd tell them, "I'm studying Tantra and will cast a spell on whoever stays."

When I got back on the road, a guy on a scooter with shades on his face and a weirdo behind him kept playing rabbit with me.

I caught up to him and shouted, "You want to stop? You want to stop?" swerving my bike toward them. Then I lost it. I yelled, "Bhagwan"—the Hindu word for God—"will strike you down." I told them, "Look in my eyes. I'm giving you the evil eye." Learning spirituality and descending into road rage. My Tantric teaching.

The sun was setting, the earth was moving when I pulled into Latif Manzil. Death confronted me downstairs. It was a war scene in the rooms where Bluebeard had kept baby chicks in a venture to start a chicken farm. He had put a screen in the window, but only three-fourths of the way up. It seemed that a mongoose had sneaked into the rooms and slaughtered the chicks. They lay dead everywhere, many decapitated.

I wondered why I'd endured hell to get here. When I unlocked the padlock on my door upstairs and stepped into my front room, I knew why. It was because I was going to have a glimpse of heaven. In contrast to the scene downstairs, upstairs we celebrated life. Cheenie Bhai chewed on a branch, stirring it. Cheenie's friends were visiting, three *jungli bhais* and one *apa,* chirping and joyous. Oh! their song! It was so loving. I didn't think it was just the grapes.

A bird hid behind a bale branch climbing toward a *jungli bhai.* Her yellow beak was visible. Fly, I thought, so I can see your silhouette and know what you are. It flew. It wasn't a *bhai* or *apa.* I watched these birds fly, glide, fly, swoop. Four flew west in a U-turn back to the bael tree. Birds in the distance hopped from one branch to the next. I heard a *bhai* before I saw him, singing as a man in a nearby *masjid* broke the air just before sunset with the *magrib azan.* The *junglis* flew away, scattering like the wind. Why?

I wondered so many things about these mountain creatures of flight that had found Jaigahan. Would they die in the summer heat of the village plains? Would I? Would they ever learn to love? Would I?

The voices of societal pressure spoke to me.

Bluebeard's wife told me it was *zaruri,* necessary, for a woman to get married. Yes, I thought unkindly, so I could get plump like so many women making babies for their slacker husbands. The year before, I'd let these pressures get to me. This time I simply told her that if she cared, it was her *zimmeydaari,* or responsibility, to find me a husband, and then I walked away. A *naga baba* sitting on the banks of the Ganga told me to seek shanti, or peace, from others, but if they didn't offer it, to walk away. Another afternoon, Bluebeard's best friend darted into my room and started rifling through the top drawers of my dressers. "Is the Qur'an here?" he asked.

"Why?"

"I just want to know if the Qur'an is here."

He finally told me what he was doing. I found a Kali statue that Rachel Momani had packed into one of her trunks. It was a stunning clay piece with the image of Kali stomping men, symbolizing her destruction, not of men but rather of evil and ignorance. I put it on a dresser. Bluebeard's friend worried that a Qur'an he remembered in the drawers was sitting *below* the statue, a sin to many. I tried to practice nonattachment and packed the Kali statue away, but as the days spilled into other expressions of oppressiveness, I searched for Kali again, sad that I had misplaced her.

I had a disaster when my Shyam Voltage Stabilizer from Jaunpur burned from a burst of high voltage. It didn't cut off, as the stabilizer *walla* said it would. I documented my case to Mr. Prakash, the stabilizer *walla,* and pulled out all the stops, even quoting Hindu mythology to tell him that the goddess Lakshmi wouldn't be pleased with his lack of professionalism. I remembered that five hundred rupees I owed the druggie *naga baba.* "Along with your worldly responsibility to me, you have a karmic debt to pay."

Bluebeard was back to his negative self. "The stabilizer *walla* made a fool out of you." I told him he wasn't being supportive, calling me a fool. He responded, "But he *did* make a fool out of you."

Thinking I was being too bold doing things on my own, I accepted Bluebeard's recommendation and bought a stabilizer from a distant relative with a shop in Khetasari. By morning, even this stabilizer turned out to be a piece of junk. They were all scam artists, these bazaar *wallas.* I sought solace from the one man I could trust, my father. "Asra *bayti,*" he told me over the phone, "don't be frustrated. You can't even buy pure milk in India. You can't even find pure red pepper."

I left Jaighan to escort Rashida Khala from Lucknow to Hyderabad, where her daughter lived. I visited my kind cousin-aunt, Najma Khala, and her husband one last time. They'd been a pillar of positive energy in Jaigahan, always smiling and encouraging. I couldn't stop the tears of frustration from spilling when I sat with Najma Khala. "It's so hard to do alone," I cried, "with everyone trying to rip you off." The other day I'd even found Bluebeard's nephew going through my wallet when he was supposed to be searching for grapes for the Cheenies. I knew he was just a boy, but the frustrations ran so deep. Najma Khala couldn't endure me crying. She wept with me. I wiped my face and returned to Latif Manzil to pack the Cheenies and my boxes of books.

As I pulled away in a Mahindra Jeep with our driver, Abu Saad, Bluebeard stated the obvious. "She is mentally upset."

I didn't contest his assessment. I had created a calm and peaceful place for myself here, and I wondered why I'd engulfed myself in trouble and suffering. I knew it was because I had a vision. I wanted this house to be a home. If I, daring of heart, could not make it a successful home, then how could my Safiyyah and Samir? I wanted this to be a place where they could live and prosper. I wanted this to be a place where the young of heart, the old in age, the vibrant in spirit, the dejected in spirit all could prosper and enjoy the sunsets so much that they, too, would be prompted to learn that the sun didn't really set. Oh, the sun was a beacon. It was telling me that life could sustain itself. Its orange blaze announced that I could conquer. Or, yes, I could flame out.

CHAPTER 20

Wannabe Goddesses Cry

I T WAS SOMETHING to be back in civilization.

The Baskin-Robbins sign greeted me as I entered Jahingarabad Palace in Lucknow again. My aunt, Rashida Khala, welcomed me in her quiet way, eager to hear my latest tales from the village. We sat at the dining table, and I told her about the railroad tracks, the birds, Bluebeard, the stabilizers, and Najma Khala's tears of empathy. Lucy called me in the night and cheered on my efforts in the village. "They haven't had a woman shake things up like this," she told me in her singsong voice. "Go for it. Fight. Make it right. Just don't get emotional. Don't raise your voice." She learned this traveling through Asia. "Walk with an air about you. Have a sense of arrogance." It's just what my brother advised. Have enough arrogance so that no one pushes you around.

I needed to hear this advice as Khala and I planned our travels to Hyderabad, the city of my father, where I had lived before crossing the Atlantic for America. Before we went, I had a day of tasks. The first was getting our train tickets. Before I'd left for my first journey to India a year before, my father had spun horror stories about the hassles of buying train tickets—long lines and seats never confirmed. But Akhtarul Uncle had shown me the counter at the Lucknow station where they book tickets for foreign travelers, journalists, military soldiers, and freedom fighters, Indians who fought the British. It was a short line, plus you got priority confirmations on bookings. I got my booking, but they wouldn't confirm Khala's seat. I climbed into another bicycle rickshaw to go back to Hazratganj to the local Indian Railways headquarters. For twenty rupees, about fifty cents, the rickshaw *walla* exerted every muscle in his body to carry me more than a mile through traffic.

At the headquarters, I was told to go into an office. I found a woman behind the desk. I stood there in her office and just admired her.

She was only thirty, but she ran a department overseeing a thousand employees, virtually all of them male. From her name, I could tell she was Hindu. I asked her to whom her *mandir* was dedicated.

"Durga," she said. She had gone to a Durga temple in Madhya Pradesh just a week earlier with her husband and child. I thought about my tears in Jaigahan.

"Do you cry?" I asked her.

She nodded her head. She cried.

"Did the goddesses cry?"

"Of course not. But we are not goddesses. We aspire to be like the goddesses, but we are human."

That was true, wasn't it? We weren't goddesses despite all the best intentions and marketing pitches. I thought of the T-shirts for sale the year before at Gabriel Brothers, a Morgantown discount store that dressed our small town in high fashion, with "Goddess" across the chest, hanging next to the T-shirts we bought for Safiyyah and her birthday slumber party girlfriends with "Princess" across their fronts. There was all the talk about the goddess within us. She was there, to be awakened, but the truth was we were ultimately defined, too, by human frailties. It was ego and *maya,* illusion, to think anything more. We didn't have to feel guilty about crying.

I secured Khala's seat, and I also got the order sent from a railway official to fix the train track outside my village that had caused me to topple. I felt a great sense of accomplishment, and, having forgotten to eat lunch and having run myself ragged all day, I promptly went back to Jahingarabad Palace to do what I had permission to do: cry.

Khala and I boarded our train to Hyderabad, along with the Cheenies. Together, we made the one-night journey to Hyderabad and settled into a cabin, where Khala slept elegantly with a Lucknowi *chikan dupatta* turned into a bed sheet. In lower berth number 19, I read Indian news magazines and trash magazines to discover that there was a sex life to India, even if I was too shy to talk to anyone about it. *Savvy,* a women's magazine, told the tales of Barmy Swami, who taught Tantra in Delhi with his wife, like the Mr. and Mrs. Tantra of America whom I'd met in Santa Cruz, having sex with people to heal them. *The Week,* a newsweekly, told me about Bengali poet Rabindranath Tagore's love lives chronicled in a sexy new novel by a Calcutta novelist who was candid about sexuality in a way I hadn't read about before in India:

> I hate pretensions in the sexual context. I am aware of the Indian ethos that always tries to suppress all these things as if it is filthy. But I have no hesitation in mentioning in my autobiography that I have gone to brothels. Rabindranath was a normal human being, with all his instincts and urges intact till he breathed his last.

The Week also had an interview with Sudhir Kakar, described as India's "best known psychoanalyst," who had just released *Ecstasy,* a novel that examined the mystical experience woven loosely through the lives of Indian yogis Ramakrishna Paramhansa and Swami Vivekananda. He said, "There are only two subjects worth writing about: God and sex."

India was a place where sexuality spilled out of the breasts of women whose sari blouses embraced them like the skin that peels so easily off ripe mangos, but yet we pretended they didn't and looked the other way, after digesting an eyeful.

Hyderabad was an oasis like I hadn't yet experienced in India.

Khala's daughter, Nafees Apa, lived in a sprawling two-story house on a quiet road in Banjara Hills with her husband, Munna Bhai, a businessman. The postal code was 500034. Like Beverly Hills 90210, life there could be out of episodes from *Banjara Hills 500034.* The city had gotten new money with its rise as "Cyberabad," the high-tech capital of the state of Andhra Pradesh. Former President Clinton had stopped there in his stint through India the year before, the local government folks sweeping beggars off the street for his visit. One of Nafees Apa's daughters lived in London, wed in an arranged marriage to a rich investment banker. The other divided her time between the U.S. and Calcutta, wed in an arranged marriage to the son of a tea plantation tycoon. Her son worked as an investment banker in Manhattan. Inside, Bally shoes sat by a doorway, Shakespeare lined a bookshelf, along with translations of the Qur'an, and a wide-screen TV dominated an upstairs sitting area.

Nafees Apa decorated her house with the gentle touches of Ikebana, a style of Japanese flower arranging she studied in courses in Hyderabad, although she would not show up for her organization's photo shoot with the chief minister of Andhra Pradesh, so strict was she about purdah. But she was also a modern Muslim woman and ran a boutique out of her house, for which I created a Web site.

Munna Bhai named his house here at Banjara Hills 500034 after his mother, calling it Tahira Manzil, Tahira meaning pure, *manzil*, also meaning "a resting place." Instead of an ashram, I found my own *madrassa*, a Muslim place of learning, here with a lush tropical garden in the backyard.

Our day started with the *azan*, or call, for the morning's *fajr* prayer from a clock marked "Made in Taiwan." It was barely 5 A.M. The sun hadn't yet risen. The curtains were drawn closed. It was quiet in the house. I laid my *janamaz*, my prayer rug, next to Khala, a bundle of white, praying as she did seated on her *janamaz*, her joints too worn for her to prostrate from a standing position. When she touched her forehead to the ground she was the image of a white kitten curled up before God.

Our prayers done, Choti Momani, Munna Bhai's mother, drew the curtains open. She was known as "small aunt" to me because she was the younger matriarch ruling the roost in our family hill station house of Panchgani. I went outside and laid a cloth and did yoga, as Khala walked slowly around the garden, moving her lips silently as she did *zikr* on her *tasbi*, her fingers methodically moving her prayer beads with each utterance. I bathed and wrote till breakfast at 9 A.M., when we gathered to eat together at the dining table.

All around me in Hyderabad I saw reminders of how a girl's life can be so different from the one that I'd had.

One morning, I read the *Deccan Chronicle* to Khala. Andhra Pradesh villagers were selling their newborn daughters to an adoption agency who resold the girls to Westerners. One doctor allegedly removed a girl's cornea to make her a more sympathetic adoption and presumably make money off the cornea, too.

"*Tawba. Tawba*," said Khala disapprovingly, using the Arabic word from the Qur'an for seeking forgiveness. She quoted from another part of the Qur'an where it states that baby girls are to be valued. She wasn't amused at the antics of the woman who ran the ring that bought baby girls and sold them. "Stupid. Doesn't she know? Women are made from girls."

Khala had never borne the son so valued in traditional Indian culture. "What did you feel about having all girls?"

"I didn't think anything. I just prayed to God that they become responsible and good."

Did she want sons?

"I thought of every son as my son."

Another day, the newspaper told us about a Pakistani-born woman in the United States who divorced her husband and won *Working Woman's* annual award as a single mother juggling her job as a scientist and her care for her young daughter. Khala smirked listening to the story. "In America, they give women awards. In India, they destroy even their *jhopris,*" makeshift homes made of cardboard and tin.

She reminded me of a woman I met in Jahingarabad Palace. She was sitting on the terrace in a black *burqa,* a widow who embroidered Lucknowi *chikan* for Rehan Bhai, despite fingers bent awkwardly from a birth deformity. She was a single mother supporting herself and her three sons because she refused to accept the condition from her husband's brother that she live in the village if she wanted support from his family. Her boys wouldn't get an education there. Alas, as it was, they were all under the age of twelve and working. She was constantly harassed, her *jhopri* of a home regularly destroyed because it was built illegally.

Many mornings, a fifteen-year-old girl named Kulsum lingered when she came to sweep the floor in my bedroom. Nafees Apa had raised her since she was young, training her for her job as a maidservant and trying, as best she could, to teach her how to read and write. Kulsum was bright enough to say phrases like, "You are stupid!" to the *bua,* an elderly woman servent, in the kitchen and curious enough to follow me as I found photos of her favorite Bollywood actor, Shah Rukh Khan, on the Internet. She had a fiery spirit not found in a lot of girls. One day she told me about her visits back to her village in the state of Karnataka, just across the border, where girls started to wear saris at the age of ten. She pranced around in *shalwar kameezes* and dared to ride her younger brother's bike and talked with the quick yap that she had learned in the big city.

"Is she a girl or a boy?" villagers asked about her. I'd heard that before, said about me.

Another morning I read another story about a fifteen-year-old Muslim girl, Fareeda, whose parents sold her to a broker for five hundred rupees, about ten dollars, and the promise of a house, to be married to a Saudi. They thought her husband might be a Saudi sheikh. These sales were usually rackets for one-night stands where men from Saudi Arabia and the Gulf States wed women in "temporary marriages."

I ventured into the narrow alleys of old Hyderabad to meet this girl with a local Muslim woman, Rehana Sultana, who was an attorney and advocate for Muslim girls and women. The lawyer ran a school trying to educate the local girls. She said the story of this bridal sale was common among families who saw no option other than making an income from their daughters. The fifteen-year-old girl lived in one room with her parents and eight brothers and sisters. Her father was feeble with tuberculosis and sat in the corner, keeping to himself. I talked to her about her journey to Bombay. She giggled about all the firsts she did—riding the train, watching TV, and eating food cooked for her.

A Saudi saw her but rejected her. She was too dark skinned. Police raided the operation and returned her home.

There were sacrifices of the female in so many forms. On the road the year before, I had read in the newspaper about a tigress named Saki who had lived in captivity in the Hyderabad zoo. One night culprits sneaked in and slaughtered her, some said for her blood, others said as part of a Tantric ritual. I went to the zoo one day to pay my respects. The Safari Park bus slipped through a gate that sat beside the cage where Saki had lived and died. The gate closed behind us. It reminded me of the maximum-security prison I'd visited in Minnesota to interview murderers who belonged to a bonsai club where they twisted and turned plants into the creations they wanted. Seeing how Saki was a captive in life and death made me sad, for such a fate could meet any one of our wild spirits if evil came our way.

I had last visited Hyderabad for my brother's wedding. There, I'd met for the first time the glorious blend of innocence, smiles, and kindness that made up my sister-in-law's family.

Her family still lived in the same narrow apartment flat above the Life Café that her father ran in a neighborhood of Hyderabad, Dilsukhnagr, which had become a busy bazaar with a rush of traffic outside. Sadly, Bhabi's father had died suddenly earlier in the year from a stroke, leaving behind his widow and nine children, six daughters and three sons. The married daughters converged on the apartment when I visited, and I was engulfed in their sincerity, her brother dashing off to bring me back Cokes, her mother cooking my favorite foods, *tamatar* chutney, a tomato chutney, and kebab, and her sisters dressing me up as a bride to take photos on the roof. They were facing struggles to survive as a family after the death of their patriarch. As in most traditional families, Bhabi's married sisters lived at their husbands' houses with their in-laws. One of Bhabi's sisters tearfully told me the tale of her domineering in-laws and rushed to watch a soap opera to try to learn how to assert herself at her husband's house. Their father ran their house as an orthodox Muslim home, the girls and women behind a literal purdah, or curtain, through which they had to sneak peeks of the street downstairs. One night I taught one of Bhabi's sisters how to use the Internet. She was smart enough to set up a Yahoo chat ID as "Sony," not her real name.

One afternoon we answered an advertisement for a possible bride for one of Bhabi's brothers. Her parents advertised her as a twenty-two-year-old divorcee. "Her husband wasn't a man," the prospective bride's aunt told my sister-in-law's aunt over the phone.

"What does that mean?" I asked. Nobody seemed to know for sure, but it was supposed to suggest the bride was still a virgin, although married.

We went to a house that looked auspicious. It was painted soft pink with doors the kind of blue they used everywhere on the island of Santorins in Greece. We sat in the front room. The aunt looked plain and weary. Her husband had just gotten his U.S. visitor's visa application rejected. Bhabi's aunt asked to see the girl. She walked into the room. I was shocked. She was draped in a stop-sign red sari with gold fringe, and she looked more like a weary forty-year-old than a twenty-two-year-old maybe-virgin. It was all quite sad.

One of Bhabi's sisters sat down next to her, talking to her about her studies. There was nothing virginal about this bride. Even the red told us

so. Another of Bhabi's sisters asked to see the possible bride's hair. I didn't
get it. Then she asked her to stand up so she could survey her height. She
tried to look under the gold border of the sari.

"Heels?" she asked.

It reminded me of a slave auction. I felt sad.

Not that I had any better alternatives. I was searching for love in a
cyberworld where *are* is *r, for* is *4,* and a "Paki boy" looks for a girl from
Ireland, America, or France. I was searching the Yahoo personals.

46. Looking for a sizzling hot female.
Age: 25;
arif515
I am a smart and sexy male from Pakistan. I am not too practicing as
far as religion is concerened. Out going activities and nice ladies
attract me a lot. So if u want to enjoy a special relationship with me,
come and lets have a try. u will love it . . .

51. Seeking Friends & Love
Age: 29; Pocono Pines
jamilahmedbhatti
It's me Jamil Bhatti, Whom you look, you may not find me the best
one but will find me a different one. I am Friendly & Frankly to
every person who is a person indeed. Come-on you are being
waited. . . .

56. Asian Boy seeks French/Amerincan/Ireland
Age: 26; Jamaica
momintariq
HI, I am male/26 in Pakistan, I am looking for a sweet girl from
France/American/ireland. if you are from any of these countries,
please emai me, you can see my pictures. . . .

Khala often visited when I retreated upstairs to write, shuffling
upstairs in sandals marked "Chips." As I tried one morning to tug a bottle
of hair oil out of her hands so I could rub the oil into her hair, I asked her,
"Why not open your heart?"

She gave me a playful smile and responded, "You should keep your heart closed."

I knew why she said this. We had to protect our hearts. The newspapers in India were filled with spiritual teachings, and one day, tucked between advice from tarot card readings, astrological horoscopes, and feng shui, I found an article that examined a book about desire by a man named J. Cornfield. He was actually Jack Kornfield, a popular Buddhist teacher in the West. He said there were two types of desire, skillful desire inspired by love, compassion, creativity, and wisdom and painful desire, which was defined by greed, grasping, inadequacy, and longing. I had painful desire down. He suggested following the advice of the shamans and Buddha and naming what we feared as a step toward gaining power over it.

Buddha had done it, saying, "I know you, Mara," to the god of darkness.

I thought about this idea. I settled on calling the loneliness and despair that I felt and feared "Jungli Apa," inspired by the wild parakeets of Jaigahan. I knew I wasn't alone when I read an e-mail from Kirsten, the cook at the West Virginia forest monastery who had taught me death meditation as a way of bringing reality to expectations so that, conceivably, we can love with skillful desire. She was trying to apply this strategy in her latest relationship with the man who had invited her to vacation with him almost a year earlier while I was at the monastery. She admitted that it had been a painful relationship. She cried every day for four months because the relationship with her boyfriend wasn't calm.

The year before, I thought that maybe I would take a path alone in this world, having failed to find a romance in which to safely and fully love. But this year had shown me the lone path wasn't easy. I wanted a supportive, fruitful, spiritual relationship in which I could create a family, children, an inspiration for myself and my husband. Maybe even a little Sunday sex. I was thinking, maybe, that I wanted to pursue an arranged marriage, modern style. One morning as Khala lay on her bed, I told her that I thought this world was too difficult to traverse alone. She listened quietly. I lay down on a bedroll below her, the ceiling fan whirring slowly above our heads. We both slept.

I wrote most days until 1 P.M. when Kulsum called me for lunch. Then, it was *azan* for *zohar* prayer when supposedly anything you ask for is received. Then, a nap. I wrote for another hour, followed by *asr,* my favorite *namaz,* because it sounded so much like my name.

Khala and I walked around the block at 6 P.M. She said prayers to keep a stray dog away from her. We were back for *magrib azan* at sunset. I sat. I wrote. *Isha azan.* Dinner. Sleep. The order was soothing. All the while, Choti Momani crocheted and Khala shuffled with her *tasbi,* pushing the beads with the edge of her fingers with every silent utterance. After a couple of weeks, I awakened at 5 A.M. feeling so strong and so full of energy it was as if God himself had touched me. The anxieties that plagued me had dissipated in the order of this home.

"How did you get your strength?" I asked Choti Momani one afternoon as she crocheted. She and another aunt, named Bari Momani, meaning "elder aunt," had raised two generations of children, educating them with matriarchal power in Panchgani, the boys for careers from Wall Street to London and the girls for successful marriages. She looked up at me and smiled. "From all of you. From the children. From God." She told me that she left her worries with God when she prayed. I wondered aloud about her experience when she prayed.

Khala snapped at me in her gentle way. "Stop thinking about things that happen in the mind when you pray. Just pray."

One morning, I didn't come down for prayer. Khala said she came upstairs to check on me twice. I lay in bed, wondering how to find contentment in my love life. I hadn't yet found the answer on this journey. Khala didn't know what I was thinking about. But she knew that ruminations weren't productive. "Sit wastefully, and wasteful thoughts come to you," Khala told me. "The devil is always there to show you the wrong path."

I always lost my bearings after a relationship ended, the most recent being a dalliance with a man I'd met at the Maha Kumbh Mela, an American surfer living in Costa Rica. I had gone to Gujarat with him to an ashram, where I climbed great heights to a Tantric shrine in the Girnar Hills and wept at his departure, even though I actually was relieved to see him go. In my meditations at the ashram, I could feel the spirit of the women of my family and ancestry from whose destiny I was so different because of the sexual freedom I enjoyed. My mother said I gave so much of myself up in relationships. Lucy gave me the gift of clarity in an e-mail.

"You must believe in your wings," she wrote to me. "They will take you to beautiful places, but when the air gets stale, you must fly from those places where the currents pull you towards the rocks. Not avoidance, no, you need to leave with the winds of change. When those winds change and you have dealt with these emotions, then leave."

Her words took me back to cliffs upon which I had stood some years earlier in a corner of the island of Oahu in the state of Hawaii. I had hit the road without any plan with two Canadian journalists I had befriended at the Asian American Journalists Association conference. We turned down a road that led us to a rocky embankment, where a group of new friends who were U.S. Marines were enjoying their day off. They were bounding from the cliffs, screaming, "Geronimo!" with each leap.

I looked down from the cliffs. It was a scary sight, the water seemed fifty yards below. Ever since an elementary school teacher made me jump off a diving board, to be engulfed in a rush of white water, I'd had a fear of the water, which I was always trying to overcome. My friend Lynn Hoverman, a California surfer girl whom I had befriended at the D.C. volleyball courts, literally held my hand one summer afternoon to teach me how to pounce into the Atlantic Ocean waves off Dewey Beach in Delaware. But one of the Marines, a woman, encouraged me and urged me to my own jumps off the cliffs. I loved the flight.

As I sat in my room, I saw myself flying above those cliffs, a choice facing me to crash into the rocks or fly free into the ocean. In my mind, I changed the direction of my flight so that I flew toward the ocean, free.

I was facing a philosophical dilemma. I had waited three months for Cheenie Bhai's feathers to grow back, but they hadn't. To continue to wait? Or to keep him caged? When I saw myself flying free, I knew that one day it was only right that he, too, should also fly free.

I'd been in Hyderabad for weeks, but I'd avoided returning to that place that stored the deepest memories for me, the house where I'd lived for the first four years of my life, before leaving it and my grandparents to go to America.

I went to the house on my last day in Hyderabad, slipping through the narrow roads of the old neighborhood. I ducked through a doorway and into a courtyard around which sat the rooms where we used to live. Everything was in ruins. A man stood on the roof with a pickax, dismantling what remained of the house. Dadi had sold the house when her sons convinced her to move to Pakistan, and now the house was being demolished. I stood in the courtyard, peeking into the dark rooms.

"This is where you used to sleep," the woman with me told me, gently. She was Zaheda Aunty, the wife of my father's friend, Aftab Uncle, who went to the U.S. with my father, watching him read my mother's letters late into the night. He had returned to Hyderabad and remained there, unlike my father. Rubble lay crumbled inside the rooms. I stood there and realized a deep truth: this was what yesterday's difficult memories should be within me—ruins.

I returned to Jaigahan. If I needed a sign that it was right for me to return, Jungli Apa gave it to me in the morning. She arrived on the branch of the bale tree.

What an amazing thing. She had waited for us all these weeks that we were away? I didn't see the other birds. I didn't hear them either. She forgave the Cheenies their absence, it seemed. She didn't sit with them on their cage as she did before. Now, Cheenie Apa's cries pierced the air like the plaintive cry of a child departed from its mother. A mother departed from her child. The sweat poured down my forehead. I spent little time this stay with Bluebeard. I had exerted the energy to befriend him and now knew that he was a drain of energy. He had a destructive effect on everything around him.

I came back to the village with a stabilizer custom-made by a Hyderabad manufacturer, the wiring assembled in a factory dominated by women with ginger fingers. My salesman was a gentle man who listened carefully to all of my instructions, a convert to Christianity who broke boundaries to marry a Hindu woman. He proudly brought my stabilizer with its functioning cutoff switch just before I left Hyderabad, wrapped snugly into a box.

Shakti was finally flowing here at Latif Manzil without obstruction. I had done it.

CHAPTER 21

Out of Morgantown

I MADE IT HOME for my guru's tenth birthday. Safiyyah and Samir both took the day off school, and we explored through tall grass that led to a farm beside the new house my parents had bought. A white horse stood in a stable with rolling Appalachian hills behind him. It was beautiful to be home. Here I brought home what I had learned in the world. Here I absorbed the great lessons about life, love, and liberation.

The children were growing. Samir was eight. He remembered one day how he wanted to marry a girl in kindergarten, Shahira. "She helped me up when I fell," Samir remembered, "and she taught me how to make S's." Life could be that complete.

One afternoon, Samir's ten-year-old friend Spencer visited my childhood home. "What do you think at night when you put your head to sleep?" I asked Spencer.

"The kittens." He, like me, was still consumed by Jaz's litter, plus the kitten named Special. They'd been given away to families far-flung, and we missed them.

Anything else?

"Well, I knew that I liked this girl named Laurel because I started seeing her when I went to sleep at night."

How did he know he liked her?

"She is as funny as me." Love was as simple as that.

"I love her, and she loves me."

I was home, peaceful in the land where shakti ran free and love was pure. I fell into the easy rhythms of Morgantown.

Tuesdays, I was Lunch Lady, collecting tickets at the North Elementary cafeteria. Tuesday, September 11, transformed reality. My mother called me at home with the news of planes crashing into the World Trade Center. I didn't believe her. Yahoo confirmed the truth.

I walked down Headlee Avenue, the sun warming me, for one of the last moments of unadulterated innocence I was to enjoy. I whispered the news to Samir and Safiyyah, as mothers and fathers swept into the building to take their children home early. When I got them home, the reports started coming in from my mother at her boutique on High Street. Ali Baba, a restaurant with mosquito netting over a booth and hummus on the menu, shut down because of a suspected bomb threat that turned out to be a vulgar phone call. Two Muslim women wearing *hijabs,* the head scarves tightly wrapped around the hair, had them ripped off their heads at the West Virginia University student union with the shouts, "We're going to get you!"

I had never been motivated to cover my head in public in America. To me, it was an unnecessary symbol of modesty in a place where not wearing a halter top in the summertime seemed like an act of conservatism. The weekend before, as I'd stood near the Doritos at Wal-Mart, an Arab woman walked by me with a full covering that cloaked her body and face. All that was visible were eyes that could study price tags. Now, suddenly, I wanted to cover myself. Proclaim to the world that Muslims weren't all terrorists. We were also good, balanced humanitarians, as my mother and father had taught me to be. I pulled out a long white cotton *dupatta* my dadi had sent home with my father, just returned from a trip to Pakistan. She wrote a message in the corner in Urdu, urging me to use it to do my *namaz.* I knotted the *dupatta* around me and unfurled it so only my eyes were visible.

Did I look menacing? I checked with the only one around, nudging awake my cat Billlie. He opened his eyes to a slit, yawned, and returned to sleep.

My inquiry into identity wasn't complete. I plucked an American flag Samir had gotten from his Cub Scout troop, ventured outside with the scarf pulled down from over my nose so the mailman could see my face, lest he drive by, and planted the American flag in a pot of geraniums on our front porch.

That night, a Muslim brother called my father. "It's urgent."

When my father called back, he told him that the board of the Islamic Center should cancel the *jummah* prayer, the Friday afternoon prayer. For

Muslims, Friday is what Sunday is to Christians and Saturday to Jews. I stood in the background, bobbing between my father's phone call and Samir's reading of *Mulan,* the Chinese girl warrior. "Don't cancel!" I urged him.

"No, we will not cancel," my father insisted. "Why should we be afraid?"

Two days later, I went to New York to keep my dear friend Dan Costello, a *Journal* colleague, company. A universe that I had known intimately had been destroyed. I used to disembark for work from the N/R subway stop in the basement of the World Trade Center. With airports shut down, the best way to get to New York was the Greyhound bus. I planned to go with my head covered. My sister-in-law's eyes widened when she saw the *dupatta* wrapped over me. This was the past she had outgrown, of being wrapped in a *burqa* and then engulfed by a faint as she rushed to catch buses in the heat of India's summer. Married to my brother, she was liberated from this religious expectation, maintaining her sense of modesty but wearing a new wardrobe of cotton shirts and stretch pants from the Limited.

She was worried. She, too, had heard the reports of Muslim women under attack. She told my mother, "Write *al-Hafiz* in the air on her forehead," so that I would have the protection of God. My mother took her finger to the air, staring over my left temple, and crossed my forehead with Arabic script. She blew a breath toward me, a *phoonk.* It was a blessing. We went to the Greyhound station. I slipped into a seat beside a woman. "Phoopu has already found a friend," Safiyyah told her dadi, mother, and brother as she waved to me from below.

In New York, I realized that I had a duty to return to Pakistan, to write from there and try to dismantle the misperceptions in the West about the Muslim world.

My friend Kerry Lauerman, and editor at Salon.com, asked me to go there and write for the Internet magazine. "You have a story to tell," he told me, giving me for the first time affirmation that I had a unique voice with which to speak. I went to the Pakistani consulate with my friend Sumita's sleeveless *kameez* flowing over my black pants, a black sweater on top so I wouldn't offend any Muslims who considered it immodest for a woman to bare her arms. I wore Dadi's *dupatta.* What a goof. It was sort of like my arrival in Kathmandu revisited. The press attaché's assistant was a Filipina veteran of the consulate since the 1960s by the name of Connie. I should have just gone in the Abercrombie & Fitch cargo pants that I usually wore. Connie told me over the phone that it would take only a day to process a visa, but when I called the next day she told me the consulate wasn't issuing visas anymore. There were too many foreign journalists in Pakistan to keep them safe. I was confused.

I wrote the press counsellor to explain my mission, telling her that my roots were in Islam with my name coming from the seventeenth surah of the Qur'an and my ties ran deep in Pakistan, with my family's presence there and my marriage, albeit a failed one. In America, we thought that folks from that part of the world were all basically the same. Even I, a Muslim with family throughout Pakistan and many trips there stamped into my passport, didn't see a divide for myself with Pakistan. But that's not what I learned as I stood outside the Pakistani consulate, the rain pouring upon me as I tried to convince the press attaché I wasn't a threat to Pakistan just because I was born in India. She let me know that was an issue of concern, even with my Pakistani visa stamped into my passport from my ride on the Peace Bus the year before.

I found out later from other officials that the Pakistani government had put up a red flag for Indian-born visa applicants, even if they had foreign passports, like from the U.S. She suggested I apply on a tourist visa. I was promptly rejected.

I ended up traveling to Washington, where I met my Salon.com editor, Kerry, who escorted me as an official white guy in a suit. The press attaché at the Pakistani embassy talked to me and saw that I wasn't going to be a threat to the state of Pakistan. He asked me in Urdu whether I was Muslim. I told him my family history with Pakistan. He cleared my visa. I talked to my mother amid the delays. She told me what we are taught as Muslims from our earliest days: "Everything happens for a reason."

My reason was the pause. Facing an obstacle that didn't allow adrenaline to make my decision, I pondered whether I really wanted to go to Pakistan. It would be a psychic journey as much as physical one. I was a bit afraid. My brother tried to relax me: "Oh! Go have a vacation!" But my previous trips to Pakistan had certainly never qualified as vacations. On my return to Morgantown on the Greyhound, I sought refuge next to a woman who looked like a nun. Turned out that I, who had been searching India to meet a Tantrika, had found one on the Greyhound from Washington, D.C., to Hagerstown, Maryland. She left me with a guiding principle. She was in America to give lectures on yoga and meditation. We talked about September 11 and the hatred from which it spawned. I told her about my mission to Pakistan and my fear. She reminded me of the mandate that propelled me to stand in front of the Pakistani consulate in New York in the rain, in my effort to do work that would dismantle barriers to understanding. "We must learn to melt each other so we are just human beings before each other."

It took me thirty-nine hours to journey from Morgantown to Lahore, where Dadi still lived with my eldest uncle. She told me she had dropped from 110 to 92 pounds in recent months. I'd traveled across the ocean with only Lonely Planet's *Pakistan: A Travel Survival Kit,* a new padded laptop backpack from Office Depot, and a JFK Airport shopping bag filled with World Trade Center key chains, New York Police Department pencils, and two New York Fire Department stuffed bears (one red, one blue) to give away as gifts. War loomed as a reality. When I'd gone to Pakistan in 1983, my gifts had been Smurf key chains.

I was returning to Pakistan, this time with voice, not the silence I'd accepted as a young bride. I set off for Islamabad on Pakistan's Greyhound, a luxury shuttle bus that carried me along the highway built not long before by former prime minister Nawaz Sharif. I'd traveled alone for the first time in Pakistan. As I stood with Sumita's North Face backpack and my Office Depot laptop bag, I wasn't sure who would greet me. A svelte figure slipped toward me, and I recognized her face though her body was draped in a cream-colored fabric that descended from her head, where she had draped it tightly around her face.

"Hello!" I yelled.

"As-salam alaykum," she answered, smiling.

We had traveled on separate paths since the days when we were childhood pen pals. I'd met her when I was about twelve. She and her family had come to India from Islamabad, where her mother, my father's sister, had settled after marriage. I loved this cousin-sister of mine. She was vibrant, beautiful, and radiant. We took pictures of ourselves on my cousin's rooftop in Bombay before it became Mumbai, throwing our hair back and laughing at the sky.

I'd seen her six years later when I took my summer trip to visit her and my other relatives in Pakistan. That summer, she had traveled with me and other cousins on a train to the frontier land of Pakistan, Peshawar. It was the wild, wild West of Pakistan. Villages were dedicated to building weaponry. Afghan refugees were spilling over the border from the Soviet invasion of their country. And tribal feudal lords cut off the arm of the law. On that ride, a man commented loudly that I, a product of the West, kept my hair long, as Muslim girls were supposed to do, but my pen pal cousin, a homegrown Pakistani girl, had shorn off her locks. It was a turning point. In Peshawar, when I asked her to trim my hair, she went to chop it off. I spent the nights playing rummy with my boy cousins, while my pen pal cousin sat in prayer and looked disapprovingly at my freedom with the opposite sex. Over time, she became more religious, eschewing the playfulness that I had so loved in her.

Now, she stood before me at the busy bus terminal in Islamabad, wearing a broad smile as she stepped toward me, a young girl in tow. "This is Khadijah," she said. It was her young daughter.

She got behind the steering wheel of her car and drove me to the house of her mother; this was my phuppi, with whom I had traveled with Dadi on the Peace Bus from Delhi. She also covered her hair. Her younger daughter came home just about then from her job as an architect. Her hair swung freely and uncovered. Gap lotion sat in her bathroom.

I revisited the Pakistan of my past, returning to the Marriott Islamabad, not as a bride but as a veteran journalist this time. I even passed the Margala Motel, where I had walked stutter steps on my wedding day. I immersed myself in a conservative Muslim world that I'd never known so intimately. I spent hours in the Qur'an study groups of my Islamabad phuppi's friends. I sipped green tea with the Taliban's deputy ambassador to Pakistan and his two wives, the younger one a fan of Bollywood actor Salman Khan.

I had as a model of orthodox Islam a nephew-cousin of my mother, whom I called Bhai Sahib. He lived in Bombay, but I'd last seen him when our paths crossed in Lucknow earlier in the year. He had sleepy eyes and a gray beard. Although he and I lived differently, Bhai Sahib always gave me a sense of calm. When I was a child he had told my brother and me that food tasted better when you eat it with your hands. I reminded him of this lesson that I'd followed—in appropriate company—ever since. He'd told me on our last visit that an elder had taught him that it was best also to wash your hands with just water, not soap, because the aroma and oils of the food are absorbed into your hand. After that, I sometimes didn't wash my hands with soap after dinner. When he left, Bhai Sahib and I walked along the train tracks. He was a slow and gentle walker. I wanted to know more about his spiritual practice. "What do you use as your point of focus in meditation?" I could hardly believe I would ask such a bizarre question. And earnestly. He answered with earnestness. His point of meditation: "The divine presence of God in all things."

Hatred had never spewed from his mouth or from that of my father. Both were religious Muslims, rational and fair men. Now, in the midst of this war that America was launching in retaliation for the World Trade Center attacks, I heard the voice of hatred coming from other circles of devout Muslims. And they weren't strangers. They were my relatives and their friends, preaching about the virtues of Islam and the fraternity and sorority of Muslims. One morning, about a hundred women gathered in a two-story house off a neat lane. They wore head scarves and sat cross-legged, listening to a woman guiding them through a translation of a Qur'anic surah. Inside a small room off to the side, about a dozen organizers of this Islamic educational organization sat on the floor, listening to a woman sitting on a bed. They were impassioned, like others, about the U.S. decision to bomb Afghanistan. They too prayed *duas* against the enemy in time of war.

One of them grabbed my elbow. "You must write about the Jewish conspiracy," she pleaded. "They are evil. They want to destroy us." I

furrowed my brows and grimaced, for the first time shedding my jour-
nalistic tolerance and getting visibly irritated at this rhetoric of hatred.

I went to Karachi, where I got a window into the bifurcated society that
was Pakistan. Karachi was a crowded metropolis where I reported on the
culture of hopelessness and helplessness that was driving record numbers
of Pakistanis to suicide, even though the Qur'an warned the act was a
one-way ticket to hell. The family of the man I married had called me
crazy because of the depression I suffered after my marriage. I saw the
irony in the fact that I was now slipping in and out of psych wards in the
country of my wedding, very much empowered and not ashamed of an
illness that should be treated, not judged.

Even now, though, I was being judged. I wrote a profile about
Pakistan President General Pervez Musharraf, expressing my admiration
for a man who dared to challenge traditional Islam by photographing
himself with his pet dogs and drinking alcohol, both of which were
deemed *haram,* or illegal, in Muslim culture. I got an angry missive from
the cousin, now settled in America, who had told me not to ride a bicycle
when I was eighteen years old. "Everyone in Pakistan knows about
Musharraf's drinking, but even Islam also says to cover up things like
that, as it is between Allah and him." He had already attacked me once
for taking one of my adult cousins with me for my tea with the Taliban.
"You don't mix with these kinds of people if you want to live in peace in
Pakistan." He was arguing for hypocrisy over truth and fear over action.
Yet his argument hit an emotional chord within me because I knew all
too intimately the path of deception this society would prefer over the
truth about itself. I sat quietly in my hotel room at the Karachi Sheraton
Hotel and Towers and wept over the lies and cowardice that defined this
culture in which I was rooted.

I saw the other side of Karachi when I reported on the world of sex,
drugs, and rock and roll in this Muslim land. I saw a side to Pakistan and
the Muslim world that I didn't know existed, and I felt connected to it
because it so resembled the world I had come to know in the West, traipsing through Eighteenth Street bars, dance clubs, and restaurants in
Washington's Adams Morgan neighborhood and zipping around in yel-

low cabs in Manhattan. A nineteen-year-old Casanova told me about getting busted by local police when he took a girlfriend to a hut at a place called French Beach. A friend of a relative suggested that I talk to his twenty-something son to find out more. I met the son, and he invited me to join him and his friends at French Beach. I knew a beach existed in Karachi. During the trip of 1983, I had plunged into the waters off Karachi with my relatives, but only to my knees, to where I had rolled up my *shalwar*.

On a late Sunday morning, I hired a Eurocar for the trek to this place called French Beach. We drove out of Karachi past the port on a busy road crowded with stalls and traffic until we got to the hut, not far from a nuclear power plant down the beach. I saw two figures in the water below a cascade of boulders. I climbed over the boulders, kicking off my black sandals. I approached the water and saw that it was my new friend, along with a man I hadn't yet met, both wading carefree in the water. I turned back to tell the driver he could go and waded into the Arabian Sea fully clad in my mother's black pants and her gray sweater. The water enveloped me, and a smile broke out over my face. When I looked at the stranger before me, I felt something remarkable. Whenever I turned toward him and gazed into his eyes, a smile crept across not only my face, but also my heart. I wondered about this recognition that transpired between us. The Tantric teachings said that contact between the sexes was experienced in so many ways from the glance of an eye to intimacy. Everything preceding intimacy was dedicated to raising consciousness and relieving tensions. Consciousness was definitely raised, as we spent the afternoon together.

The next day, my friend Danny flew into town for a day of reporting. It had been so long since I'd seen him, almost two years, although we had continued to e-mail to each other about the bizarre nature of our travels. He had become the *Journal*'s South Asia Bureau Chief, politely asking me if I was interested in the job before raising his hand. I never visited him and his wife, Mariane, in Bombay, however, because the city was such a congested and depressing memory from my childhood days.

The days were over when I would travel to parties with an entourage. So, even though my new friend from the day before had invited me over to his house with other friends, I made plans to go to dinner with Danny at a restaurant called Haveli, the Urdu word for a large house like our Latif Manzil in Jaigahan. When Danny arrived at the Sheraton, we were so happy to see each other, embracing in the hugs of friends who had scraped their knees on the same playground. We talked through dinner of the possibilities for books that he could write. Mariane called from Paris during dinner, and Danny spoke with uninterrupted affection to her. I told Danny we could get together with a friend I'd just met.

"A guuuuuuuy?" Danny knew me too well.

The stranger whom I had met the day before had told me to call him if I was free. I called him now to see what he might be doing. He said he could pick us up from the restaurant in ten minutes. Danny smiled. Looked like he would be my chaperone for the night. "Okay, what'll be our sign for me to go?" he asked.

"I'll go like this," I showed him, running my fingers through my hair.

The three of us returned to my room at the Sheraton, where I pulled out a water bottle of Scotch that my friend's friend had brought me, thinking I actually drank hard liquor.

"Well, I think I'll be going," Danny said awhile later, stretching his legs.

I was relieved to see my new friend didn't move.

We were alone. I suggested that we try again to see if I could inhale a cigarette, something we had practiced the day before. We sat on the floor across from each other. I could feel a magnetic pull bringing us closer together.

"I have another way we can try," my new friend suggested.

He leaned toward me and brought his lips gently toward me, resting them like the gentlest flutter upon my lips. I was supposed to inhale his breath. I held my breath instead.

As I was writing my article about the secret world of sex, drugs, and rock and roll in Pakistan, I'd forgotten the word for "illegal sex" in Islam.

I called my new friend to ask him. *"Zina,"* he told me, and I scribbled the word on my notebook cover, perchance above his name.

> *The woman and the man*
> *Guilty of adultery or fornication—*

Flog each of them
With a hundred stripes.
QUR'AN, 24, AL NUR, "The Light"

We weren't married, which we both knew would make our sex illegal in the eyes of Islam and the state of Pakistan. But he talked to me about getting married. "I want us to start making babies right away," he told me. He was a man unlike any I thought I'd find and, certainly, wasn't looking to find. He was not only dashingly handsome but also smart, navigating through balance sheets and privatization efforts, working on Karachi's Wall Street. And when we gazed into each other's eyes, I was reminded of something I'd learned in Hyderabad. The doors of heaven opened to a husband and wife gazing into each other's eyes. I told him. He smiled and looked into my eyes even more deeply.

Ramadan started. We found ourselves driving through Karachi as the hour approached to break fast for the first day of Ramadan. He planned to go to his khala's house. Unexpectedly, he invited me to join him. "Is it okay?" I asked him, my hand always seeming to stroke his arm as he shifted gears. I came from a family in Pakistan where none of my cousin-brothers could bring a woman home except as his bride.

He assured me it would be fine. I played Ping-Pong on the dining table with his young cousins and helped his khala put dishes out for *ifthar,* the meal with which we break fast.

I knew the meaning of *zina* with him for the first time on the fourth day of Ramadan in a cove that was the shore off the Arabian Sea waters where our gaze first locked.

Our legs entangled around each other. We looked into each other's eyes. It was a coincidence, but we eased into the mystical posture encouraged by the Tantric texts. The gods and goddesses made love this way. But I didn't think they got sand up their *muladhara* chakras. It was the sea breeze that clothed us, and the boulders that were our walls. The waves of the Arabian Sea crashed behind us. The stars were our canopy, as they had been mine in Latif Manzil. I was so in love with him. And he continued to gaze deeply into my eyes, writing poetry to me about his love for me.

While the world made war, we made love. U.S. planes dropped bombs just about every day over Afghanistan. I didn't understand this war. I didn't accept President Bush's amorphous enemy called "al-Qaeda." I did know that each day I fell more deeply in love with this man who pressed me against the mirrors in the Karachi Sheraton elevators to kiss me deeply. "I've met the woman I'm going to marry!" he yelled into his phone one day, answering a phone call from a friend as we got onto the elevators.

He introduced me to a world in which it seemed my dualities could coexist. For once, I didn't have to choose between them. He took me every night to play volleyball at Alliance Française. One night, we stopped by his house first so he could get a change of clothes. I was nervous about going inside. I would be meeting his parents for the first time. I was wearing pants and a T-shirt. And strangely enough, we were with a former girlfriend of my new boyfriend. She was thin and bouncy. He was relaxed and comfortable as the three of us walked inside. I was in shock that he so freely walked into his home with a former girlfriend and a new girlfriend, but I tried my best to be at ease. I talked to his parents with warmth, wondering all the while if I was breaking a taboo.

We started visiting his house regularly. I didn't know if he had told his parents about our relationship, but I figured they must know. I so appreciated that we could be honest about it. I was wary about getting involved again with a Pakistani, but my boyfriend's life didn't seem impinged by values separate from mine. I was so touched when I saw his father sitting next to his mother, holding her hands gently.

One night his father asked me, "What do you see as your identity?"

I was taken back to that awful moment after my wedding when the father of the man I married told me my identity. I slipped back into the present moment, impressed that my boyfriend's father was so curious about that which I had much reflected upon. "I am a Muslim born in India and raised in America. The pulse of my ancestors courses through me, but I have values of modern-day America," I told him. I knew I hadn't expressed myself well, but I was breathless in wonder that I had even tried to express my own identity with some clarity.

It was Friday. My boyfriend got off work early for *jummah namaz,* Friday prayer.

He worshiped instead with me. Husbands and wives were allowed to kiss while they fasted, as long as they didn't cross a line. "Are we allowed to do this?" I asked. First of all, we weren't married. Second, we crossed the line.

We went on a road trip to a place where blind dolphins swim.

We crossed the Indus River to camp upon its banks, guests of one of the feudal lords of New Jatoi, a village tucked into the deep interior of the Sindh province in central Pakistan. The canopy of stars under which we fell asleep beside a gentle fire transformed the morn into a clear blue sky with petals of clouds whisking overhead. When I awakened, the Indus River flowed before me, a sleepy current of brown water washing against rocky banks. I stretched my body into a cartwheel on these shores.

My boyfriend wasn't happy that I flew upside down in the air in front of the gunmen with Kalashnikovs who were our escorts.

"You don't do that here."

It was the first time he had drawn a line for me. I studied his face to see if he was serious. He was serious. I felt hurt.

I swallowed my hurt and went for a walk along the banks to reflect. The Indus River was the last place I expected to find myself but the first place that I had planned to go when I had embarked on my journey to the subcontinent of my ancestors two and a half years earlier. The mysterious Tantric practice was said to have sprung from goddess worship in the ancient Indus Valley civilization, India's first major civilization, born on the banks of this mighty Indus River. From here, historians and archeologists say, Tantra wove its way into Hinduism and spread to Tibet, China, and other parts of Asia with Buddhism. Now, I was here at the wellspring of the civilization with the first documented presence of Tantric teachings. Along the banks of the Indus River, Tantra taught that disciplined minds could reach liberation through sexual intercourse, sensual living, and other joys that would give disciples a boundless ecstasy. For me, it was a place where I had to spend the night on a separate *charpai* from my love so that the guards wouldn't be offended.

The long grass stirred around me as I walked. In their wind dance I could see my soul stir. I had flown far not only in body but also in spirit to walk along these banks. I concluded it wasn't important for me to cling to the notion of doing a cartwheel with my body as long as I was free to do cartwheels in my mind. That was where true liberation lay, wasn't it? I turned around with this realization, and I willed my boyfriend to walk toward me. I gazed forward, imagining his figure, imagining and imagining, until I blinked and he was actually there, pacing toward me. I ran toward him. I was so happy to see him.

"I was afraid you were angry," he told me.

"How can I be angry? I love you." He embraced me, relieved.

This was a land of forests and underbrush where *dacoits,* the hardened robbers of the Indian subcontinent, hid from the law. The gunmen armed with Kalashnikovs guarded our every move like sentries. They had ridden with us the night before in the darkness as we bounced over the rocky terrain to hunt. By day, they walked with us as we climbed into a wooden boat to cross the Indus River to the other bank. As the boat glided through the waters, a man guiding our way with a single oar, I searched for the blind dolphins that swam here but saw only my reflection.

As we left, my boyfriend asked the driver to stop, grabbed a rifle from one of the guards, and shot a soaring white bird out of the sky. The armed guards looked at it. "It's *haram,"* one said, meaning it wasn't kosher to eat in Islam. We had to leave this beautiful white bird behind, dying. Its death haunted me, but I wasn't sure why.

On assignment, I left my boyfriend for a few days and headed for Afghanistan. When I was in Pakistan as a teenager, I had only jumped across the border into Afghanistan. This time I wanted to venture deeper into this land from which the Sufi poet Rumi hailed.

The day after Christmas I walked into Afghanistan. Less than an hour later I walked straight out. The Afghani soldiers at the border, allied with the Northern Alliance leaders who had taken over the country, were clearly running an extortion racket.

Liberation, I discovered, came in strange forms. A volleyball streaked through the clear night sky in Karachi.

Across the net, an athletic player in spectacles and Nike shorts threw his body across the dirt court to save a hit from touching the ground. His team set the save and scored. "Bravo!" his teammates yelled to their defensive hero. "Well done!"

He wiped a layer of dirt from his shorts and shyly smiled.

It was a long journey that had brought me across the net from my pal Danny on a dirt court at Alliance Française in Karachi, on Saturday, December 29, the last weekend before New Year's 2002. It happened to be the anniversary of my wedding. In the summer of my divorce, Danny had tossed me a volleyball at Modell's Sporting Goods on L Street in Washington, D.C. I had turned the ball in my hands and seen its scarlet letter: "Made in Pakistan."

"No way," I'd said, hurling the ball back to Danny. "Made in Pakistan" conjured up too many memories of boundaries eschewed when I flung my Speedo bikini-clad body for a shanked pass.

Days earlier, one afternoon just before Christmas, I had found myself standing on a ridge outside the Shamshato Afghan refugee camp, looking over a dirt valley tucked between the rugged hills outside the northern Pakistani town of Peshawar. That morning, I had left a traditional Pakthun home with a *dupatta,* a head scarf, worn so that only my eyes would peer out as I interviewed allies of the Taliban and Northern Alliance. I stood looking down at a game of volleyball played only by Afghan refugee men. I turned back to the car, certain that I couldn't cross this barrier. I looked toward one of my companions, a burly, bearded Pakthun Pakistani Muslim, Shaukat Ali, with two wives at home.

"I'd really like to play," I told him.

"Let's go," he said in Urdu, to my shock, rolling up his sleeves.

I ran down the hill. I kicked off my sandals and walked onto the court in bare feet, crossing more than the lines drawn in the dirt.

In Karachi, my boyfriend had zipped Danny and me to the Nike store to outfit Danny in new shorts and running shoes before dropping us off at Alliance Française. Danny played according to the character that defined him off the court with the indefatigable fire and goodwill he had taught me. "Nice save!" I yelled to Danny across the net.

"Did the ball say, 'Made in Pakistan'?" Danny asked as we walked off the court.

"I don't know," I said, realizing that on this path on which my great friend had taught me so many lessons, it really didn't matter after all.

I was reminded of the superficial judgment made in this society, where people rejected others without even knowing them. My boyfriend told me one night when he visited me in my room at the Pearl-Continental that two of his former girlfriends commented disapprovingly on our age difference, not surprising in a society where a woman is most marketable as a young virgin. He was twenty-eight. I was thirty-six.

"But look at the Prophet Muhammad and his wife Khadija," I told him. She was forty and he was twenty-five when they married."

"That's right," he assured me. "It doesn't matter to me. You're the only woman I know who can do cartwheels."

But, sure enough, the daggers were out for me. "She looks older than you," said the former girlfriend who had gone into his house with me.

He used our argument. "So what? The Prophet Muhammad married a woman older than he."

"Well, you're not the Prophet Muhammad," came her reply.

The other former girlfriend called from Ithaca, New York, where she was studying for her master's in business at Cornell University, angry that he sent her an e-mail that he was in love with someone else and wouldn't spend New Year's with her, as he'd agreed.

"She's too old for you," she told him. "It's not practical."

He hung up the phone on her. She called back to apologize.

"What does it mean my age isn't practical?" I asked my boyfriend.

"That it'll be difficult to have a baby. I told her, 'I've been smoking since I've been fourteen. I'm probably the one who's infertile.' Anyway, we'll adopt."

"Really? That's sweet." He had confided to me once that he wanted one day to open an orphanage in Pakistan.

I draped my legs over my boyfriend and settled my head upon his chest, as he drew me closer. I thought I couldn't have been happier.

CHAPTER 22
Parrots over a Safe House

"**B**OY!" the message flashed.

My Nokia handset had just beeped, breaking the quiet of an afternoon in Karachi, as my friend Danny sent me a text message from Islamabad. He and his wife, Mariane, had just emerged from having a sonogram done on the baby they were expecting.

"Ibn Pearl!" I wrote back, using the Arabic for "son of Pearl."

A smile crossed my face. After so many years of the dating scene, Danny had found true love with Mariane. She was eclectic and a practicing Buddhist, just the right combination, it seemed, to enrapture Danny without threatening his delicate sense of space and endearing spaciness. Just three weeks before, Mariane had jetted to Karachi on New Year's Eve, and I had spent my first time together with them since their wedding in August, 1999. I still owed them the wedding gift I was cross-stitching for them. After the wedding, I'd accidentally left it at the Parisian boutique hotel where I'd been staying up the street from their apartment in the cute Montmartre neighborhood. Danny sent it back to me with his familiar scrawl on the front.

"Hi, I was so curious but I 'restrained' myself from looking."

Danny had come into Karachi a few days before New Year's for our volleyball game, and he was intent on finding Mariane the perfect New Year's gift as we meandered through Park Towers, a mall right out of Americana except for the drivers outside waiting for their elite lady bosses to emerge with their shopping.

"I don't know," Danny had said, studying a smooth-toned silver choker he'd spread out on a glass counter. "It looks crooked. What do you think?"

I had studied the choker. "Looks okay."

"I don't know . . . " Danny had said, trailing off.

I had studied the choker some more He had been right. It was crooked.

Mariane had arrived with her belly full with their unborn baby and socks with a colorful animation at the ankles, part of her New Year's gift for Danny. He had pulled them on right away and danced on his toes in their hotel room. "I love them!"

We had returned together to the mall. I had known Danny had great tales to weave from his travels. "You've got to write them all down!" I had told him as he, Mariane, and I had plucked three spiral notebooks off the shelves at an office supply store.

We had all tumbled into my boyfriend's car for New Year's. The last time I had spent New Year's with Danny he was a foreign correspondent in the *Journal*'s London bureau, traipsing through the Arab world, interviewing kings and revolutionaries, but never forgetting to send me additions to the barf bags I'd been collecting for years for an article I never wrote. My cousin-sisters Lucy and Esther had come in from Maidenhead to meet us at a London club to see a band called Egg, and I had helped Danny throw a New Year's breakfast party at his apartment in a London mew. At the stove, Danny had respected his and my religious ban on pork, frying sausages made from everything but pork, even pulling vegetarian sausages out of his fridge.

"Voilà!" he had proclaimed, spinning in his kitchen, using the little French he knew until he met Mariane.

It was a different scene in Pakistan. For the first time in that country, I had worn a dress, a sleek long number I had borrowed from Mariane, a funny "Save The Queen" label at the nape of my neck. We had thrown shawls over our dresses.

"There could be trouble," my boyfriend had said, behind the wheel of his Honda. Islamic fundamentalist groups didn't think highly of the alcohol and dancing at the parties of the elite. Danny had tucked into his pocket a business card from an official at the conservative Islamic group Jamaat-e-Islami just in case we needed a friend. Indeed, the ringing of Danny's mobile phone had broken our chatter as we drove through town to go from one party to another. A bomb had gone off at a bowling alley, Area 51. I'd bowled there with my boyfriend during Ramadan when it was open all night, whipping Brunswick bowling balls down a lane, wearing a T-shirt with "PAKISTAN" across my chest.

"Don't get close," Danny had warned me as we'd stepped out of the car. "They often plant two bombs, one to go off after the other."

Subdued, we'd continued jotting notes along the way. On the way, my boyfriend had gotten directions from a woman friend.

"Okay, *jaan!*" he had yelled into his mobile to his friend.

Jaan? My ears had prickled as I sat beside him. *Jaan* was the term of endearment my boyfriend had taught me. It literally meant life. I thought it was a term we'd reserved only for each other. I had become sensitive. The realities of having a Western relationship in an Eastern world had started to catch up with us. My boyfriend had started cutting short his visits to me to get home for dinner with his parents. "I don't want them to hate you," he had tried to explain to me. So why, since I'd met them, couldn't I join him? I didn't understand. He'd had many girlfriends. He had taken me to his house. I'd spent time with his parents. Since I moved out of my childhood home and into a rental with a lopsided floor, I'd spent nights freely with my boyfriends. It was a different existence here, I knew. This was a world where I'd discovered all things of the West happened. Men and women played strip poker, frolicked in ménage à trois bedroom scenes, danced at a nightclub called Equinox, and freely smoked hashish, but boyfriends and girlfriends often met on the sly. They rarely spent nights together even if they were having sex. Our Saturday nights at French Beach were a luxury. But now he was calling someone else *jaan*.

We had dropped Danny and Mariane off at the party to go park. "*Jaan* just means dear," my boyfriend had insisted. "It's nothing."

I'd felt even more slighted. I had gone to cuff him on the side of the head to mime a hit for digging such a deep hole. Instead, I'd boxed his ears. Hard.

Both of us stinging, we'd lost each other at the party. I had peeked outside. Danny and Mariane were snuggling heads, oblivious to the thumping music and swirl of men and women around them in black on black. I'd wished that I felt so happily in love.

Until Danny met Mariane, he had never been a model of an attentive boyfriend, but this striking and beautiful woman of Dutch and Cuban

ancestry had transformed him. I had surprised myself the next day, seeking relationship guidance from him.

"Can I ask you something?" I had asked in the lobby of the Pearl-
Continental.

"Sure."

"How do you become patient?"

He'd smiled his askew Danny smile. "You can't learn to be patient,
but because you love someone you can pretend to be patient."

Oh. "There are times when you get impatient, but you don't show it?"

"Because it's not worth upsetting Mariane."

I tried, but I had started to worry. My boyfriend flirted with a woman,
both of them drunk at one of the many Karachi balls thrown around the
city after New Year's. He had gotten on his knees to apologize to me. Still,
things had been getting strained. He had told me that it would be best if I
returned to the States, because he wouldn't be able to spend as much time
with me as he had during the shortened work days of Ramadan when he
could juggle work and family with our budding relationship. He had
thought it best if we continued long distance for six months until we
could be together.

"No, it'll be okay," I had said, optimistically.

On New Year's Day, before setting off for Islamabad, Mariane had
looked at an unfurnished house that I was thinking about renting in
which I could write my book and nurture my romance. "You'll even have
to buy air conditioners," Mariane had warned. "Get a furnished apartment. Make your life simple."

That day, I had found a beautiful home on a posh lane next to the
Clifton neighborhood where my boyfriend lived. Bright flowers, trees,
and *chowkidars,* or guards, lined the street called Zamzama after the
name given to holy water that supposedly sprang out of the parched
desert outside the revered Muslim city of Mecca at the time of the prophet
Abraham. Wide carved doors opened into an immaculately furnished
three-bedroom home with everything down to a table clock with a
golfer's club as a second hand, swinging to mark each passing moment. I
envisioned it as the perfect home to which I could beckon my family so
they could see the life I'd built for myself on the subcontinent, comfort-

able, fun, and independent. I had gotten my second set of keys to a home on the subcontinent. I always kept my keys to Latif Manzil with me. I also had signed the lease with a mind to see more of Danny and Mariane.

"It's got a great guest bedroom!" I had told Danny.

He was no pushover. "Does it get sun?"

Now, they were planning to come to Karachi on their way back to India. I needed friends. The city had turned lonely for me. My boyfriend had been right. He was spending less time with me, and somehow I wasn't welcome at his home anymore. Although I had enough confidence to know my self-worth, I also knew that I wasn't the ideal pick for his parents. I was older. I was divorced. I came from India. And, to top it all off, I was a woman who had her own home without a chaperone, and their son stayed out late alone with me. I was not Islam's girl next door.

I had found myself getting depressed and isolated. I went to Pakistan to bridge misunderstanding between people with sincerity and honesty, and both my work and I were being attacked. I had found myself weeping every day, and I had started contemplating the darkest thoughts. When Danny and Mariane's car pulled up outside my gate, I jumped out of my seat to run into the sunshine to greet them. Somehow I felt they could give me a reprieve from the depression into which I had sunk.

I led Danny and Mariane upstairs. "Look," I told them, opening the screen door onto the veranda. Four parrots that lived across the street were gliding through the sky. Their twerps filled the air, transporting me to those magical moments where the *junglis* would fill the sky over Jaigahan with their chatter.

Danny set up his Toshiba laptop at my rolltop desk. "Have you seen one of the Nikes I bought to play volleyball?" he asked.

Uh, no. "Why?"

"I lost it."

Goofy Danny. By night we listened to Phil Collins, Bruce Springsteen, and the sufi Pakistani rock band, Junoon, and I escaped for some time alone with my boyfriend.

Danny was in Karachi to do an interview with a Muslim leader. The day after he and Mariane arrived, he set off for the interview. The Sheraton didn't have any cars available to send over. Danny was getting anxious about being late. I asked the *chowkidar* guarding my house, Shabeer, to find taxis for Danny and Mariane, who was setting off for a separate interview. In the bright shine of an early Wednesday evening, shortly after 5 P.M., Danny slipped into his yellow taxi, fumbling with his notebook, mobile phone, and shoulder bag, as he was prone to do. I waved to my dear friend as the taxi pulled away.

"See you later!"

He returned my good-bye with a gentle wave and smile.

Daylight turned to darkness, but Danny didn't return home. Mariane had cooked a Cuban dinner that night to which I'd invited my boyfriend and some of his friends. She and I spent the evening calling Danny's mobile. "It's still turned off," Mariane said after each try. She remained calm, but with each passing hour the tension rose.

"I'm worried," she admitted. Danny never turned his phone off. He always wanted Mariane to be able to reach him.

We wondered aloud if he'd gone to a *madrassa,* a Muslim religious school, outside Karachi. I remembered that Danny had told me he might spend some time with the religious leaders' disciples. "Maybe he's out of range."

After the last guest left, Mariane and I climbed the stairs to peck for clues in Danny's e-mails and Palm Pilot on his computer. We found the name of the man he was supposed to meet: Gilani. I tapped the name into a Google search. What we found was frightening. The FBI wanted Gilani for bomb attacks in the U.S., staged from an organization called Muslims of America that converted many black Americans to Islam. He and the organization denied any wrongdoing. We found a *Boston Globe* article in Danny's e-mails about Gilani. I couldn't believe my eyes. It quoted one of the friends of the family whom I'd met in Islamabad, a man named Khalid Khawaja, as a close friend of Gilani.

The night was slipping into dawn. My boyfriend had fallen asleep as we had trolled for clues. Each passing car had given us hope that one would stop in front of our gate and Danny would emerge, kept overnight by overeager hosts. But the new day's first light arrived without Danny.

I called this man I'd found quoted by the *Boston Globe,* a fundamentalist Muslim whom I'd spent hours interviewing, as other Western journalists including Danny had done, because he was an educated and articulate spokesman for the cause of not only the Taliban but also Osama bin Laden, whom he claimed was his friend. When I called him, as the cry broke out for the sunrise prayer, he preached to me about the destruction America was causing Afghanis instead of agreeing to help. I wondered about these Muslim values of goodwill that he preached. He knew Danny, but still he was balking at helping.

That day, my writer's retreat became the command center for the hunt to find Danny. Mariane and I steered the police through all that we knew. I didn't bother wearing a *dupatta,* as I did when I met elders or more conservative Muslims than my boyfriend's crowd. I didn't even clear away the Murree Brewery beer bottles that littered the house from the night before.

The police asked me questions about my life and work. "I'm an open book," I told Inspector General Kamal Shah, the police chief for the province of Sindh, in which Karachi sits as the capital.

Yes, I was born in India. Yes, I lived in this house alone. Yes, I was writing a book, and, yes, I was on leave from the *Wall Street Journal.*

He tapped his walking stick. "We don't suspect you."

I didn't know what to think about Danny's disappearance. I went to the gate in the early evening. Two of my boyfriend's friends were standing there, looking anxiously for my boyfriend. "Is he here?"

"He isn't." I told them I had just talked to his boss, and he said he expected him back soon. "Do you want to come inside?"

"No, we'll be going," they said and rushed off.

My boyfriend soon appeared in his dark business suit and a clipped walk. His face had fallen. I'd never seen him like that before. He looked afraid. He sat at the dining table with two of the Pakistani investigators. My boyfriend thanked one of them. "You got the people off my back."

We went upstairs. My boyfriend looked intently at me. "I can't come over much."

"Why?"

"You'll have a lot of things happening here. You shouldn't have just anybody walking through here."

"You're not just anybody."

He told me that he had gotten a phone call from Pakistani intelligence. We knew he and I were on their radar screen because he had gotten stopped once after visiting me at the Sheraton by a man who said he belonged to Pakistan's Inter-Services Intelligence, known as ISI, a group with a dark side of torture and harassment in the country's history books. "I talked to my parents. They don't want me coming over." He told me that a mamoo, one of his maternal uncles, disappeared some years back for days, and his family didn't want the same to happen to him. I couldn't believe my ears. I actually thought this crisis would give him the opportunity to stand by my side, even stay with Mariane and me as male protection. Didn't he understand what we were going through in this land foreign to us? He was adamant. "I have to leave."

"How can you do this?" I screamed.

"I have no choice," he responded.

"You always have a choice." I could only think of the many times I had chosen to displease my parents for my own independent judgment. What about his love for me? He responded with a finality that pierced my heart with a dagger unimaginable.

"I've made my choice."

"Your family?"

"Yes."

I closed the door and retreated upstairs to the closet that was my meditation chamber. I wept.

The outside world sees Pakistan as a monolithic Muslim nation, but it isn't. When I had been in Lahore the year before, a relative had told me, "We don't have our Urdu-speaking girls marry Punjabis."

When I wed I thought I was satisfying the desires of my culture and religion to marry one of my own. I had no idea about the identity trap into which I was walking. My family is Urdu-speaking Muslims from India, a minority called *mohajirs,* or immigrants. We are culturally and linguistically different from the Punjabi-speaking Muslims of the region of Punjab that dominates Pakistan politics, military, and bureaucracy. While the two often get along, there is also often a divide of distrust. I married into a Punjabi family, and now I was dating a man from a Punjabi family.

My relative told me, "It's often said that a Punjabi man will give a Punjabi woman a chauffeur-driven car, a house, a refrigerator, and all the luxuries in the world. She will use the luxuries to appease herself while she looks the other way as he has affairs. But an Urdu-speaking girl will say, 'Take all your luxuries but give me your loyalty.'"

The headline said, "Baffling Questions about Indian Lady in Pearl Case," when it showed up in *The News*, an English-language newspaper related to Jang, the country's largest circulation newspaper with an estimated two million readers.

From that moment on, I became "the baffling Indian lady." I read the allegations with both horror and amusement. It said that I was denied my visa twice, that I arrived in Pakistan and then simply disappeared. The article was a direct plant from the Pakistani consulate in New York. It quoted from the letter I had written to Rizwan Khan, the New York press counselor, everything about my vision to cross cultures, my failed marriage to a Pakistani, even my phone number at Sumita's apartment in Brooklyn—the contact number I'd left for the consulate—and the address of Latif Manzil, gotten from the back of my business card. I couldn't understand why they were going after me. So what if I was born in India? With Pakistan's current leader, General Musharraf, born in Delhi, did they judge me an enemy just because of my birthplace? I became enraged at their judgments, but I remained quiet, because our mission was only one: to find Danny.

I remembered the bespectacled manager of the Kwality Restaurant and Fun Foods off Montieth Road in Chennai, a man by the name of Ravindar Visht. Lucy, Esther, and I were waiting at his restaurant for our car, overdue for our trip to Pondicherry. He didn't have to help us, but he repeatedly called the car service to check on our reservation and, then, Indian Railways for our future train trip to Lucknow.

"Thank you," I told him.

"It is my *farz,*" he told me. His duty.

That's how I felt now. It was my duty as Danny's friend to find him. In choosing to protect Danny, Mariane, and their unborn son, I chose to aspire to values of selflessness, *nairatmya* in Sanskrit, the name of a Tantric Tibetan Buddhist female deity, "No-Self." It meant I had to risk losing my own identity. Ego couldn't define me. Fear couldn't deter me. My own questions couldn't hinder me. Mariane and I were beyond fear, anyway, suspended in a place past terror where there were no rules. We had to persevere. We became powerful beyond tears. I had made my choice.

My boyfriend, meanwhile, would not be swayed from his choice. He returned on the second night, again after work. I couldn't understand why.

We went upstairs again to the room in which Mariane and I had held our vigil the night of Danny's kidnapping. He asked me for the book contract my literary agent's assistant faxed to his office for me days before Danny's kidnapping.

"Could you rip the top off?" he asked.

What was he talking about? I asked, but I knew the answer. He wanted to discard any trace of his company's name on the transmission record at the top of the page.

I rifled through my papers, angry and again humiliated. I thrust the paper at him. It didn't even have his company's name across the top, just the sender's identification. I walked away without saying good-bye. After he left, I looked at the paper upstairs. He had torn the top line off.

In the kitchen one day, I confided my personal troubles to a chief Pakistani police investigator whom Mariane and I had started calling Captain and whom we trusted. "Captain, the police have cost me love."

He listened carefully, looked me in the eye, and said matter-of-factly, "It's in times of crisis that you discover the true nature of a person's character." It was true. I was learning this lesson through a crash course.

The first night after Danny's disappearance I had curled onto a sofa in my living room so I could be near my home phone in case Danny called and, better yet, near the front door, if Danny should walk through it. Instead, a Pakistani stringer who had helped Danny make contact with the man who set up his Karachi interview had walked through the door, summoned by the police. Before law enforcement got to him, Mariane and I had drilled him for every bit of information. Danny had met his contact at a Rawalpindi hotel. We had already found the trail of e-mails that followed. The man had called himself Bashir. My Urdu from bad Bollywood movies told me that he was trouble. He had put "nobadmashi" in his e-mail address. *Badmashi,* literally, meant troublemaking. Who was he?

The stringer had linked the man to a dangerous militant Islamic group, Harkatul Mujahadin, fighting Indian troops in the state of Kashmir in northern India. Pakistan claimed the state as its territory ever since partition.

"You never told Danny!" Mariane had exclaimed.

The stringer had admitted that he hadn't.

The Sunday morning after Danny's disappearance, Mariane and I readied to go to Pakistan Interior Minister Moinuddin Haider's house with a cadre of police officials who looked like overgrown boys dressed for Sunday church. Haider oversaw law enforcement. We needed him on our side. The day's early quiet was broken by a phone call.

"We've got a ransom letter with pictures," a *Journal* colleague told me.

We ran to Danny's laptop. I opened my Yahoo account. A *Journal* bureau chief had forwarded the letter. It came from an e-mail with "kid-napperguy" in the address. It claimed Danny was a spy for the CIA, later spinning him into a spy for Israel's Mossad intelligence agency. The charges were ironic. Danny had been one of the first to document the widespread feeling in Pakistan that September 11 was a Jewish conspiracy to pin the attack on Muslims. As we drove around on New Year's Danny had joked about the notion of a Jewish conspiracy: "I missed the last meeting."

The photos showed Danny with a gun to his head.

"Is it Danny?" Captain asked. Mariane looked for his wedding ring.

"It's Danny," she said without a cry. There was no room for emotion to overtake us.

"We'll find Danny," I told her.

"I know we will," Mariane replied.

We created a surrogate family in my house, Mariane and I, the only women in this investigation, joined by John Bussey, the *Journal*'s foreign editor and Danny's boss, and Steve LeVine, a *Wall Street Journal* reporter who worked with Danny in Pakistan. We hunted for every clue. Mariane stuck a yellow Post-It on a computer disc and marked it, "Danny's floppy not checked," until we could check it. I installed a chart on the wall to map a family tree of the links between suspects, the same kind of family tree I'd used to understand the teachers of American Tantra. In that case,

I included ties between men and women who had slept together. Now I was studying ties between militant Islamic groups.

A regular visitor from Pakistan's ISI came by our house. He described himself only as Major.

"How can we help?" he asked one day.

We asked him to research two suspects for us. He came back to us with useless information. I sat on the glass coffee table opposite him and told him so. His eyes widened. This was an agency that wasn't used to being challenged by civilians, but we didn't have room to be anything but efficient. Our surrogate family took to talking secretly on the veranda where Danny had once gazed at the parrots. We didn't know whom to trust as we swung between moments of worry, hope, and even levity when gallant, burly men from the French consulate delivered crepes homemade by their wives after I told them Mariane needed home cooking.

My boyfriend begged me to see him. I consented. When he arrived, I led him to the stairs by the servants' quarters. We climbed the narrow circular stairs to the roof, where I figured we could talk without surveillance from Pakistani intelligence, and I sat down on the cold cement. He sat down beside me.

He was irritatingly silent. The kidnappers had sent their demands and the wretched photos of Danny with a gun to his head and bound in shackles. I couldn't indulge my boyfriend.

"What do you want?" I scowled.

"I don't know."

"Why are you here?"

"I miss you."

I couldn't take his weakness. His mobile phone was blinking, turned on. I was just waiting for it to ring. I was so used to enduring the sound of his mother's voice on the other end, cajoling him home. I started punching his shoulders, my blows so hard they forced him to fly backward, spread-eagled. I threw the key chain I'd bought for him across the roof. I threw his phone across the roof. And I kept pounding him.

"You're an idiot!" I screamed, happy to release my wrath into the dark sky that surrounded us. "A coward and an idiot."

"I am."

I sat again in silence. I started to cry, my body convulsing from his torture and the cold night air seeping through my thin shirt.

"I would have died for you," I told him before wiping my face defiantly, forcing myself to my feet and leading him downstairs and out of my home in silence.

Our battle to find Danny continued. We fought to track down clues and plotted strategy. Meanwhile, it wasn't just my boyfriend who abandoned me. The friends whom Mariane had cooked for the night of Danny's kidnapping disappeared. And I heard not a peep of support from my relatives in Pakistan who had lectured me so much about the values of being a good Muslim, praying five times a day, and giving *zakat* to the poor. I heard from only two of my cousins, one through e-mail, the other through text messages on my mobile phone. They said they couldn't phone me for fear of being investigated by the police or Pakistani intelligence.

I felt alone except for my family in West Virginia and my mother's cousin-sister in Alaska, Anjum Khala, who had visited me once in Chicago with her American husband, Tim. Through e-mail, she was a lone voice in our extended family, encouraging and supporting me. As with the implosions during the journey through India, my family in Morgantown stood by me and encouraged me. My parents quietly worried about my safety but never asked me to return. "You are doing the right thing for your friend," my father told me.

Safiyyah sent me an e-mail, "You'll find Danny because you're cool."

A realization hit me. I seemed to have missed a period. I didn't have a calendar, so I created one in my Winnie-the-Pooh book. I was late.

I sat alone on the striped sofa in the sitting room, curled up with the classic *The Little Prince*. Mariane saw me and sat beside me. Unspoken words crossed between us. "Is it your period?" she asked.

"It is. I think I missed it."

Her eyes widened. She sent me in the Eurocar on John and Steve's nightly ride back to the Sheraton. A police escort followed me up the stairs to the night counter at Sani's. I prayed he wouldn't stand right beside me.

"A pregnancy test," I asked the clerk. I considered buying all the tests on the shelves but left with just one. Mariane waited at home in anticipation. I was nervous. Scared. I opened the box. We studied the instructions. She forced me to leave my seat on the sofa and venture into her bathroom. The drops fell. I returned with the Band Aid–sized test. We watched a pink line come across. "It's negative," I sighed. Then with only my expressed relief as a pause, the next line came across making a very distinguishable cross, a positive result.

"You're pregnant!" Mariane yelled. I was dazed when Mariane started laughing hysterically. She covered up her face, apologizing unnecessarily. "I can't wait to see the look on John Bussey's face," she said, continuing her gales of laughter. I had to laugh, too. It was the best response we could have had.

I had been pregnant, then, when Danny was kidnapped, and spent the first month of my child's creation trying to find terrorists. I didn't have any of the symptoms of morning sickness or fatigue. How could I, in the face of horrors more awful than hormonal imbalances? A Muslim scholar in Islamabad had told me that women were *jihadis* from the time of conception to the time of delivery, waging a battle for their child's health. I didn't know what to do. Mariane was clear in her vision for me. "I don't think everyone who gets pregnant should keep their baby. It's not that. But you'll be a beautiful mother. You must keep the baby."

I told my boyfriend the next night. "I'm carrying your child."

He stared back in silence. I should have made the first words from his mouth his last. "I have to go." He told me he had to pick up dinner from his nani's house for his mother.

"You have to go?" I screamed. "I tell you something like this, and your response is that you have to go? Get someone else to pick up the dinner from your nani's house. Skip dinner!"

"I can't. I'll be back."

He left. Downstairs, they couldn't believe it. I invented that he was picking up *biryani* from his grandmother's house. In my mind, such an important mission had to be for a dish of feasts like *biryani*. He returned, still stunned. He couldn't talk about the baby. And, again, he had to leave quickly. "I have work tomorrow."

We talked over the phone into the night. He was inarticulate and frustrated me. I couldn't forgive his decision to leave me to pick up dinner from his nani. It seemed a warning to me of things to come. As if I needed any more warnings.

"You're pushing me against a wall," he shouted at me. "I don't want this baby. I don't want it this way. I didn't really love you. It was just about the sex." I couldn't believe my ears. I hung up the phone on him.

He sent me an e-mail, repeating himself like a mantra. He didn't want the baby. He didn't want it this way.

I remembered a woman I'd met in Delhi over a year ago before I embarked on my motorcycle ride through the Himalayan foothills. She wore tight white jeans with pink flowers embroidered, stretching up the right calf up to the right pocket.

She was the tall and flamboyant Brazilian wife of a diplomat in the embassy of Denmark, long-legged and slender with a long mane of thick black hair. She paid no attention to the taxi *wallas* assembled at the corner of Khan Market, staring at her as she glided by them. As we sat, first at a friend's bookstore in Khan Market and then at the Yellow Brick Restaurant at the Hotel Ambassador, she espoused breathlessly her views on motherhood and Buddhism. She had twin teenage sons. She was a great admirer of the peace activist Aung San Suu Kyi under house arrest in Burma and pulled out her biography from her purse.

"Being a mother is the ultimate expression of oneness with the universe," she said. "To love a child is the greatest exercise in unconditional love. To leave a child to the forces of the universe is the greatest exercise in nonattachment. You could not separate from your child unless you believed your child was one with the universe."

I understood the awesome truth that this baby chose me to be its mother. My boyfriend had told me that he didn't want me to continue the pregnancy. This forced me to ask myself whether or not I did. I turned to the written word. When asked about coitus interruptus, called *azl* in Arabic, the Prophet Muhammad was said to have declared that it was lawful for individuals to do as they will, but if God intended for a child to be born, the child would be born.

My boyfriend told me he would visit me around 9 P.M. I tried to look nice. Mariane, a devout Buddhist, sat upstairs chanting. I sat beside her. I was distraught, watching the time slip by without a word from my boyfriend.

Her Buddhism was a different branch from the one I had been studying the last two years. Instead of internal meditation, she chanted, her eyes focused on a scroll with a special mantra written in Japanese and Sanskrit, representing the highest ideals of Buddhahood. I had joined Mariane on the third day after Danny's disappearance, sitting slightly behind her every day. Now, as I waited for my boyfriend, we chanted to again overcome fear and to surround Danny with strength.

It was on the Sunday morning after Mariane and Danny's wedding at a chateau in Normandy that I'd first uttered the words she chanted, *"Nam-myoho-renge-kyo."* They represented the ideals of loving and compassion written about in a scripture called the Lotus Sutra. I was sharing a room with a friend of Mariane's, Rebecca, a pretty and tall blond woman whose striking good looks had the attention of several men at the wedding. She invited me to chant with her. I walked into a quiet corner past the grassy lawn on which I had led the children and adults through picnic games. Mariane and Danny had giggled as they ran down the lawn with their legs tied together in the three-legged race.

Rebecca and I sat on a stone bench, and she pulled out the small scroll that she used when she was traveling. She wrote the chant in red pen in my address book and chanted slowly so I could keep up.

I raised my hands together beside Mariane as we sat together in Karachi, uttering the same words. Mariane told me again she wanted me to have the baby because she believed in me as a mother. "Danny would be so happy."

The toll of the mystery of Danny's whereabouts was starting to kill us.

"This is a matter of life and death," she said to me with a clear gaze. "If Danny dies, I die."

"That's why we have to win," I said.

"I have no other choice," she said.

I watched the clock turn past 11 P.M. I swallowed my pride once again, locked the door to my bedroom, embarrassed to call my boyfriend, and dialed his mobile number. He answered his mobile. "Where are you?" I asked, trying to sound as calm as I could. My voice trembled.

"At a friend's party."

"A friend's party?" I answered, my voice cracking from the pain. What friend?

"A friend of my ex-fiancée's sister."

"You told me you were going to be here at 9 P.M. And you're at a party?" I spoke through my anguish, my voice cracking even more. He talked about obligations. About being polite. He finally offered an explanation that seemed plausible. His parents weren't allowing him to visit me. He was allowed only to go this party. "I'll come over later." I could only offer him my mental defeat: "We'll see."

I slumped into my chair at the dining table, my fingers poised on the keyboard, trying to find some relief. Steve asked me about my boyfriend. I started to explain. John rushed into the room, fiddling with his mobile in his hand.

"Let's go," he commanded Steve.

"Asra was just getting her time," Steve offered.

"It can wait until tomorrow," John answered briskly.

The rejection felt personal for the moment it took me to realize that in fact something had to be terribly wrong. They stuck around only long enough for John to offer that they were going to see the U.S. consul general in Karachi, a kind man by the name of John Bauman, for an update. After 1 A.M.? Something was definitely wrong. Mariane entered the room after they left.

"Something is wrong," I told her, explaining the scene that had just unfolded.

I called Randall Bennett, the regional security officer at the U.S. consulate in Karachi, the Rambo of our investigation. "What's going on?"

He tried to explain that John and Steve were coming over for a regular briefing.

"That doesn't make sense," I said.

He shouted at me. "You want me to be so callous that I tell you something like this over the phone?" Something was clearly wrong. Everything was wrong.

I pushed the dial pad on my mobile for every mobile number we had. Turned off. Turned off. Turned off. Turned off. Where to turn? I called former cricket star Imran Khan's cousin, the dashing new police chief of Karachi. I could hear the sound of a TV in the background. He sounded tired. "What's going on?"

"I'm out of the loop."

We had to move. I called Eurocar to send us a car immediately. We'd go to the consulate ourselves. Mariane was ready to go. We were about to walk out the door. John walked in. Everyone walked in.

John walked to Mariane. He told her something in a very serious voice. It fell on my ears garbled, but I knew what he was saying. Captain was the one to put it clearly. He put his arm around Mariane. "I'm sorry, Mariane. I couldn't bring your Danny home to you." This reality was never possible in our minds in the four weeks of sleepless nights and constant vigil we'd kept for Danny. It couldn't be true. Mariane was six months pregnant. Danny still had to meet his son.

My mobile rang in the darkness before dawn. My boyfriend. "My mother finally went to sleep. I'm coming over."

"It's not a good time."

"Why?"

I was silent.

"Why?" the question came again.

How could I explain? "Danny is gone."

I fell asleep beside Mariane under the softness of a gray jersey cotton comforter. John awakened me. My boyfriend had come over.

I led him upstairs, stunned, groggy, wondering if he had come over because he cared or so he could tell his friends about his witness to history, but so sad and tired I hardly cared.

I heard the rain before I saw it. I had missed rain so much that when I had called home not long before, Safiyyah had put the phone receiver to the window so I could hear the rain pouring in Morgantown. Sure enough, the heavens had suddenly opened, and rain poured upon the parched earth before me. Danny was dead. The heavens were crying.

I sat on the carpet before the window, a sheet wrapped around me. Until the end, Danny, who had taught me how to have fun, had been planning parties. We planned to return to the site of my ill-fated wedding, the Margala Motel in Islamabad, and throw a bash—our way.

"Let's call it I Slama Jama bad Party," Danny had said. It took me a long time to fully appreciate his wordplay on *Islamabad*.

Now, my boyfriend embraced my shoulders, leaned me against his body as a buttress.

Too little too late. But I needed comfort. The weeping erupted from within me as if the veneer of my soul had transformed itself into dark rain clouds. I thought I heard the doorbell ring. I walked quietly past a sleeping Steve onto the veranda where we had our picnic lunches to swap theories about Pakistani intelligence. The rains were real. They mingled with my tears. I returned to my bed.

My boyfriend held me. I allowed him to make love to me. I needed to know life. The lovemaking slipped into hallucinations as I drifted between wakefulness and sleep, and he slipped into me, morphing into a penetration unrecognizable. I escaped into a sensibility as Rabia of Basra. I was beyond the existence of my body.

Before we left Karachi, I neatly packed Danny's garment bag for Mariane and stumbled upon a reminder of the great spirit of play that defined this man who flew through the air to dig balls others would let drop. Inside was his one Nike waiting to find its mate.

We walked the steps into President Musharraf's residence on this clear sunny day. Guards in turbans stood on both sides of the carpeted steps.

I pondered these steps I was taking into the home of the leader of this Muslim nation, this shirt of Mariane's with paisleys snug upon my breasts ripening from pregnancy. With each step in my black sandals, the swoosh of my black Nike pants sashayed just slightly. Under the code of Pakistan's *sharia* law, I could be arrested with one pregnancy test as evidence against me. As the Jamaat-e-Islami leader had once told me, *sharia* normally requires four witnesses to testify to the act of penetration. In the case of a pregnancy, a prosecutor wouldn't even have to rely on four witnesses. A prosecutor could use confirmation of my pregnancy and the absence of a *nikah nama* as evidence of my act of *zina*.

I was a lawbreaker entering the residence of the army general who was the leader of the Islamic Republic of Pakistan.

General Musharraf turned to Mariane. "Can I ask you a question?" She nodded.

He described the Western perception of Pakistanis as fundamentalists and countered with his perception of most Pakistanis as moderates. "What have you seen?"

As Mariane delicately described the many moderates she had met, I knew what I wanted to tell him. The words spilled out of my mind without my lips giving voice to them. Yes, many Pakistanis were moderate. Maybe most. I had a family of educated engineers, doctors, and professionals. Yet they were held hostage by one great deterrent to power: fear. Except for a teenage cousin in Karachi, none called me to offer me condolences upon news of Danny's death. They were a majority made silent by fear—and the fear was related to the absence of a civil society where they trusted neither government nor law enforcement. I wanted to tell him how I was targeted for political propaganda that came straight from within his government, just because I was a child of the same country from which he was born, India. The message I wanted to send to Musharraf was simple: "Remove the fear, and you will give voice to the silent."

Instead, I sat voiceless at the edge of my seat. The dismantling of my self was done.

In the regal office of Jacques Chirac, the president of France, the press secretary searched for the official presidential photographer.

It was getting late on Friday evening. He had gone home already. The press secretary got President Chirac's point-and-shoot camera, and he started directing her, as if he was a wedding photographer. "One with the brother," he said, throwing his arms around Mariane and Satchi, Mariane's brother. "Now, one with the journalists," he said, drawing John, Steve, and me into the photograph.

Somewhere, Danny was laughing, and, in this unexpected place among French antiques, I was beginning to recognize myself again. It was all *maya*.

I went with Mariane to Los Angeles where Danny had grown up in the suburb of Encino. It was a rolling neighborhood where no one seemed to walk the sidewalks.

Danny's family was hosting a memorial service at the newly built Jewish Skirball Center. I sat beside Mariane and listened to the addresses. A rabbi stepped to the podium. He talked about the clash of civilizations that Danny's murder represented. Danny's murderers made him declare, "I am a Jew," before his slaughter, as if that was the only thing that defined him. The *Wall Street Journal* had done an amazing job of communicating the human being that made Danny a remarkable man, defined not just by race, religion, or even gender, but rather by his personality. I knew him as one who would send me postcards from his travels; one time he'd compared my profile to the Queen of Sheba. I listened and couldn't see Danny's life through the prism of a clash of civilizations.

When it was my turn to speak, I forgot to introduce myself, as if it didn't really matter who I was but rather what I had to say. I spoke my heart. "There is a lot that is said about the so-called clash of civilizations," I started, looking at the sea of faces, many of them familiar. "I am a Muslim daughter of India. Danny was a Jewish son of Israel. We should have been the clash of civilizations. But let me tell you about our friendship. I have not even admitted this to my parents, but it was the summer that we met that Danny introduced me to beer at outings at the Big Hunt. Our friendship was about volleyball. Danny was a man who transcended his identity so that we were simply two human beings drawn together in friendship."

Danny crossed the boundaries of his identity to cover the Muslim world but, ultimately, was murdered for his identity. The fact that his murderers severed his head was an act of horror in our world. But it was, in its own gruesome way, the symbolic representation of how he had lived his life, for in Buddhism, as with the Severed-Head Vajrayogini, to sever the head from the body meant to slice duality, ego, and the other trappings from which Danny, in fact, had freed himself during his lifetime. He didn't succumb to legitimate fears, and he gave voice to his thoughts before his murderers slit his throat. I realized it was a deep responsibility we carried when we worked to free ourselves from convention. This freedom led us into darkness, just as my Nepali friend Deepak had been warned it would do. I didn't find my darkness on cremation grounds or in Tantric temples but, rather, in realities much more gruesome—of betrayal, dishonesty, and murder.

CHAPTER 23

Child of Truth

I STRUGGLED WITH the question of whether or not to keep my baby.
The only answer I could find among the Islamic scholars to the question of abortion seemed to relate to pregnancies within a marriage, not outside marriage, as if *zina* never led to such realities. That wasn't helpful. I read on anyway. Early Muslim legal scholars said abortion was lawful for a variety of reasons until forty to one hundred twenty days after conception, basically the first trimester. I remembered Mariane's and my discovery of the Muslim concept of *nafh al-ruh*. I'd even asked my boyfriend, before I knew I was pregnant, to help me define this Arabic concept. We'd decided *nafh al-ruh* meant "living soul." When did my baby's "living soul" take birth? That was the deadline I gave myself to decide.

Most Muslim scholars said that an abortion could occur only if a mother's life was significantly endangered. It was not my physical well-being about which I worried. It was my mental health. I knew that I could collapse under the weight of keeping the baby alone. My boyfriend sent me loving e-mails, promising to one day be with me, but I was in such a haze of trauma I couldn't understand him. I distrusted him. I wondered if I even loved him. Most of all, I didn't know how I could survive each day.

Mariane got early contractions in Washington. We spent the night at Georgetown Hospital, I lying in a chair that stretched into a bed. Before we left Karachi, I had promised Mariane I'd see her through the baby's birth. "You won't be alone," I assured Mariane, in a thinly veiled reassurance to myself as well. At the hospital, I watched a husband pacing up and down the hall with his very pregnant wife. We returned to the Mayflower Hotel. The contractions started again. We returned to Georgetown Hospital, where the husband was still pacing the hall. I wondered if I could do this without the father of my baby.

Back at the Mayflower, I tried to talk to my boyfriend, but I was filled with loathing. "Are you sure you want to keep the baby?" he asked me.

"Do you want me to kill her?" I screamed at him. I was convinced the baby was a girl.

We couldn't communicate. I felt as if everything I had learned over almost five years of spiritual lessons had gone down the drain. I ended up in tears. My despair over my baby and my boyfriend allowed me to release my anguish over Danny's death.

A dear friend, Pam, drove me home to Morgantown for the weekend.

Life was such suffering on so many levels. I was consumed in depression. I retreated to Safiyyah's room. A white lace valance hung from her closet. I curled up on her bed and started weeping. I didn't know who discovered me first, but within a few minutes everyone had gathered around to comfort me. My sister-in-law, Bhabi, put oil in my hair. Safiyyah rubbed my head. Mummy pressed my calves. My friend held my hand. Samir brought me water. My brother tried to comfort me.

My father started talking. He talked about the madness of violence, how U.S. foreign policy, like terrorism by Muslim *jihadis,* murdered innocents, like Danny. I had lost touch with compassion. "Kill them all!" I screamed. "They're all animals, anyway." My father tried to argue logically with me. My mother tried to quiet him. I kept screaming. My father argued more. My mother kicked my father out of the room. I kept crying for the darkness of slaughter and sadness in which I found myself. My body convulsed with the pain and anguish I had felt but little expressed in the months since that fateful day on January 23.

I wrote to my boyfriend to encourage him to be thoughtful and reflective while confessing that I had a great trauma from which I had to heal. In the thirty days in our safe house in Karachi, we had confronted the worst of humanity and, at times of compassion, the best of humanity. It was the darkness that was my companion in the quiet of my mind.

I feared I would lose the baby in a miscarriage. The baby chose to enter my universe, and I was choosing to respect this divine creation's decision. My boyfriend made me wonder if an abortion wouldn't be an easier solution. I had only two weeks until the baby would become *nafh al-ruh,* a living soul, after which time Muslim scholars said an abortion couldn't be performed, even to save a mother's life. I didn't want to capitulate to fear, however, and take the easy route.

My boyfriend's doubts and fears sparked within me a voice of shame and dishonor that I heard from no one but myself. I felt like a loser. A failure. I knew this was a voice that I had to simply observe and allow to dissolve, but the self-doubt buried me in discontent. To me, the father of my child did not consider me beautiful enough, young enough, acceptable enough, inspiring enough to embrace me and legitimize me in marriage and family. What did this do to me? I had to confront feelings of shame, insecurity, and failure. I had crossed these *haduds,* these boundaries, of our culture. While the society and its people could not stone me, I felt as if I was experiencing a stoning on a psychic level. It came in the form of the barbs from the Monas, Zains, and Shakirs of my boyfriend's world, his friends who judged me. They came, too, from even him in his decision not to legitimize me. I did not want my child to inherit the legacy of shame and self-hate that our society and culture inflicted upon us. I wanted to protect this child from the torment that I had endured and offer the baby, instead, affirmation and unconditional love.

Each convulsion of my body in tears sent shock waves through me about the damage I could be doing my baby. My boyfriend had asked me why I wanted to keep the baby. I knew that it was because she was created at a time of love between him and me. Ultimately, I believed in life and love, even if it didn't come with the proper rubber stamps.

When I packed my bags to return to Paris with Mariane, I searched for my other Nike running shoe. It was missing. Danny. Playing another practical joke on me. I packed the one Nike, just in case.

In Paris, I lived with Mariane in a cute pied-à-terre that Danny and she had bought in the neighborhood of Montmartre.

In Paris, the investigation continued as a trial began to prosecute four Pakistanis allegedly involved in Danny's kidnapping. I went to Karachi for the beginning of the trial. My boyfriend didn't pick me up at the airport. "I'm sorry. I'm sorry. I'm sorry. I'm sorry," he told me when he found me. "I overslept."

I read that day's *Dawn,* the country's largest English-language news-paper. A court had sentenced a Pakistani woman, allegedly raped by a brother-in-law, to death by stoning for *zina,* a word I knew all too well now. Prison officials had given her daughter to other female prisoners. Death for carrying life. I put my hand on my belly and sighed.

Two of our friends in Pakistani law enforcement visited me secretly. "You're not safe," they told me. Unknown to me, the defendants' lawyers were pointing the finger at me as a possible culprit and alleged spy for India. They claimed I had disappeared without a trace. My boyfriend vis-ited at the latest hours. He told me he had told his parents about my preg-nancy, but I felt again like an illegitimate consort.

I flung myself to the bathroom floor, chanting in desperation the words that Mariane had taught me. *"Nam-myoho-renge-kyo. Nam-myoho-renge-kyo. Nam-myoho-renge-kyo,"* I cried out, desperately trying to defeat my overwhelming sense of isolation and alienation. I left Karachi so sad.

Then, in one moment, I felt the divine love that I had been seeking.

The doctor tapped XY on the video screen. All of a sudden, all of col-lege honors biology evaporated. "XY. Does that mean boy?"

The doctor smiled.

"A boy," I whispered, smiling at Mariane, who was quietly document-ing my reaction on a camcorder. "Mariane, a boy!"

My pregnancy doctor, Dr. Gerard Strouk, had calculated my baby's due date during my last visit. Spinning a wheel around that estimated gestation, he concluded, "October 10."

"October 10?" I responded, my eyes widening.

"Oui."

I had studied Danny's documents enough to have his birthday memo-rized. It was October 10. I knew, then, that my baby wouldn't be born on that date, but this was Danny's not-so-gentle reminder that he'd be watching to make sure I raised my boy listening to good music, not the country music, Cher and Meatloaf, of my liking.

White puffs that I had learned long before to call "grandmother's hair" wafted down rue Yvonne Le Tac, past the red canopy in front of Le Durer restaurant, toward me. I was those white puffs. I was the sun. I was the wind. I was the mother goddess. I realized the truth of the path I had to forge for my baby and me. I had heard more defenses of single motherhood and the baby's life from my friends who were Western liberals. "We shall forever be connected," I told the father of my baby, "through our baby. I will honor you. I will respect your parents. I know the importance of my patrilineal heritage. I shall always strive to be good." But I knew that I could not rely on a future with a man who couldn't give me a present that was content and secure.

"You caused me suffering," I told him. "I chose happiness." Even if, despite all my hopeful talk, I still imagined him on Saturday nights seducing new women.

I called that house where only women lived in Maidenhead, England, off the banks of the Thames River where I had first met Iftikhar Mamoo. I kept Rachel Momani on the phone while I talked to Lucy. When I had told momani that I was going to have a baby, she gave me the assurance that I needed to know I was making the right choice in choosing life over death. "Your Mamoo would be very happy."

"The baby is a boy!" I told them.

My dear Lucy knew the joy of this moment.

"I feel in this one moment," I told her, "the joy of every full moon upon which I've gazed, the raindrops that fell upon us as we rode away from Beach Number 7, the wind and the sun."

What was the power of this unborn child within my being? Profound. When I heard the sound of Mariane's and Danny's son, Adam, as he entered this world, I understood how, in fact, life could emerge from darkness.

In the days we had awaited Adam's birth, we had gotten word that Danny's body had been found outside Karachi. We had always tried to imagine where he had been taken. Now, we know. We had been told Danny had been picked up as planned for his interview. The kidnappers had driven him around town, ending at a hut in the city's remote suburbs. We had been told his captors spoke little English, but when he thought they were going to poison him, he went on a hunger strike. They had convinced him to eat, bringing him fast food and soft drinks. He had apparently tried to escape once. Until the last moment, we had been told, his Pakistani captors thought he would be set free. But three Arabs had been dispatched to the hideout to kill him. We had been told Danny was blindfolded and didn't know death was upon him. It was a small consolation. I had hidden the autopsy report when it was e-mailed to us to protect Mariane as she readied for Adam's birth. The details had sent me to the hospital in the middle of one night, my abdomen cramping in excruciating pain as I imagined the place where we had been told the kidnappers had hurt Danny.

All the while, I watched as Mariane used her chanting and spiritual discipline to free herself from the trappings of anger and fear. I, meanwhile, got irritated when our assistant didn't know where to find the scissors. But even Mariane didn't pretend to be extraordinary. "It's a constant battle."

As only nature could confirm, a small bird sang outside the window the day of Adam's birth, reminding me of the beauty of all things divine. When Adam arrived in his new home, the buds on the fig tree had opened to create a lush canopy of leaves.

In Karachi, the defense claims against me continued, making the newspapers in Pakistan. The kind U.S. consul general in Karachi, John Bauman, said he had started calling me "Mata Hari" after the French exotic dancer executed for being a spy during World War II.

"It's so ridiculous," he said, trying to comfort me.

A friend of Mariane's came over one day to chant. Her name was Anne Robin, a bodhisattva in Paris for me, along with Mariane's other friends. She was a journalist and happened to be doing an article about Mata Hari. She told me the story of this French woman who married a military officer, living overseas and then returning to Paris to become one of the country's leading exotic dancers. "It was never proven that she was a spy," Anne told me.

I looked at the pictures of Mata Hari that Anne brought me. She could have been any one of us. "They executed Mata Hari because she didn't have an appropriate defense," I told Mariane, as Adam slept nearby. "I'm not going to let that happen to me."

"We won't," she said. "But you're going to Pakistan over my dead body."

There were butterflies on the wall in this room in which Mariane rested her head at night.

I stepped quietly into the room filled now with the voices of women slowly chanting the staccato of the Lotus Sutra in Japanese. I was staying in a house tucked into the hills outside Aubagne in the south of France. Here, bullfrogs croaked loudly every night in a pond with a lone lily flower, calling the female frogs to mate. The full moon was now waning. I rubbed my belly every night in my room, decorated with ceramic figures of creatures the French called *cigalle* climbing the walls, sitting on velvet branches on the wall behind beds with golden sheets. The closest Western creature to which Yves, the owner of the house, could find a comparison for the *cigalle* was the cricket. I was fighting tears. I had just read an e-mail from the father of my baby, wondering if he could afford to see me in both July and October. He had promised me since January that he would visit me in July. He had responded to my need for his support as a threat upon his independence, sending me virtually every day into a spiral of anguish, loneliness, and self-destructive thought.

We were five women, each with familiar and difficult stories of love lost and children found. Rebecca sat in front of us with her sixteen-month-old daughter, Dune, facing her on her lap. It was she with whom I had first chanted almost three years before on the morning after Mariane and Danny's wedding. I chanted the Lotus Sutra with these mother goddesses and thought about the mother goddesses who had inspired me along my path. Khala. Mummy. Bhabi. In her own way, Dadi.

I looked at Dune, and I thought about the goddesses-to-be. Safiyyah. I saw the dark blue of the Baby Bjorn carrier in which Adam rested against Mariane, and I thought of the unborn boy within me. I thought of the boys and the men trying their best to realize the power of the divine mother goddess within them, too. My father. My brother. Samir. Yes, even the father of my child. I stared ahead at the *gohonzon* upon which the Japanese and Sanskrit of the chant was written. I aspired to the highest level of its scrawl. In Paris, a friend of Mariane's, Marc Albert, had taken me to see a Buddhist leader named Betty Mori, who said we had to aspire to live with the people in our lives who rose to the top of a ladder instead of settling for the bottom.

I remembered what I learned on that rooftop in Dharamsala, and I imagined the father of my baby beside my mother and father. In that moment when I felt sadness, disappointment, abandonment, and, yes, anger, I tried to relate to him with compassion. When I was twenty-eight, like he, I was reeling from a marriage I'd entered because I wasn't honest with myself about the person within me, a truth that kept me from being honest with others. Rebecca tapped a brass bowl with a wooden stick. She chanted prayers for our teachers, our *sangha,* and the Buddha within us. She tapped the brass bowl again. The ringing filled the air as we bowed our heads. We were now in prayer for those who had died. I thought of Mamoo. Bubli. The Sherpa. Nani. Danny. Dear Danny.

It was the breath of those who no longer breathed life that I could feel in the cool wind passing through the leaves outside. My baby stirred inside as if he knew his mother was doing that which we must all do in our pursuit of the divine experience: try.

I returned to Morgantown, as I have from all of my sojourns on the road, and home embraced me.

This path upon which I ventured when I left New York almost three years earlier, had taken its toll on me. It left me exhausted with my life and my identity dismantled. I didn't even have a bed to call my own. I was living off my parents' credit card. And I certainly didn't have a ring on my finger, a symbol of the divine love I thought I might find with a man. I had just about nothing but my own self and the great divine gift of creation within me. I considered this journey a success. The destruction of my self freed me to begin a new life.

When I began this trip, I had jetted to the Best Western in Santa Cruz, California, to learn the secrets of sexual ecstasy. For a little over four years, I confronted dualities, and they confronted me. Hinduism versus Islam. East versus West. Male energy versus female. I had to choose the values with which I wanted to live. True spirituality versus false opportunism. True love versus lust. The traditional female versus the liberated woman. Purity versus hypocrisy. Ego versus heart. Fearlessness versus fear. Reality versus illusion.

The darkness of Danny's murder made me confront the limitations of life on this earth if we accept the boundaries of duality. Even in death, Danny accepted neither the boundaries nor the labels others tried to thrust upon him. When his captors made him declare himself a Jew on the video that was to document his death, he did so with the nonchalance that characterized him in life.

I, too, had chosen a path in which I rejected labels and boundaries. To do so meant venturing into darkness that we could have avoided by choosing to live comfortably within the boxes assembled for us. Rejecting those boxes meant taking on great responsibilities. For Danny, the consequence was death. For me, it meant carrying a child within me, unwed. Only the fact that I did not live in a village in Pakistan or Afghanistan spared me a similar fate.

After I had returned to Morgantown, another Pakistani publication attacked me with the headline, "Who and Where Is Asra Nomani?" It was the essential question of my identity that Vishnu Uncle posed to me in Kathmandu. The lawyer defending Omar Sheikh, the man convicted of kidnapping Danny, said he planned to focus Omar's appeal upon me, calling me an agent for RAW, India's foreign intelligence agency, innocently named Research and Analysis Wing. The newspaper claimed I had posed as a student of mysticism in an earlier trip to Pakistan, describing the trips I had made to Sufi shrines with my grandmother. The article traced my roots back to the state of Uttar Pradesh in India and led readers straight to the address of my childhood home on Cottonwood Street, listing our home phone number, too.

Almost three years earlier, I had danced around the answer to the question of my identity. This time I knew the answer. I was more than an American journalist born a Muslim in India and raised a free thinker in West Virginia. I was an independent being and spiritual warrior who wasn't going to be defined by labels. I knew my powers, sexual, spiritual, intellectual. I was a Tantrika. And, as I stood outside my childhood home, my belly swollen in front of me, my hand caressing the contour of my baby's body against my own, I saw Jaz, the mother cat who taught me an early lesson in my journey about the beauty of unconditional maternal love.

I smiled and yelled out to her, "Jaz, I'm going to be a mother, just like you!"

I was going to have a hillbilly baby born, like Safiyyah and Samir, at West Virginia University's Ruby Memorial Hospital. My family embraced me. My father, a man who had to face so many new realities because of his daughter, had sent me a simple e-mail when my mother told him about my pregnancy: "I love you." His fingernails were coated with paint as he finished a room that would be home to me and my boy. My mother, who once stood at a railway station shocked at losing her veil, guided me to release myself from the shame and alienation of a culture she had rejected because of its oppression of the female spirit. "You are free," she told me. My brother, a survivor of the demons of darkness, shook my hand and said, "Asra Boo, I love you. Everything will be all right." Bhabi walked with me in the moonlight, burdened by battles in India, trying to save a newlywed sister whose mother-in-law terrorized her, arguing with me that I didn't abandon love by choosing to live without shame. Samir, my nephew, gave me the perspective I needed to appreciate the divine nature of the baby within me, telling me, "Babies are a little bit of heaven brought down to earth." And Safiyyah, my guru, curled up beside me as I slept on her bed with clouds upon the sheets so I would know I wasn't alone.

With all of the encouragement and love, I lived with a deep sadness. The father of my child had continued to live with secrecy about the baby. He had told me in the springtime that he'd told his parents about my pregnancy. Indeed, he hadn't told them, only recently admitting the truth to his mother. After coming to Morgantown, I chose to release myself from the lies. I called his father to tell him that I was carrying his grandson. "You're brave to tell me," his father said. "But I don't want to talk about it. I'm going now. Bye-bye." With a defining click, he hung up on me. Two days later, I received an e-mail from the father of the baby. "You've ruined everything now, Asra. I know now that I will never love you."

I knew, though, that I had chosen to be free. "You have chosen to live honestly in a culture of such hypocrisy," Bhabi told me as we walked in the crisp early autumn air. I had that luxury, and it would be my horror if I squandered it. The truth was that I remembered that bird shot out of the sky not far from the banks of the Indus River, and I breathed deep gratitude that I was not it. My Muslim goddess, Arina, my cousin in Aligarh, had married a man who moved her to Saudi Arabia, a fine place according to her father's estimation. I realized that I didn't have to wonder about the merits of another's path compared to my own. Her path and the path of others were simply different from mine.

My mamoo who told me to take the bull by the horns to tackle India told me that he fully supported the baby and me but wondered if I should construct a story to make the baby acceptable to our conservative subcontinent society. "Maybe that he has been adopted? That the baby was born with artificial insemination? That you married the father and then divorced?"

I laughed. Maybe a better story would be that I conceived in a temporary marriage with a *jihadi* who became a *shaheed,* or martyr, fighting against the West? I was not hurt by his suggestions because I knew he didn't feel shame. Still, I didn't sleep well the night after our conversation. The next morning, my mamoo called me again. "I'm sorry," he said. "You must simply tell everyone, 'This is my baby.' End of story."

In the early morning, as I pen my final words of this journey that took me around the world but, most important, within myself, my little boy stirs within me. I have chosen to name him Shibli, the Arabic name of my ancestor who was a Muslim scholar. The name means "my lion cub," and his second name will be Daneel, a derivation of the Hebrew name Daniel, meaning, "God is the judge." For me, it is true. Our judgments and definitions upon this earth are capricious and arbitrary. There is a magic more sublime and divine by which we can exist.

"Jaan!" I call out to him.

This is the name of affection that the living soul, the *nafh al-ruh,* within me deserves, for *jaan* is life.

Epilogue

"WHERE IS HIS heartbeat now?"
        "One hundred and thirty."
"And now?"
"One hundred and eighteen."
"Now?"
"One hundred and ten."

My eleven-year-old niece, Safiyyah, calmly read my baby's descending heart rate off the monitor beside me as I propped my body on my arms and feet, my eyes staring straight ahead, my belly still swollen from the life within me. The doctors had just warned me that my delivery was now considered a high risk. My baby's heartbeat had dropped to danger-ous levels with each of my contractions. I needed to keep it up. I was prac-ticing every secret I'd learned over my years of Tantric journey. I inhaled deep, drawing my breath into me, filling my belly with oxygen and chan-neling this breath through me into a complete exhalation. It was the pas-sion pump that I had learned in Canada with American Tantra. I was unleashing the Kundalini serpent of Tantric yoga. I was being mindful in the Buddhist tradition. I was doing whatever I could to protect my baby's life. I reached into my Sufi tradition to sink me into the cloud upon which I needed to float in order to rise to this occasion.

"*Allahu Akbar, Allahu Akbar, Allahu Akbar,*" I recited over and over again, drawing upon the *zikr,* the remembrance of God that my aunt taught me when I was a young girl on summer vacation in Hyderabad. I counted each utterance on my fingers, inhaling the entirety and emptiness that is divine with each utterance of *Allah* and exhaling into the world the divine within me with each expression of *hu.* Could each remembrance of the divine bring new breath to my child? I turned to the chant that I learned beside Mariane as we prayed for Danny's safe return. Perhaps its memory in my baby's psyche and its vibration within me would matter even just a beat.

I couldn't panic. I was breathing for my baby. In my mind, each breath I denied my baby could cost him his life. I had worried that I would be distracted by the horrors I had experienced this year. But in this moment of life and death, there was no distraction. Omar, Danny's kidnapper, didn't loom before me. My troubles with my baby's father didn't matter.

I had spent the night before walking through our house, easing my body through the contractions that pierced my lower abdomen, lighting my path with a Martha Stewart cinnamon spice candle I held in my hands. For company, I kept near me Billluh, my gentle black-and-white cat with a mask like Zorro.

Outside, raindrops that resembled jewels twinkled in the dim light cast from inside our house. They took me back to a time when I rode with Lucy behind me on a scooter from a magical place called Beach Number 7. I saw those jewels as heaven sent by her father, my uncle. So were these. It was a crisp autumn day with reminders of the divine all around. The Appalachian mountains of our backyards and the trees of our front yards were enflamed with the colors of Starbursts candy, bright oranges and reds exploding all around.

As the sun began to rise, my family arose from slumber. Samir donned a tie printed with the image of the Three Stooges. I had bought it for one of Danny's birthdays in Washington but had never given it to him. It had landed in my father's tie collection, and for this occasion, my father tied it around Samir so he could resemble a TV reporter doing broadcasts of my baby's birth on our home video camera. Safiyyah wore the outfit she had set aside days ago for this special day and tucked butterfly clips into my hair after I had slipped into a flowing white dress. "I want to look pretty for my son," I told her.

Minutes slipped into hours in Room 601 as I practiced what a friend had recommended days earlier. Observe the experience. It felt as if my baby had invited fifty of his angel friends into the womb from heaven, handed them each a staple gun, and every six minutes told them, "Okay, now!" and they all stapled. I didn't scream but, ultimately, relinquished to an epidural. "You don't have to suffer," Mariane had advised me. Her words made me reflect on so many choices I had made in my life in which I brought suffering upon myself. This time, relief came to me, but my contractions weren't sufficiently widening my baby's passageway into this world, and my baby's heart rate was dropping with each contraction. The doctors were visibly worried. A gentle nurse named Stephanie soothed me. Bhabi, my white Tara, stroked my hands. Safiyyah, my young guru, started reading my baby's heart rate to me. The first warning that my baby was in trouble came from a Muslim doctor educated at Karachi's Aga Khan University, where the father of my baby had failed to retrieve my first blood results. The baby's heart rate kept dropping. Nurses rushed inside to wheel me into the operating room for an emergency cesarean section. I trembled as they lifted me onto the operating table. A part of me wanted to weep from fear. But I knew that to weep would be to deny my baby vital oxygen. I rejected fear. A mask floated onto my face, and I was disappeared into the ether.

In Room 602, my mother, my Vajrayogini, cried for the first time, a mother hoping to see her daughter into motherhood. "If something happens to the baby, it will be the end of Asra," she wept. My father pulled out his *janamaz,* his prayer rug, to pray for us.

Shibli Daneel Nomani emerged at 8:20 that night. He slipped first into the arms of those who were closest to heaven's touch, Safiyyah and then Samir, and then floated from arm to arm of my bhabi, mother, father, and brother, to finally rest in my arms when I emerged from the confused haze of anesthesia. As I gazed upon this creation, seven pounds and six ounces of good health swaddled into a blanket, my eyes confirmed what my niece and nephew had told me. "You're right. He is beautiful," I whispered.

Long lashes fanned toward me. His eyes so elegantly swept toward his brows it was no cliché to say his eyes resembled almonds. The turn of his lips beckoned me closer. The immaculate construction of each of his toes made me forget whether the correct count was four or five for each foot. In the coming nights, I felt his breath upon me with such awe. I gazed at the lines upon the palms of his hands so impressed. To have helped bring breath and life lines into this world was to know something more divine than I could have ever imagined. The moonlight bathed us in his beams one night. I tucked Shibli against my breasts, rested my cheek upon the warmth of his head, and sank into a place of content like none I'd known before.

The importance of Shibli's good health overtook the expectations I'd had about his birth. He was the greatest lesson in living in the present and not questioning reality. I'd had images of pulling my baby out from within me, as they allowed at the hospital, and gazing into his eyes for the first time as he lay upon my breasts. Instead, I wasn't even conscious when he emerged. On the eve of Shibli's fifth day, I sat with my breasts filling with the milk that takes a few days to be made. I imagined nourishing Shibli with the flow of milk from my breasts. I remembered the image that had moved me most in the temples of sexual images in Khajuraho, a statue of a baby nursing at his mother's breasts. The pain, however, became excruciating though in my breasts as my baby remained in slumber, unable to suckle the milk from me. I remembered the Saturday after Adam's birth when I imploded from the weight of all that I had carried to help see Adam successfully into this life. I wept my first tears since my baby's birth on this Saturday night. The nurse on duty wheeled in an electric breast-feeding machine, and my first milk flowed not into my baby's eager lips but into clear bottles. Little did it matter.

Bringing Shibli into the world was an experience like none I could have imagined. I wondered how many men, but those who go into battle, experience anything close to the trauma of childbirth. The first time I walked from my bed, I left a trail of blood behind me. Every time I nudged my body even the slightest, pain shot through this sacred place in my belly where my baby once thrived. I no longer knew the luxury of sleeping in the dark, let alone sleeping long enough to dream. A smiling resident appeared one morning to cheerfully ask, "Ready to get your staples out?" Indeed, Shibli and his pals had stapled me shut once he'd successfully emerged.

Lying in my hospital gown, wishing I had the strength to lift my own child from his bassinet at the foot of my bed, I fully appreciated the *hadith,* the saying of the Prophet Muhammad, that the woman in

Islamabad had told me about women being *mujahadeen,* freedom fighters, on a *jihad,* a holy struggle, when they became mothers.

When Mariane called, I was aghast that I could have been witness to her delivery and afterbirth but not known the terrific pains of childbirth. Her voice was ecstatic when I talked to her. But I had to ask her, "How could you do this? How could you keep this a secret from me? I've been to hell and back."

She giggled.

The affirmations for Shibli's new life spilled into Room 616. Phone calls from New York to Paris, Hong Kong, and even Tajikistan arrived. My father had sent personalized e-mails to all the friends I'd gathered together for a mailing list, signing his message, "Proud Grandpa." Shibli wasn't born on Danny's birthday, as I had known, but he arrived on Mariane's brother's birthday.

"Bisou!" Satchi told me from Paris, elated to share the birthday with my newborn. "Kiss!"

A nurse brought in a vase of a dozen red roses from my friend Nancy in Portland. "This is only the second time in my life I've gotten a dozen red roses," I told Nancy. The first time had been from my beautiful boyfriend in Chicago. "If not when you've had a baby, then when?" Nancy asked. She was right. Bursts of color from Laurie, my friend in Washington who had let me stay in her basement room after Omar walked away from our marriage. My childhood friend, Sumita, and her husband, Dariush, sent a basket of goodies, Goldfish crackers tucked inside.

I needed this affirmation. Throughout my pregnancy, I had struggled with shame and loneliness. With my family's love, I had started to reconstruct myself. I vowed not to cry as I held my baby. I had shed enough tears throughout my pregnancy. To see my baby had survived my convulsions of weeping was incentive enough not to risk emotional scars of a mother's tears upon her baby's fresh skin.

Shibli's first visitor was Yusuff Aunty, who had seen me grow, as I stood at her kitchen sink first as an eleven-year-old washing dishes after dinner parties. Her husband, Yusuff Uncle, stayed downstairs so as not to

intrude upon the woman's world. She was a practicing Muslim, and the act
of creating Shibli was wrong, but she told my mother when she first learned
I was pregnant, "The baby has done nothing wrong." Now, she came to
admire my baby, making the first contribution toward his college fund.

I feared going home. Would I implode into the postpartum depression that claims so many women? Would I cry and yell from the slightest
of frustrations? Would Shibli feel at home? He did, and I did. We took
refuge in the clouds cast upon the sheets spread across Safiyyah's bed. My
mother brought me *hareera,* the mix of almonds, pistachio, and warm
milk that her mother used to bring her after my brother's and my births.
She washed Shibli's clothes by hand, as her mother had washed my brother's and my clothes.

On Shibli's seventh day, my parents and I bundled him up for his first
venture into the world, into the arms of Dr. Indira Majumdar, the Hindu
pediatrician whose children, Bobby and Misty, I had baby-sat as a child on
Cottonwood Street. In my childhood, Dr. Majumdar had earned a positive reputation in the sari she traditionally wore underneath her white
doctor's coat. Before I saw her, I thought I would ask her about which
goddess might be the deity of her worship. But when we arrived, her
enthusiasm for Shibli's birth bubbled over without censor. A red, white,
and blue American flag pin stared back at me from her white jacket, now
covering pants and a sweater.

It didn't matter anymore which goddess she might worship. I was just
thrilled my baby had regained his birth weight and added three ounces in
the week since his birth. "Shibli will call you Dr. Nani," I told her, using
the maternal honorific in Urdu for grandmother, as she beamed at his
face, wide-eyed in the new environment.

I couldn't escape the fact that we were keeping a secret from some.

"Has anybody told Dadi?" I asked my father one night after most of
the family had gone to sleep, Shibli tucked into my arms.

"No way!" declared my father, a kind man despite his sometimes
indelicacy. "Nobody wants to give her a heart attack."

I looked down at my baby in slumber. How could this gentle being
give anyone a heart attack, least of all a woman who had loved me since
my earliest days? I felt angry again with my baby's father for making us

illegitimate in the eyes of so many. I easily could have wept. And I would have had the perfect excuse in postpartum baby blues.

"What you say makes me very sad," I told my father. But I swallowed hard, stiffened my spine, and reminded myself of the enduring truth that was my only sustenance. "It hurts me. But we will win. We have won. Life has won."

The years behind me seemed to have been lived by someone else. My blossom-headed, ring-necked parakeet, Cheenie Bhai, must have traveled the trains with another woman. Surely, it wasn't I who rode a motorcycle through shakti piths in the Himalayan foothills. And all that they said happened to Danny couldn't have been true. But one place remained real to me. My village.

I planned to return to Jaigahan one day with my aunt, Rachel Momani, cousin-sisters Esther and Lucy, and my mother, not only to take her to her ancestral home again, but to give her a ride on my motorcycle, which I had left parked there, waiting for my return. I planned to distribute to families in the village meat from the two goats traditionally sacrificed for a boy's birth. I wanted the meat also sacrificed in another place. I planned to make arrangements to distribute meat sacrificed in Shibli's name in the Karachi neighborhoods that bred the kidnappers who turned my Islam into a vehicle of hatred.

Shibli's conception forced me to choose the Islam I wished to embrace. I had learned a profound lesson in the consequence that comes with the free expression of a woman's sexuality. It's said the prophet Mohammad declared that married men and women who commit adultery should be stoned to death, and unmarried men and women who have sex should receive 100 lashes and one year exile. For so long, I believed the modern-day Muslim culture in which I conceived my child would have had me punished if I had dared to keep the child within its borders. This was the experience of Muslim women throughout the Islamic world from Pakistan to Malaysia, Saudi Arabia, and Nigeria, where Amina Lawal, six years younger than me at the age of thirty-one, was sentenced to death for committing *zina* after giving birth to a girl, Wasila. She faced a sentence of being stoned to death after her baby stopped breast-feeding. Human rights groups in Pakistan reported that as many as 80 percent of women in jail were there because of *zina* prosecutions. They are prosecuted under 1979 Hudood Ordinances, which President Zia ul-Haq passed as part of a wider legal and political system enacted to make Pakistan fit his idea of Islam. The ordinances made *zina* a crime, and women who brought charges of rape often found themselves charged with adultery or fornication, particularly when they became pregnant, a condition used as evidence of their alleged crime. In 1980, few women were imprisoned; by 2002, about 1,800 women were in prison, says the Human Rights Commission of Pakistan. Human rights experts figure as many as 1,440 women were alleged *hudood* criminals. Amid international pressure, the courts had overturned the sentencing of the mother who was to be stoned to death for *zina* during my return to Karachi earlier in the year. But the lives of other women and their children went unnoticed in prisons around the world.

My spirited Greek friend Vasia arrived at my doorstep to welcome Shibli into the world. She had reflected years earlier on the fluency of making love in her native Greek language but had eschewed national boundaries to marry a French man, with whom she had spent the last several years in Morocco's capital of Rabat. At the dining table, she told me about her experience in that Muslim country. A gifted artist, she volunteered at a women's prison in Rabat teaching art to dozens of women, many of them imprisoned after their out-of-wedlock pregnancies were discovered. The situation was bleak and uncertain for single mothers and their children in Morocco where it is a crime to have a child out of wedlock. Mothers raised their children in their prison while they were nursing, other times handing them over to orphanages. Either way, it was difficult for children to receive the proper papers that would send them to school because their fathers had never legitimized them. Women who kept their babies were still shunned by their families and often left prison only to return for prostitution. I listened quietly with Shibli on my lap.

It saddened me to be part of a religion that punished a woman when she had brought life into this world. In Islam, *zina* ranked as a major sin beside murder. That would have equated me with Danny's killers. It's said the Prophet Muhammad had a dream in which naked men and women were making horrible noises in an oven. These men and women were said to be adulterers. I searched for other unmarried Muslim women who had become pregnant. I found only the story of a woman from a place called Juhaina. It's said she became pregnant after committing *zina*.

She went to the Prophet Muhammad and said, "O Allah's Prophet, I have committed something for which a prescribed punishment is due, so execute it on me."

The prophet supposedly told her master, "Treat her well, and when she delivers bring her to me."

The master did so, and the Prophet Muhammad sentenced her to be stoned to death. After she was killed, he prayed over her body. Hazrat Omar, the second caliph of Islam, said, "Do you pray over her, O Allah's Prophet, yet she has committed fornication?"

The prophet replied, "She has repented to such an extent that if it were divided among seventy people of al-Madina, it would be enough for them all. Have you found any repentance better than she having sacrificed herself for the sake of Allah the Most High?"

There was, however, no mention of her child left without a mother. As with the father of my baby, men lived secretly with their participation in *zina* while the women carried the responsibilities of the choice they had made to realize their sexuality outside the prescribed *hudood,* or boundaries, of the religion.

I turned to my mother that night. "Shibli chose carefully in coming into my womb. If he had entered the womb of any other Muslim woman, his life would have been so different." Perhaps he would have grown up in a prison instead of a home with Peter Rabbit in his bassinet.

Shibli's father phoned when he was a week old on a six-minute call he booked through Pakistan's telephone operators. I could count the number of phone calls he made to me over the year on just one hand, but at that moment I didn't care. I had Shibli in my arms. Life had won. For the first time I understood equanimity toward my baby's father. I felt neither love nor hatred. I was content to share with him the growling sounds that made Shibli's name as a lion cub appropriate. He called two days later on Friday night as I waited for Mariane's arrival from New York, amazing myself with Safiyyah, Samir, and their friends over how cute Shibli looked in a ladybug outfit.

"I'll call you tomorrow," he told me.

"Okay," I said.

His call never came. I heard from his sister, a TV personality on an Asian programming channel based in London. She wanted me to marry her brother. I told her that her brother had left me no alternative but to choose to be a single mother. I felt comfortable until we parted. As we ended the conversation, she said, "I was just calling to claim ownership over Shibli."

At that moment I remembered the last day of the Kalachakra initiation by the Dalai Lama in the Himalayan monastery of Ki. After Lucy, Esther, and I had settled into a space under a tree, a Tibetan man had stood in front of us and yelled, "This is my space!"

Lucy had looked calmly up at the man and responded, "There is no ownership over space."

As I absorbed the words of a woman who had known of my pregnancy from the start but had done nothing for the life within me, I took inspiration in Lucy. "There is no ownership with love," I told my baby's aunt. It was a cliché, perhaps, out of my *Chicken Soup for the Soul* day timer, but I believed what I said. "I don't believe in boundaries."

If she wanted to love the baby, she was free to do so. Receiving silence from the baby's father, I had grown stronger. But with utterances from him, I was daydreaming again, calculating ten hours ahead to Karachi to imagine what he might be doing. I phoned the baby's father, wishing to answer the questions that now consumed me as I nursed Shibli at my breast. He spoke promises again. This time, he said he would be applying for MBA schools in the U.S. His constraint was money, he said, but he would make his efforts alone. "I have to prove myself to you." He did. It wasn't enough to be humble, though. He wanted to give Shibli a middle name. I told him that he had a middle name in Daneel. "How about Ali?" he asked. I was firm, and I was angry at his entitlement after having done nothing for the baby.

If I needed any reminder that I was no goddess, it came a few days later when Shibli's father wrote to tell me that he was upset that I wouldn't consider Ali as Shibli's middle name. He wrote, "I think I'll just call him Ali. So can you please send me some pics of Ali, I'm dying to see him."

I knew my bodhisattva friend would tell me to ignore this intrusion, even though she saw the arrogance in his claim. But I couldn't accept this sense of entitlement. I called him. "What have you done for the baby that you think you can make such a claim?" I asked furiously. Except for a Subway tunafish sandwich he had brought me on my return sojourn to Karachi for the trial of Danny's kidnappers, he had done nothing toward the baby's health. "You haven't even sent him one outfit to wear."

"Why do I have to do something so symbolic?"

I couldn't believe his audacity. "What are you doing for us?" I screamed.

"You want daily reports?" he screamed back. "I'm not going to give you daily reports."

"Just one report will do," I yelled. "Tell me!"

He swore at me.

He was tormenting me again. I was allowing him to torment me. I had lost control. I was screaming into the phone. My mother swept into the room. "Why are you calling him?" she screamed.

"He's driving me crazy!" I wept, sobbing as I had done so many nights in Paris during my pregnancy.

"Hang up!" she shouted. "Hang up!"

I hung up, weeping in the embrace of my bhabi, my sister-in-law, and my mother. Shibli lay fast asleep all the while.

Two days after Shibli's one-month birthday, I called his father to apologize and make peace for my utterances of the week before. Accidentally, I dialed 911. The phone rang, breaking the quiet of the night. "Hello?"

"I'm the dispatcher at the West Virginia State Police. You dialed 911 and hung up. Is everything okay?" a woman asked. I explained my mistake. "Is someone holding a gun to your head?" the woman asked.

Was someone holding a gun to my head? I sat in the dim light of a small lamp, amazed at the truth of her question. Somebody was holding a gun to my head, and she was me. I was the only one pulling myself back to this city thousands of miles away where my dear friend had been slaughtered and my baby's life had been conceived. I knew this to be true. Still, I punched the buttons to that mobile phone whose ringing had caused me so much torment.

"Hello?" Shibli's father seemed different. "I wanted to call you but I was too afraid."

"Oh." Each of us had to overcome our own fears on our own.

"I had a long talk with my mother yesterday about everything," he said. "I showed her Shibli's picture. My mother says we should get married right away. What do you think?"

I was stunned. I was getting a marriage proposal from the mother of my baby's father. He wasn't even committing to it himself.

"What do you think?" I asked.

"I want to live with the baby. I think the baby should be with his mother." It was as if I didn't matter. I wasn't about to lose my temper again and resuscitate the cycle of apologies, but I couldn't participate in this delusion any more. Why hadn't he had this conversation with his mother months ago? "I've been avoiding her. She's been going through menopause. Hormones causing depression." Hormones. Depression. They were both something I knew a little bit about. But the baby's father and his family wanted to associate with me only to claim the baby. I saw clearly the choice I was going to make. I would raise my baby alone, welcoming any emotional expression Shibli's father and his family wanted to make but allowing nothing more. I wouldn't marry his father and risk losing the life I had fought to bring into the world. I had put a gun to my head fighting for a legitimacy that would only tie me to a person and family that I neither respected nor trusted. I couldn't be defined by a society that punished a mother for choosing life.

A phone call broke a rare Saturday afternoon when I was alone in the house with only Shibli. "As-salam alaykum." It was the Muslim greeting, "Peace be upon you."

"Wa'laykum salam," I said, not even still knowing the greeting is properly said, "Wa'alaykum as-salam." "And peace be upon you."

The man on the other end introduced himself with a Muslim name and asked for my father. "He's not here."

He asked for me.

"This is she." I was slightly suspicious, wondering if he was a Muslim who read the Pakistani newspaper article with my home phone number, but he had an American accent. He said he had read a personal advertisement that I had written and figured out who I was from my Salon articles he had also read. I figured it out. He had come across one of the advertisements I had written the year before in one of my efforts to make a conscious effort at finding a good match.

"A little something has changed since I wrote that ad," I said, glancing at Shibli sleeping calmly in my lap. Except for Shibli's birth, the stranger knew the tale of my year. He understood when I told him that I wasn't yet ready for new romance. I had the little business of again centering my *muladhara* chakra, my base chakra, representing stability and roots. But his phone call was fortuitous in my effort to know the being that was my true self. An Islamic scholar, he provided me just the intellectual gems I needed to bring me the clarity I was seeking.

"Through all of your experiences," he said, "you have known surrender. And a child learns surrender from his mother. It doesn't have to mean doing what your emotions say. If you just follow your emotions, you don't mature. You're a victim of your emotions. When you develop the ability to relate to an emotion, it enters into your consciousness without you having to act upon it. It can pass through you like a cloud." This was Tantra. It was Sufism. It was the Vipassana meditation I'd learned in a Buddhist forest monastery.

My son crystallized so much for me. Through this stranger, I learned that Shibli was the name, not just of my ancestor, but also of a renowned Sufi saint of the tenth century from Baghdad. This saint believed, as I had concluded, that the rituals of religion were mere vehicles for spirituality that transcends dogmas and rites. It's said that he ran the streets carrying flaming coals proclaiming he was going to set fire to the Ka'aba, the most sacred place in Islam to which Muslims pray. The truest Ka'aba, he and other Sufi saints argued, lay within the heart of a devotee.

Another Sufi tale about Shibli underscored to me the true nature of goodness. The tale recounted how Shibli the Sufi after his death appeared to someone in a dream. In this dream God asked Shibli whether he knew why God had chosen to show him forgiveness. Shibli listed all of his prayers and good deeds. "But the Lord told me, 'Not for all this have I forgiven you!'"

Shibli asked, "But then why?"

God said, "Do you remember that winter night in Baghdad when it was snowing and you saw a tiny kitten shivering on a wall, and you took it and put it under your fur coat?"

"Yes! I remember that," Shibli responded.

"Now, because you had pity on that poor little cat, I have mercy on you."

My baby led me to discover more about my lineage. I knew Shibli Nomani, my ancestor, descended from the Hindu Rajput nobility through which our family converted to Islam. Learning more about my baby's namesake, I discovered that he was inspired by a seventh century Muslim scholar named Imam Abu Hanifa Nu'man ibn Thabit. He founded the Hanafi *madhab,* or school of jurisprudence in Arabic, in the city of Kufa in Iraq. The Hanafi *madhab* spread in India where my ancestor Shibli Nomani took the name Nu'man because of his deep respect for the teachings and life of Abu Hanifa. I learned several a *madhab* divided Islam.

I knew Islam was not practiced in a singular way, but my personal inquiries allowed me to meander in a history that helped me understand that the Muslims who wanted to stone women in the modern day for *zina* weren't part of my Islam, and they weren't part of everybody's Islam. I called Pakistan again, not as a broken woman, but as a journalist to discover more about the work of the women's moment fighting to protect women, throw out the Hudood Ordinances, and get identity cards for children born to mothers not married. A human rights lawyer in Pakistan, Asma Jehangir, and her brave sisterhood of women activists and advocates had challenged judges in Pakistan that wanted to punish women where pregnancy was a part of their guilt: "The women's movement isn't quiet," she said. In Rabat, my intellectual mentor Fatima Mernissi told me the Qur'an says God created humans and gave them free expression. "It's fantastic. You responded to God's will by expressing yourself," she said, telling me about the women in Morocco who expressed themselves to defend single Muslim mothers, pushing DNA praternity testing and empowerment of women, training them in one Casablanca organization, Association Solidarite Feminine, to earn a living.

Scholars told me that the Hanafi *madhab* was one of four schools of law, practicing Islam as a more rationalist school of thinking with credence to scholars to settle issues of debate. It allowed for an embrace of

Sufi mysticism and a school known as Wahhabi sprang up in opposition. It believed in a strict adherence to the word of the Qu'ran and gained steed with the Saud family, making it the ruling principle in the kingdom of Saudi Arabia. It was said that Shibli Nomani wandered with missionaries in an effort to understand other religions and opposed Wahhabi thinking at the turn of the twentieth century. But recent years have seen the spread of Wahhabi Islam, as well as another orthodox school called Deobandi, the growth fueled by financing from patrons in Saudi Arabia. Their momentum helped script the Hudood Ordinances that made my return to Pakistan as an unwed mother a potential for arrest. The rigid practice of Islam separated me from many of my own relatives, but I realized for the first time that I didn't have to have a guilt trip about it.

Most dramatically, it created the divide that was to set Danny's killers and their allies against me. It divided those who defined Islam in the name of al-Qaeda, Osama bin Laden, and hatred from those who sought to live peaceful lives. With knowledge, I was liberated from the boundaries some Muslims tried to put around Islam. In my inquiries about Tantra, I had heard much about the importance of finding a teacher with a lineage. My twenty-first century newborn made me realize that I had my own lineage through a brave Sufi convert born a Hindu Rajput, Shivraj Singh, and a progressive Muslim scholar, Shibli Nomani. They set me on a path of inquiry that I had just undergone with the strength of all the women who had preceded me and surrounded me.

When I drew my breath in deep to give my baby life on the day of his birth, I was, of course, nothing less or more than a woman fighting for her baby.

In one moment of sheer epiphany, as I beckoned Shibli into this world, I knew surrender. An unborn child superseded my ego. Without explanation, I knew unconditional love. All of the experiences, experiments, and adventures of the last years, all of the anguish, the joys, and the reflections converged at that one moment to dedicate my being to only one purpose, my baby's life, for he was my manifestation of divine love. I had met him without even having seen him.

As I write, country music spilling out of Safiyyah's bedroom next door, Samir bringing me a chocolate wrapped in gold paper, my baby nuzzles asleep against my breast, the delicate scent of his mother's milk upon his breath, his belly rising and falling with his every breath. He clutches one of my mother's fine black hairs, always taking a souvenir when he lies in her arms.

My shadow kisses him.

Acknowledgments

My Blessed Sangha

A parakeet, a calico, and an aunt named Rashida. They are part of the *sangha* that is the spiritual, intellectual, and inspired community who created this book.

My mother, Sajida Nomani, and father, Mohammad Zafar Alam Nomani, loved me, read my manuscript, and still loved me. My brother, Mustafa Nomani, shared with me his clarity even when I was too feeble to understand it. My sister-in-law, Azeem Nomani, always cheered me to stay strong. Ah, my gurus, Safiyyah and Samir. You welcomed me into your sacred childhoods so I could know my own.

I am grateful to the beautiful people in Morgantown who have prepared me for *samsara,* the worldly life, and helped me also forget it. First, the children for their beauty, wisdom, and grace: Spencer Lindsay, Tali and Tasha Soccorsi, Dayshia and Daniel Johnson, Ryan Bell, Breanna Woods, Natasha Nickles, Neha Gupta, Gary and Emily Scopel, Kate Blobaum, Youseph, Adam, and Heba Kassar; and all of their parents for letting their children hang out with me even when I brought them home late. The teachers, parents, and staff at North Elementary School and Suncrest Middle School; Jeanne DeVincent for worrying about me while I was on the road in emails with type in more colors than I knew existed. *The Dominion Post* for starting my publishing career with a letter-to-the-editor. Morgantown High journalism teacher, Earl Straight, who let me put my first interviews in print in the *Red and Blue Journal.* The elders, the Yusuffs, the Majumdars, the Sinhas, and all the immigrant families that made Morgantown a melting pot. The customers of my mother's boutique, Ain's International, and the erstwhile Louiga Audia for praying for me while I was on the road.

The Nomani family, far and wide, when I thought I was so different you reminded me with your hospitality and kinetic energy that it is from the same cloth that we are cut. The Ansari family and all extensions, you enveloped me in your quiet grace and gave my soul a place to rest. Rachel, Lucy, and Esther Ansari, my companions in this life's *safar,* Arabic for spiritual journey. To all those who opened their doors to me and made me feel at home in this world.

To fly as a *dakini* you have to have a strong home base from which to soar. The *Wall Street Journal* gave me that. I'm grateful to Paul Steiger for his leadership and support and to the editors who pushed me, each in special ways, Byron Calame, Joanne Lipman, Rich Regis, Jonathan Dahl, and Tim Schellhardt. John Koten, my Chicago bureau chief, who recognized how much I was doing to prove my parents' migration right, Alan Murray, my second Washington bureau chief, who pegged me an enigma before I got on the radar of Pakistani intelligence agents, Al Hunt, my first Washington bureau chief, who bought a Coke for me during a dark moment and told me, "Get well. Your job will be waiting." Greg Hill, my San Francisco bureau chief, the first to tell me to: Write about that which you know. And Mary Nese and Cathy Reynolds, who always helped me sign the papers that set me free.

There are *hudud* everywhere. You don't simply have to live in a harem to know boundaries. The special family of friends I've made at the *Wall Street Journal* are all breakers of *hudud.* I am so grateful to them for always cheering me on. Nancy Keates, my Gemini twin. Tina Duff for her friendship. Ken Wells for showing the unorthodox can succeed. Dan Kelly who was as crazy as me to travel to Shanghai, China, for a party. Marcus Brauchli for throwing the party. Dan Costello and his brother Sean Costello for being chaperones in my life. Vicki Parker who cheered me as an enigma. Laurie McGinley for showing me the grace of professional generosity. And all my dear friends, Robert Frank, Phil Kuntz, Holly Neumann, Kemba Dunham, Bridget O'Brian, Tom Herman, Charlie Gasparino, Nik Doegun, Charlie McCoy, Liz McDonald, Kim Strassel, Ron Shafer, David Rogers, Jill Abramson, Peter Waldman, Marilyn Chase, Mary Lu Carnevale, Rachel Kessler, Michelle Higgins, Laurie Campos, and Liz Yeh. Jeff Bailey, an early teacher in the craft of daily journalism, who showed me Old School is the best school. Finally

Rochelle Sharpe who taught me to end sentences with a punchy word, wow!

My *dakini* friends, Sumita Ashrafi, who wrote this book with me as teens, Pam Norick for infinite wisdom and compassion, and Vasia Deliyianni for her global vision. We once thought it was a big deal to call ourselves women of the nineties. Lynn Hoverman because I was wrong. I didn't have enough friends when I met you. Mark Kukis for making me laugh so hard in Pakistan. And my friends Nancy Snow, Ellyce Johnson, Chiyo Kobayashi, Dariush Ashrafi, and Larry Paul, for teaching me about friendship even if I wasn't cool enough to hang out with the McCroskey twins at Suncrest Junior High.

I've been lucky to have had gems passed to me. At the 1981 Ball State University high school journalism workshop, Bruce Watterson told us that it was important to talk to everybody, principals or janitors. After September 11, 2001, my friend Kerry Lauerman told me my voice, too, had worth and sent me to Pakistan for Salon. Salon's chief David Talbot for trusting Kerry's judgment. Salon editor Joan Walsh and Salon readers for being so appreciative.

In my new incarnation, I am indebted to my compassionate agent Kris Dahl for conceiving of the vision that became this book and supporting me so unflinchingly while it was being realized. My editor Liz Perle who taught me by trusting me. Liz Farrell for spreading the word. Jud Laghi for being so kind. And, finally, all of the inspired people at HarperSanFrancisco and HarperCollins who were so kind to this first-time author, Anne Connolly, Tom Ward. Eric Brandt, my new editor, for caring enough to ask me, "Are you happy with us?" Chris Hafner for staying calm amidst my panic. Calla Devlin for caring about the message. Any errors on these pages are mine to claim, but I am so appreciative to Islamic scholar Alan Godlas for scouring my manuscript and telling me about intellectual truths in history, language, religion, and culture I couldn't have even imagined. And I am so grateful to my kindred spirit, my cousin-aunt Shehla Anjum, who knew not only Latif Manzil and my culture, but also the past perfect tense, making this book and life so much richer.

The year 2002 was the hardest in my life. I thank John Bussey and Steve LeVine who brought humanity to our war in the trenches in Karachi. And all those friends from Karachi who must go unnamed, I thank you. My dear new friends in Paris who cared for me when my child was unborn, Anne Robin, Marc Albert, Frederique Lambert, Satchi Van Neyenhoff, "Ben" Benguezzou, Marie de Banville, Aurélie Ducasse, Ouhid Essid, and all those who allowed me to join with them in prayer.

Finally, a gratitude deeper than I could ever express goes to my dear friend Danny Pearl whose absence I don't believe even as I write. You saved my life in so many ways, and you blessed me Danny by leaving me with the friendship of your dear wife Mariane whose gifts to me touch my soul.

I am indebted to everyone, named and unnamed, including you dear reader, who gave me strength so that I could deliver my greatest package, my son Shibli, who waited six days so I could meet my editor's deadline. My lion cub Shibli, I am indebted to you for giving me the inspiration to not only write but to live.

It's said that no intersections are without purpose. May you dear readers be blessed in your life as I have been in mine, with a *sangha* that helps you fly.